D1605988

American Politics in the Postwar Sunbelt
Conservative Growth in a Battleground Region

This book analyzes the political culture of the American Sunbelt since the end of World War II. It highlights and explains the Sunbelt's emergence during the second half of the twentieth century as the undisputed geographic epicenter for conservative Republican power in the United States. However, the book also investigates the ongoing nature of political contestation within the postwar Sunbelt, often highlighting the underappreciated persistence of liberal and progressive influences across the region. Sean P. Cunningham argues that the conservative Republican ascendancy that many have identified as almost synonymous with the rise of the postwar American Sunbelt was hardly an easy, unobstructed victory march. Rather, it was consistently challenged and never foreordained. The history of American politics in the postwar Sunbelt resembles a rollercoaster of partisan and ideological adaptation and transformation.

Sean P. Cunningham is Associate Professor of History at Texas Tech University. A decorated teacher, he holds a Ph.D. in Modern American History from the University of Florida and teaches broadly in twentieth-century U.S. history, while specializing in the history of post–1945 American political culture. His first book, *Cowboy Conservatism: Texas and the Rise of the Modern Right*, was published in 2010.

Cambridge Essential Histories

Series Editor

Donald Critchlow, *Arizona State University*

Cambridge Essential Histories is devoted to introducing critical events, periods, or individuals in history to students. Volumes in this series emphasize narrative as a means of familiarizing students with historical analysis. In this series leading scholars focus on topics in European, American, Asian, Latin American, Middle Eastern, African, and world history through thesis-driven, concise volumes designed for survey and upper-division undergraduate history courses. The books contain an introduction that acquaints readers with the historical event and reveals the book's thesis; narrative chapters that cover the chronology of the event or problem; and a concluding summary that provides the historical interpretation and analysis.

Titles in the Series

Edward D. Berkowitz, *Mass Appeal: The Formative Age of the Movies, Radio, and TV*

Sean P. Cunningham, *American Politics in the Postwar Sunbelt: Conservative Growth in a Battleground Region*

Ian Dowbiggin, *The Quest for Mental Health: A Tale of Science, Medicine, Scandal, Sorrow, and Mass Society*

John Earl Haynes and Harvey Klehr, *Early Cold War Spies: The Espionage Trials that Shaped American Politics*

James H. Hutson, *Church and State in America: The First Two Centuries*

Maury Klein, *The Genesis of Industrial America, 1870–1920*

John Lauritz Larson, *The Market Revolution in America: Liberty, Ambition, and the Eclipse of the Common Good*

Wilson D. Miscamble, *The Most Controversial Decision: Truman, the Atomic Bombs, and the Defeat of Japan*

Charles H. Parker, *Global Interactions in the Early Modern Age, 1400–1800*

Stanley G. Payne, *The Spanish Civil War*

American Politics in the Postwar Sunbelt

Conservative Growth in a Battleground Region

SEAN P. CUNNINGHAM

Texas Tech University

CAMBRIDGE
UNIVERSITY PRESS

Shaftesbury Road, Cambridge CB2 8EA, United Kingdom

One Liberty Plaza, 20th Floor, New York, NY 10006, USA

477 Williamstown Road, Port Melbourne, VIC 3207, Australia

314–321, 3rd Floor, Plot 3, Splendor Forum, Jasola District Centre, New Delhi – 110025, India

103 Penang Road, #05–06/07, Visioncrest Commercial, Singapore 238467

Cambridge University Press is part of Cambridge University Press & Assessment, a department of the University of Cambridge.

We share the University's mission to contribute to society through the pursuit of education, learning and research at the highest international levels of excellence.

www.cambridge.org
Information on this title: www.cambridge.org/9781107024526

First published 2014

A catalogue record for this publication is available from the British Library

Library of Congress Cataloging-in-Publication data
Cunningham, Sean P.
American politics in the postwar sunbelt : conservative growth in a battleground region / Sean P. Cunningham.
    pages cm – (Cambridge essential histories)
ISBN 978-1-107-02452-6 (hardback)
1. Sunbelt States – Politics and government. 2. United States – Politics and government. 3. Conservatism – Sunbelt States. 4. Republican Party (U.S. : 1854–) I. Title.
JS437.C86 2014
320.97309´045–dc23   2013044947

ISBN   978-1-107-02452-6   Hardback
ISBN   978-1-107-67234-5   Paperback

For Caitlin and Samantha

Contents

Acknowledgments

This book would not exist without the guidance and support of numerous friends and colleagues. Don Critchlow is at the top of that list. In February 2011, Don asked me to consider writing a study about Sunbelt politics for Cambridge's Essential Histories series. It goes without saying that I jumped at the invitation and have never once regretted doing so. Don's expertise in the field of post–1945 American politics and the history of modern conservatism was especially invaluable, as was his guidance during the initial stages of the proposal and publication process. I also want to thank Lew Bateman, who stepped in to shepherd this project after Eric Crahan – whose support was also invaluable – left for a new position at Oxford University Press in June 2012. Thanks also go to Shaun Vigil, whose patience with me during the production process was greatly appreciated, as well as Abigail Zorbaugh, Linda Benson, Sumitha Nithyanandan, and everyone else associated with Cambridge University Press – in my experience, a truly first-class organization.

I also want to thank Texas Tech University for supporting me and this project through a Faculty Development Leave, which I was awarded during the spring 2013 semester. That award allowed me to temporarily step away from teaching responsibilities to focus on the final stages of research and writing. I also want to thank my colleagues in the Department of History at Texas Tech for their support, wisdom, and input throughout the various stages of this project. I am thankful to work in a department whose members celebrate with and consistently support one another – a rarity, I think, in the world of modern academia.

I also want to thank Bill Link, Brian Ward, Kevin Kruse, Matthew Lassiter, Darren Dochuk, Kyle Longley, Dan Williams, Walter Buenger, Alwyn Barr, Donald Walker, and Randy McBee for constructively critiquing my earlier scholarship on the Texas Right, thereby influencing my approach to this study. Their work is among the very best in the field, and I relied heavily on both their scholarship and previous advice as I wrote *American Politics in the Postwar Sunbelt*.

I am also thankful for the love and support of my wonderful family, including notably my parents, Kirk and Kay Cunningham. I also want to thank my brother, Eric Cunningham, for the always enjoyable and often challenging political discussions we've had in recent years, usually while drinking some very good beer. Those conversations have helped me clarify several of the arguments I make in this book. A particular word of thanks also goes to my uncle and aunt, Al and Cindy Cunningham, for allowing me to occupy their mountain home in Angel Fire, New Mexico, for an extended stay during the final stages of the writing process. The uninterrupted solitude and crisp mountain air were particularly motivating.

Finally, I want to thank my wife, Laura, and my two daughters, Caitlin and Samantha. Without their patience, love, and encouragement, this book would not exist, nor would my career. I dedicated my first book, *Cowboy Conservatism*, to Laura, and I dedicate this one to Caitlin and Samantha, and do so with much love.

Introduction

What Is the Sunbelt – and Why Is It Important?

This book is about the political culture of the American Sunbelt since the end of World War II. At the heart of this story is the rise of a powerful Republican Party, increasingly detached from its establishment roots on the East Coast, shaped by grassroots organizers and business leaders in rapidly growing metropolitan communities, and fueled by an ideological conservatism that employed a populist style to champion an agenda for free enterprise, limited government, low taxes, strong national defense, fervent patriotism, and traditional family values. As a result of these and other converging factors, the Sunbelt emerged during the second half of the twentieth century as the undisputed geographic epicenter for conservative Republican power in the United States.

Yet, at the same time, the political culture of the American Sunbelt – or perhaps more accurately, the history of American politics in the postwar Sunbelt – is also a story of contestation. At different moments and with varying degrees of success, leftist radicals, reformist progressives, establishment liberals, pragmatic moderates, and even some conservatives used the Democratic Party, as well as other organizations, to fight against this Republican ascendancy. Sometimes these groups were successful. Sometimes they were not. But the conservative Republican ascendancy that so many have identified as almost synonymous with the rise of the postwar American Sunbelt was hardly an easy, unobstructed victory march. Rather, it was consistently challenged and never foreordained. The history of American politics in the postwar Sunbelt resembles a rollercoaster of partisan and ideological adaptation and transformation. This book seeks to tell that story.

WHAT IS THE SUNBELT?

One of this book's central arguments is that the emergence of the Sunbelt has been a pivotal factor in the evolving nature of modern American politics since 1945. It is not the first book to make such an argument. Journalists and political analysts have been discussing the growing power of the Sunbelt since at least the late 1970s, if not earlier. Social scientists began to examine these trends more frequently during the 1980s and early 1990s. Then, beginning in the mid-1990s – but especially since 2001 – the Sunbelt began to receive significantly more attention from historians. This was particularly true among historians interested in explaining the rise of modern American conservatism and the growth of the Republican Party. In fact, during most of the 2000s, the study of modern conservatism, principally as it evolved in the Sunbelt, was one of the trendiest research fields in all of academia.[1]

---

[1] Studies of the Republican ascendancy have generally seen Reagan's victory in 1980 as a climactic moment in the rise of modern conservatism. The literature on this political shift is vast. For examples, see John A. Andrew III, *The Other Side of the Sixties: Young Americans for Freedom and the Rise of Conservative Politics* (New Brunswick, NJ: Rutgers University Press, 1997); Michael D. Bowen, *The Roots of Modern Conservatism: Dewey, Taft, and the Battle for the Soul of the Republican Party* (Chapel Hill: University of North Carolina Press, 2011); Mary C. Brennan, *Turning Right in the Sixties: The Conservative Capture of the GOP* (Chapel Hill: University of North Carolina Press, 1995); Jennifer Burns, *Goddess of the Market: Ayn Rand and the American Right* (New York: Oxford University Press, 2011); Joseph Crespino, *In Search of Another Country: Mississippi and the Conservative Counterrevolution* (Princeton: Princeton University Press, 2007); Donald T. Critchlow, *Phyllis Schlafly and Grassroots Conservatism: A Woman's Crusade* (Princeton, NJ: Princeton University Press, 2005); Donald T. Critchlow, *The Conservative Ascendancy: How the GOP Right Made Political History* (Cambridge, MA: Harvard University Press, 2007); Sean P. Cunningham, *Cowboy Conservatism: Texas and the Rise of the Modern*

Such trendiness aside, the recent attention scholars have paid to
the relationship between political change and regional identity – in
this case, the relationship between conservatism and the Sunbelt –
hardly represents a new approach to the study of political history
in the United States. On the contrary, scholars have been interested in the regional dynamics of American politics for as long
as there has been scholarly interest in America. Take, for instance,
studies of the U.S. South. As a region with a distinctive culture,
character, economy, and political history, the South – commonly
defined as the collection of states that seceded from the Union
in 1860 and 1861 – has received enormous scholarly attention
over the decades, and deservedly so. After all, the nation fought a
bloody civil war from 1861 to 1865 in reaction to that secession,
and it did so largely because of unresolved competition and incom-
patibility between two seemingly distinct regions – the North and
the South.[2] Meanwhile, scholars have also paid considerable

Right (Lexington: University Press of Kentucky, 2010); David Farber, *The Rise and Fall of Modern American Conservatism: A Short History* (Princeton: Princeton University Press, 2010); Laura Kalman, *Right Star Rising: A New Politics, 1974–1980* (New York: W.W. Norton & Co., 2010); Kevin M. Kruse, *White Flight: Atlanta and the Making of Modern Conservatism* (Princeton: Princeton University Press, 2005); Matthew D. Lassiter, *The Silent Majority: Suburban Politics in the Sunbelt South* (Princeton, NJ: Princeton University Press, 2006); William A. Link, *Righteous Warrior: Jesse Helms and the Rise of Modern Conservatism* (New York: St. Martin's Press, 2008); Robert Mason, *The Republican Party and American Politics from Hoover to Reagan* (New York: Cambridge University Press, 2012); Lisa McGirr, *Suburban Warriors: The Origins of the New American Right* (Princeton: Princeton University Press, 2001); Michelle M. Nickerson, *Mothers of Conservatism: Women and the Postwar Right* (Princeton: Princeton University Press, 2012); Gregory L. Schneider, *The Conservative Century: From Reaction to Revolution* (New York: Rowman & Littlefield, 2009); Jonathan Schoenwald, *A Time for Choosing: The Rise of Modern American Conservatism* (New York: Oxford University Press, 2001); and Daniel K. Williams, *God's Own Party: The Making of the Christian Right* (New York: Oxford University Press, 2010). For a comprehensive examination of this literature, see Kim Phillips-Fein et al., "Conservatism: A Roundtable." *Journal of American History*, Vol. 98, No. 3 (December 2011), pp. 723–773.
[2] The historiography on the South is also vast, and the literature on the South's experience during the Civil War even more so. For more on southern identity and heritage before, during, and after the Civil War, see among many others, David W. Blight, *Race and Reunion: The Civil War in American History* (Cambridge,

attention to the unique regional identity of the American West. Rarely, however, have those scholars managed to agree on what "West" actually means. In fact, competing definitions of "West" – in the sense of both its geographical borders and its intangible character – have been the driving force behind much of the ongoing research into that region's history. That research not only reflects the conversation that historians continue to have about the true nature of the West, but in many ways also frames the almost never-ending debate about the character and identity of the United States as a whole.[3]

In many ways, the historical construction of an identifiable "Sunbelt" owes a debt of gratitude to these scholarly traditions. Today, thanks in part to academic interest in competing regional identities within the United States, most contemporaries at least recognize the existence of a region known as the Sunbelt; journalists still refer to it regularly, political analysts still account for its influence, and scholars have now written about it extensively. But

MA: Harvard University Press, 2001); James Cobb, *Away Down South: A History of Southern Identity* (New York: Oxford University Press, 2005); John McCardell, *The Idea of a Southern Nation: Southern Nationalists and Southern Nationalism* (New York: W.W. Norton & Co., 1979); Lacy K. Ford Jr., *Origins of Southern Radicalism: The South Carolina Upcountry, 1800–1860* (New York: Oxford University Press, 1988); William W. Freehling, *The Road to Disunion: Secessionists at Bay, 1776–1854* (New York: Oxford University Press, 1990); Steven Hahn, *A Nation Under Our Feet: Black Political Struggles in the Rural South from Slavery to the Great Migration* (Cambridge, MA: Harvard University Press, 2004); Michael F. Holt, *The Political Crisis of the 1850s* (New York: John Wiley & Sons, 1978); William A. Link, *Atlanta, Cradle of the New South: Race and Remembering in the Civil War's Aftermath* (Chapel Hill: University of North Carolina Press, 2013); Eric Walther, *The Fire-Eaters* (Baton Rouge: Louisiana State University Press, 1992); Bertram Wyatt-Brown, *Southern Honor: Ethics and Behavior in the Old South* (New York: Oxford University Press, 1982).

[3] For examples, see Gerald D. Nash, *Creating the West: Historical Interpretations, 1890–1990* (Albuquerque: University of New Mexico Press, 1993); Gary J. Hausladen, *Western Places, American Myths: How We Think About the West* (Reno: University of Nevada Press, 2006); Robert V. Hine and John Mack Faragher, *The American West: A New Interpretive History* (New Haven, CT: Yale University Press, 2000); and Richard White, *"It's Your Misfortune and None of My Own": A New History of the American West* (Norman: University of Oklahoma Press, 1991). For a specific example of the "New Western" historiography, see among others, Patricia Nelson Limerick, *The Legacy of Conquest: The Unbroken Past of the American West* (New York: W.W. Norton & Co., 1987).

acknowledging its existence or even researching its history and culture is not the same as providing a clear definition. Therefore, it is still important to ask and answer a deceptively complex question: What is the Sunbelt?

The term "Sunbelt" first became part of America's mainstream political lexicon in 1969 when Kevin Phillips coined it in his highly influential book, *The Emerging Republican Majority*. Phillips, a former campaign strategist for Richard Nixon, used the term to describe an ambiguously defined southern half of the continental United States that stretched from the Atlantic to the Pacific and shared common economic interests in oil, agribusiness, defense, and technology. At its simplest level, this definition works. When most Americans think of the Sunbelt, they usually picture a loose merger of the South and the West, highlighted by modern and economically vibrant states such as California, Texas, and Florida, as well as young but growing cities such as Los Angeles, Phoenix, Dallas, and Atlanta.[4]

On a deeper level, however, this definition lacks complexity. It is easy enough to highlight broad swathes of the American map, recognize a few common characteristics, and assume that some sort of coherent regional identity exists. But the reality is not so simple. Take, for instance, the Sunbelt's geographic dimensions. Does an unbroken region that connects California to Florida require that all parts in between share a common political, social, or economic culture? Is New Mexico part of the Sunbelt? What about Mississippi or Alabama? How far north does the Sunbelt extend? Does it include Utah, Colorado, Arkansas, or Virginia? After all, Richmond – the capital of Virginia – is much closer to

[4] Kevin P. Phillips, *The Emerging Republican Majority* (New Rochelle, NY: Arlington House, 1969). The Sunbelt as a regional concept was also promoted with some lasting significance in Kirkpatrick Sale, *Power Shift: The Rise of the Southern Rim and Its Challenges to the Eastern Establishment* (New York: Random House, 1975). For a more nuanced discussion of these two works and of the Sunbelt as a regional concept, see Michelle Nickerson and Darren Dochuk, eds., *Sunbelt Rising: The Politics of Space, Place, and Region* (Philadelphia: University of Pennsylvania Press, 2011), 1–28.

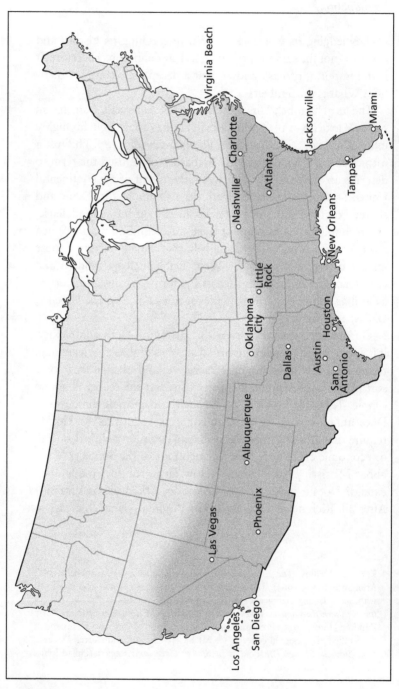

Major Cities of the Sunbelt

New York City in terms of mileage than it is to Atlanta, Georgia, the city on the East Coast most widely considered to be quintessentially Sunbelt.

In response to these and similar questions, it could be suggested that the Sunbelt's geographic identity is actually rooted in the similarities of its largest and most dynamic metropolitan centers. Texas, for instance, is always included in popular conceptions of the Sunbelt, not because of its mostly unsettled trans-Pecos frontier or the agricultural quilting of its Panhandle, but rather because of the expansive growth of megalopolises such as Dallas and Houston, which have thrived because of developments in oil, finance, real estate, and technology. Other metropolitan centers typically identified as Sunbelt include San Diego, Los Angeles, Las Vegas, Phoenix, Miami, and Atlanta. Cities such as Tucson, Austin, San Antonio, Oklahoma City, Nashville, Jacksonville, Tampa, and Charlotte are also often included on such lists, as are many others. Thinking in these terms, the Sunbelt seems less like a vast region of connected states and more like an archipelago of metropolises that have experienced rapid growth during roughly the same decades as a result of roughly the same economic forces, populated by individuals living in roughly similar suburban and exurban developments.[5]

If the Sunbelt's existence as an identifiable region depends on the shared characteristics of its largest cities, then it is also fair to ask whether a proper understanding of the Sunbelt might actually depend more on economics than geography. Certainly the term "Sunbelt" implies that warm weather is an important aspect of the region's identity. But heat and lack of water have long been impediments to population growth and economic

---

[5] Additional studies dealing with the question of Sunbelt identity include Carl Abbott, *The New Urban America: Growth and Politics in Sunbelt Cities* (Chapel Hill: University of North Carolina Press, 1981); Richard M. Bernard and Bradley R. Rice, eds., *Sunbelt Cities: Politics and Growth Since World War II* (Austin: University of Texas Press, 1983); Nickerson and Dochuk, *Sunbelt Rising*; and Bernard L. Weinstein and Robert E. Firestine, *Regional Growth and Decline in the United States: The Rise of the Sunbelt and the Decline of the Northeast* (New York: Praeger, 1978).

diversification, at least so far as the arid West (especially Southwest) was concerned. What changed after 1945? One of the many technological developments that undoubtedly contributed to the Sunbelt's formation and economic growth was the advent of air conditioning. Taming the heat was a prerequisite for significant population growth, and population growth was a corequisite for economic development. There is little question that managed cold air – along with advances in hydroelectric power, water conservation, and irrigation – helped make Sunbelt growth possible.

Technological advancements such as these provided an economic boon to the Sunbelt, but such advancements were not alone in shaping regional economic expansion. Federal defense contracts were also critically important. The Sunbelt cities and states that experienced the most significant population growth in the decades after World War II also typically shared a stronger-than-average reliance on federal defense contracts. Those contracts were most often awarded to companies located in metropolitan areas where proactive civic leaders and economic developers had taken a more aggressive approach to attracting new businesses by creating entrepreneurial climates popularly perceived as conducive to free enterprise. Despite being characteristically hostile to labor unions, the cities, states, and companies that won these contracts attracted tens of thousands of new employees for jobs in high-tech, aerospace, and defense industries.

Many of these industries were designed, at least in part, to strengthen national security. When workers in these industries moved from other parts of the country into Sunbelt cities, they also typically used federally subsidized loans to purchase new houses, many of which had been mass-produced in modern tract developments. In turn, the booming housing market fueled new retail and commercial construction, which required new and expanded banking and financial markets and, cyclically, new jobs. Responding to the region's population growth and related need for new housing, the federal government also subsidized the construction of new highways. Those highways were quickly crowded with new automobiles, all of which required lots of gasoline, thereby increasing the demand for – and contributing to the rising price of – oil.[6]

As a result of these combined factors, Sunbelt cities grew quickly in the decades after World War II as metropolitan economies diversified, modernized, and expanded. And unlike older cities in the Northeast such as New York, Boston, and Philadelphia, these Sunbelt metropolises became more expansively broad than tall; they tended to spread out, not up. This, too, became a hallmark of Sunbelt modernity – vast, sprawling, commercial, and residential development generously networked by federally funded highways and abundantly dotted with automobiles, all of which made concerns such as the traveling distance between home and workplace far less relevant than such concerns had been for earlier generations. These growing distances between home and work also widened the expanding cultural chasm between the daily experiences of those living in suburbs and those left behind in the inner cities.[7]

It seems, therefore, that defining the Sunbelt along both geographic and economic lines makes sense, at least to a certain point. Warm-weather states in the southern half of the continental United States disproportionately benefited from wartime and postwar

[6] Bruce J. Schulman, *The Seventies: The Great Shift in American Culture, Society, and Politics* (New York: The Free Press, 2001), 106–109.

[7] The best recent study of the relationship between business and politics is Kim Phillips-Fein, *Invisible Hands: The Businessmen's Crusade Against the New Deal* (New York: W.W. Norton & Co., 2009). For more on the general economic development of the Sunbelt South and West, see, for example, Numan V. Bartley, *The New South, 1945–1980: The Story of the South's Modernization* (Baton Rouge: Louisiana State University Press, 1995); Roger W. Lotchin, *Fortress California, 1910–1961: From Warfare to Welfare* (Urbana and Chicago: University of Illinois Press, 2002); Gerald D. Nash, *The Federal Landscape: An Economic History of the Twentieth-Century West* (Tucson: University of Arizona Press, 1999); and Bruce J. Schulman, *From Cotton Belt to Sunbelt: Federal Policy, Economic Development, & the Transformation of the South, 1938–1980* (New York: Oxford University Press, 1991). For more on suburbanization, see Kenneth T. Jackson, *Crabgrass Frontier: The Suburbanization of the United States* (New York: Oxford University Press, 1985); Adam Rome, *The Bulldozer in the Countryside: Suburban Sprawl and the Rise of American Environmentalism* (New York: Cambridge University Press, 2001); and Kevin M. Kruse and Thomas Sugrue, eds., *The New Suburban History* (Chicago: University of Chicago Press, 2006).

defense contracts, federally funded research and development, new housing construction, and technological advances like air conditioning, all of which combined to result in a significant infusion of both population and economic power to previously underdeveloped areas. As those cities and states become larger and more economically modern, the Sunbelt developed a semblance of regional identity and gained political power.

But geographic and economic commonalities across the Sunbelt can be overstated. Sunbelt cities and states no doubt looked similar when seen from a distance, but a tighter focus reveals important distinctions. The Sunbelt's heterogeneity is reflected, for instance, in Arizona's proximity to the Mexican border, along with its substantial and largely impoverished Native American population. These unique traits have created a multiethnic political and socioeconomic environment very different from Georgia's, for example – just one case of a former Confederate state that has long functioned within a much more rigidly "black-white" racial context than has Arizona or any other state in the Southwest, for that matter. Or, one could look at Florida. Since 1945, the Sunshine State's economy has been far more dependent on tourism, leisure, and the relocation of retirees than that of most other Sunbelt states. Meanwhile in Texas, oil functioned like an economic Goliath, creating pockets of extravagant wealth and power that functioned in ways largely unique to the rest of the region and country. Elsewhere, North Carolina's federally supported Research Triangle – which connected powerful corporations with universities in Chapel Hill, Durham, and Raleigh – did not stifle or limit the proliferation of diverse political ideas – quite the opposite, in fact. A mere decade into the twenty-first century, the North Carolina Research Triangle – dotted with what John B. Judis and Ruy Teixeira have called "postindustrial metropolises" – was one of the most solidly Democratic areas in the nation, emblematic of the emerging "progressive centrism" at the heart of Barack Obama's popular appeal with young, middle-class voters in both 2008 and 2012. The same could be said of similar postindustrial metropolises elsewhere in the Sunbelt, including those near Silicon Valley – California's high-tech hub. Analogous political cultures have developed for comparable reasons in Austin, Texas, and Boulder, Colorado. Such communities suggest that categories like "urban" and "suburban" no longer mean as much in the twenty-first-century world of telecommunications, sprawling office parks, and virtual workplaces. Meanwhile, despite the region's widespread metropolitan growth and relative material abundance, millions of nonwhite Sunbelt residents remained stuck in poverty, without access to education or job opportunities, largely excluded from the region's culture of sprawling material abundance. Successful and economically attractive on so many levels, the postwar Sunbelt also struggled, as did the nation, with deep and enduring poverty and inequality.[8]

Clearly, geographic and economic commonalities have contributed to the Sunbelt's image as a distinct region, even as geographic and economic variances have simultaneously implied the existence not of a single Sunbelt, but of many different Sunbelts. What ultimately coalesced these cities and states into a more coherent region during the second half of the twentieth century, therefore, had less to do with geography or economics than with the development of a vibrant and contested political culture – one that from roughly 1945 until at least the end of the century also typified the evolving political culture of the United States as a whole. That political culture was largely defined by a basic set of principles posited in response to the question of what relationship government should have with its citizens. In this view, the Sunbelt came to exist not simply as region popularly (if loosely) defined by geography and economics; it also came to exist as a political sensibility – as a "state of mind." More than anything else, this state of mind – and the political culture that informed it – was increasingly associated in the decades after World War II with an evolving brand of modern conservatism, and especially the Sunbelt public's social and cultural engagement with that conservatism.

[8] For more on the Sunbelt and its diverse and ever-changing economic and political landscape, see John B. Judis and Ruy Teixeira, *The Emerging Democratic Majority* (New York: Scribner, 2002).

Put more simply, modern conservatism flourished in and helped define the postwar Sunbelt. That conservatism was anchored by preexisting notions of entrepreneurialism; rugged individualism; self-help or "bootstrap politics"; limited and local government (sometimes referred to as "states' rights"); and traditional social mores informed by Protestant interpretations of the Judeo-Christian ethic, broadly defined. These notions were, in turn, fortified by an at least partially imagined past in which brave and enterprising citizens had fought a lost cause to preserve their way of life against a tyrannical northeastern majority, had civilized the uncivilized and settled the western frontier, and had done all of it by God's grace and the sweat of their own brow, and never with the assistance of the federal government. Strongest in the Sunbelt's metropolitan areas, this brand of conservatism easily gelled with that of areas less intimately connected to major cities – both smaller towns and cities across the region, as well as the region's vast and still quite rural hinterlands. Such places had long been dedicated to certain propositions about hard work and traditional values, but they became more reliably Republican when modern politicians seeking to foment widespread partisan realignment repackaged those propositions.

In essence, this was the Sunbelt's creation story. Recast for the modern era, Sunbelt boosters, politicians, and residents worked together to construct an image of a thriving, entrepreneurial, future-oriented, growth-dedicated, individualistic, color-blind, and typically union-free place for citizens to unabashedly pursue the comforts of the American Dream. In some ways, this image was an accurate reflection of the modern, postwar Sunbelt. In many other ways – and for most nonwhites – it was a figment of the conservative imagination, and one that demanded a response. Regardless, the image of such a world certainly sounded appealing to the millions of Americans who decided to make the Sunbelt home during the second half of the twentieth century.

So what, then, is the Sunbelt? At the end of the day, the Sunbelt is both a collection of places across the southern half of the continental United States that share certain economic commonalities, as well as an imagined place best understood through its dynamic and multifaceted political culture. That political culture has often been dominated by an evolving brand of modern conservatism, but it has also often been contested by competing interests on both sides of the liberal/conservative divide. Ultimately then, one cannot define the postwar Sunbelt without simultaneously exploring the region's political history, the dynamics of which center on the rise of modern conservatism, the persistence of contestation, and the ways in which that tenuous balance both challenged and reinforced competing worldviews in the decades following World War II.[9]

WHY IS THE SUNBELT IMPORTANT?

Having dealt with the question of defining the Sunbelt, it is also important to ask why the Sunbelt is important. In short, the history of American politics in the postwar Sunbelt is important because, in so many ways, the region has both reflected and shaped the trajectory of postwar American politics. For one thing, the Sunbelt's exponential growth – best reflected in its three largest states, California, Texas, and Florida – has resulted in a quantifiable increase of political power at the national level. As evidence, simply look at the Electoral College. In the presidential election of 1944, California, Texas, and Florida accounted for a combined 56 electoral votes. In 2012, those three states accounted for a combined 122 electoral votes.

This is just one way to envision the Sunbelt's growing influence. Since 1945, Sunbelt politicians have also reconfigured the House of Representatives, dictated legislative agendas, altered party platforms, and fueled widespread partisan realignment. Many of the nation's fiercest and most controversial political debates – for

---

[9] The best recent study of the formation of Sunbelt identity seen through a South to West migration is Darren Dochuk, *From Bible Belt to Sunbelt: Plain-Folk Religion, Grassroots Politics, and the Rise of Evangelical Conservatism* (New York: W.W. Norton & Co., 2011). For more on the formation of Western attitudes, identities, and memories, see again Limerick, *The Legacy of Conquest*, and Nickerson and Dochuk, *Sunbelt Rising*, 1–28. See also White, *"It's Your Misfortune and None of My Own,"* and Hal K. Rothman, *Devil's Bargains: Tourism in the Twentieth-Century American West* (Lawrence: University Press of Kansas, 1998).

instance, those on civil rights, abortion, labor, taxes, and the environment – have been most fiercely waged on Sunbelt soil. But perhaps nothing reflects the growth of postwar Sunbelt political power more than the conspicuous presence of Sunbelt presidential and vice-presidential candidates running every four years on major party national tickets. In every presidential election from 1952 to 2008, at least one of the four candidates representing either the Republican or Democratic Party tickets was from a Sunbelt state. Even more striking, from 1964 to 2004, the winning candidate in every presidential election hailed from a Sunbelt state. Four of those – Richard Nixon (California), Ronald Reagan (California), George H. W. Bush (Texas), and George W. Bush (Texas) – leaned to the ideological Right, whereas three – Lyndon Johnson (Texas), Jimmy Carter (Georgia), and Bill Clinton (Arkansas) – leaned, more or less, to the ideological Left.

This somewhat surprising balance speaks to yet another aspect of the region's influence on national politics. In a world of "red states" and "blue states," agenda-driven cable news networks, never-ending reelection campaigns, endless streams of money, and unlimited access to unedited opinion via the Internet, the Sunbelt has shown remarkable flexibility and moderation as it continues to reflect a nation that, while seemingly polarized along the lines of Left and Right, has almost always gravitated to the pragmatic middle.[10]

Take Texas, for instance. At the national level, Texas has been a bedrock of conservative Republicanism since 1980. But before that, it was a battleground state in postwar presidential elections and remained loyally Democratic in state and local races through at least the mid-1990s. And although still conservative and loyally Republican at the dawn of the twenty-first century, demographic changes suggest that Texas's future could be far more competitively balanced. Meanwhile, on three separate occasions – 1960, 1968, and 1972 – California gave its electoral votes to Richard

---

[10] For more on the debate about American political divisions, see, for instance, Morris P. Fiorina, Samuel J. Abrams, and Jeremy C. Pope, *Culture War?: The Myth of a Polarized America* (New York: Pearson Longman, 2004).

Nixon. It also produced and supported Ronald Reagan (in 1980 and 1984), before supporting his vice-president, George H. W. Bush, in the presidential election of 1988. But California has not voted for a GOP presidential candidate since 1988 and is, today, one of the nation's most solidly liberal and Democratic states. Perhaps most dramatically and schizophrenically, Florida voted for the conservative George W. Bush twice, in 2000 and 2004, before voting for the liberal Barack Obama twice, in 2008 and 2012. At times, Florida has seemed southern and quite red. At other times, politicians have looked to Florida for guidance on how to pursue a national agenda, viewing the economically, demographically, and ideologically diverse Sunshine State as a microcosm of the country as a whole.

All told, there is no such thing as a "Solid Sunbelt," a fact that only adds to the region's importance. Rather, the history of Sunbelt politics since 1945 is important because it provides a window into the world of American politics during those years. The issues, personalities, and struggles waged in that region since the end of World War II have transformed the landscape of modern American politics. The history of Sunbelt politics since 1945 is, therefore, an American story.

A SHORT WORD ON METHOD

The chief aim of this book is to provide a concise and accessible narrative of the Sunbelt's political culture and development since 1945, and to do so within the contextual framework of national politics. Rather than breaking new ground or exploring the previously unexplored, *American Politics in the Postwar Sunbelt* is designed to construct a clear image of the Sunbelt's vast and multi-faceted political history. The chapters following this Introduction tell that history by highlighting many of the salient issues, personalities, events, and moments that best reflect that narrative and its multiple subplots. As a whole, the book draws on the substantial body of historical scholarship that has been produced on the Sunbelt as a region, the rise of modern conservatism (both nationally and regionally), and postwar American politics more broadly.

For the purposes of this study, the term "politics" is used to describe the process by which leaders are elected to public office; how those leaders serve once in office; how political parties shape everything from campaign strategy to policy implementation; and how ordinary individuals, typically far from the corridors of elected power, have often mobilized at the grass roots to affect change at national, state, and local levels. The various ways in which Americans engage the political process further shape the nation's political culture – meaning the collective opinions, attitudes, and values that people in a given space have about politics. By illustrating how people in the Sunbelt thought about, reacted to, and shaped their political world, this book hopes to say something valuable about where American political culture is today, and why.

Ultimately, the story of American politics in the postwar Sunbelt is a multifaceted story about political change and contestation, and it is to that story that this book now turns.

I

Convergence, Metropolitanization, and Anticommunism

World War II transformed the modern American Sunbelt. That war – or more specifically, the massive amount of money spent by the federal government to mobilize the nation and fight that war – accelerated the regional convergence and economic development of metropolitan communities across the South and West. Much of that economic development was rooted in industrial growth connected to national security interests, defense contracts, military expansion, and technology. It was concurrently fueled by and cyclically reflected in the rapid growth of related but increasingly postindustrial sectors such as higher education, finance, real estate, retail, and tourism. Economic expansion across the Sunbelt resulted in population growth, and population growth contributed to greater political significance.

The Sunbelt's early growth also coincided with the development of a national political culture that was powerfully shaped by anticommunism. During the late 1940s and early 1950s, as cities across the South and West were booming, Americans everywhere – whether liberal or conservative – operated within a contextual framework that prioritized the containment (and eventual defeat) of communism. Seen by many as both a challenge to U.S. interests abroad as well as American values at home, communism – in all its loosely defined and fearfully imagined forms – quickly became the nation's top perceived threat.

The long-term political ramifications of anticommunism in the Sunbelt were significant. As the Sunbelt grew, many of its residents became increasingly committed to fighting communism abroad by protecting the free market at home. Such protection, many of these men and women believed, depended on the preservation of individuals' ability to pursue economic independence without government interference. For these people, economic independence also meant rejecting organized labor. Most entrepreneurs and civic boosters across the South and West had long been hostile to labor unions. But within an anticommunist context, the fear that such organizations would breed socialist radicalism and undermine profitability seemed more urgent. Anticommunism also revitalized much of the public's gravitation toward religion while reducing widespread tolerance for state-supported reform. In short, virtually everything during the early postwar period was processed through some form of anticommunist lens.

This was especially true in the Sunbelt, where the twin engines of metropolitanization and anticommunism eventually merged into the driving force behind the development of dozens of economically vibrant and fiercely patriotic Sunbelt cities and states. Yet, despite the acceleration of such trends during the early postwar period, it would be several years before these inclinations coalesced into the operational and ideological bases for a Republican-led conservative ascendancy. On the contrary, by the end of the 1950s, Cold War liberalism – seemingly more rational, technocratic, and responsibly anticommunist than most brands of conservatism at the time – remained well entrenched as the ideological heart of American political power. Democrats continued to win most local, state, and national elections, even in the emerging Sunbelt.

The persistence of Democratic power notwithstanding, the nascent convergence of these economic and political forces nevertheless catalyzed the rapid development of the Sunbelt between 1945 and 1960. That development set the stage for the seismic shifts in power that would eventually transform the region into the nation's pacesetter by the end of the twentieth century.

CONVERGENCE

Understanding the nature of American politics in the postwar Sunbelt depends, in part, on appreciating the geographic, economic, cultural, and political convergence of South and West after 1945. After all, South and West had very little in common prior to World War II, at least according to the popular imagination. Even contemporary perceptions of the historical Old South tend to recall images that look like a scene out of *Gone with the Wind*, whereas common perceptions of the Old West often look more like a John Wayne classic, such as *Stagecoach* or *The Searchers*. Blending fact with fiction to create convenient and entertaining history, Hollywood filmmakers have often unintentionally reinforced long-standing perceptions about southern and western history – perceptions that have flourished in both academic and nonacademic settings for decades.[1]

Such images can be deceiving. Despite many obvious differences, the political cultures of these apparently disparate regions have often shared or been coinfluenced by several factors. The first is related to simple demographics. Southern whites have been moving into the West ever since Thomas Jefferson finalized the Louisiana Purchase in 1803. Thereafter, these southerners continued to flow into the West in search of new financial opportunities, often bringing their slaves with them. As they moved, they also carried deeply ingrained attitudes about race, religion, economics, and politics. Such attitudes helped shape the character of the West. Also, common to both South and West was a spirit of popular rebellion and a related zeal for independence. These attitudes have historically manifested as deep-seated hostilities toward established power, especially power perceived as centralized in the East Coast, particularly in New York City and Washington, D.C. In the South, the most obvious example of rebellion against the federal government is the Civil War. From the perspective of an

---

[1] For an overview of Western identity in the twentieth century, specifically using film and television as a lens for analysis, see Richard Slotkin, *Gunfighter Nation: The Myth of the Frontier in Twentieth-Century America* (Norman: University of Oklahoma Press, 1998).

unreconstructed ex-Confederate, the Civil War was about states' rights – and more specifically, the right of (white) individuals to control their own destiny (and the destiny of their slaves), apart from federal regulation or domination. Before the Civil War and for generations thereafter, white southerners typically interpreted almost all forms of federal intervention as an encroachment on their liberty.[2]

Similar resentments have shaped the history of the West. Most of what Americans think of as the West was almost entirely unchallenged Indian Territory until at least the 1820s. By 1835, enough southerners had migrated into Texas to foment a revolution with Mexico. From 1846 to 1848, the United States fought a war against Mexico in large part to resolve the Texas issue. By winning that war, the United States formally acquired most of what is now the American West and Southwest. A year after the Mexican–American War ended, gold was discovered in California. Waves of fortune-seeking Americans, including many from the South, did whatever they could to cross the country in search of riches. Most of them did not get rich panning for gold, but many of them did establish lives as farmers, small business owners, or commercial investors. Attracted to the hope of unregulated financial opportunity, railroad magnates, entrepreneurs, civic boosters, and outlaws all moved west during the nineteenth century. This process continued well after the historian Frederick Jackson Turner famously declared the frontier "closed" in 1893.[3]

These migrants no doubt shaped much of the region's popular image and character. But the federal government was often just as influential. The federal government did not simply advertise the West as a place where dreams for independence and security

---

[2] For more on southern identity and heritage before, during, and after the Civil War, see among many others, Blight, *Race and Reunion*; Cobb, *Away Down South*; Ford, *Origins of Southern Radicalism*; Freehling, *The Road to Disunion*; Hahn, *A Nation Under our Feet*; Holt, *The Political Crisis of the 1850s*; Link, *Atlanta, Cradle of the New South*; McCardell, *The Idea of a Southern Nation*; Walther, *The Fire-Eaters*; Wyatt-Brown, *Southern Honor*.

[3] Frederick Jackson Turner, "The Significance of the Frontier in American History," *Annual Report of the American Historical Association*, 1893.

came true; it also subsidized those dreams through massive programs such as the Homestead Act of 1862, which gave away land to millions of Americans willing to uproot their families and move west. As a result, the West came to reflect a place of uneasy tensions. On the one hand, it was a place for pursuing dreams of independence. On the other, it was a place that depended deeply on the federal government. To at least some degree, therefore, the Sunbelt that emerged in the decades after World War II was shaped by a worldview rooted in both historical contradiction and regional convergence. That worldview emphasized settlers' pioneering spirit and rugged individualism, as well as the virtues of local authority. At the same time, this worldview commonly decried the same federal "intrusions" that ironically subsidized the region's economy.

Within this framework, white southerners could claim a history in which they had fought to preserve racial hierarchies under the auspices of states' rights and local control, whereas white westerners could point to their struggle to break free of the East Coast's colonial subjugation of their region. For both white southerners and white westerners, life came to be understood as a story of hardship, survival, and resistance to centralized power. These shared struggles and worldviews shaped much of what eventually gave the postwar Sunbelt its sense of political heritage and identity.[4]

Seen in this way, the convergence of South and West suggests that conservatism has long been a powerful, if not dominant, force

---

[4] The literature on nineteenth-century westward expansion and the Civil War is also vast. The field of Western history owes a debt of thanks to Frederick Jackson Turner, whose "Frontier Thesis" has created more than a century's worth of debate. The Frontier – or "Turner" Thesis – has been discussed at length in any number of texts on the American West, the list of which would be too long to recount. For examples, see Nash, *Creating the West*; and Hausladen, *Western Places, American Myths*. For specific examples of the West and its political culture, see among others, Hine and Faragher, *The American West*; Limerick, *The Legacy of Conquest*; Michael A. Morrison, *Slavery and the American West: The Eclipse of Manifest Destiny and the Coming of the Civil War* (Chapel Hill: University of North Carolina Press, 1997); and White, *"It's Your Misfortune and None of My Own."*

in the social, cultural, economic, and political history of what eventually became the Sunbelt. However, as eventually became true in the postwar Sunbelt, this early convergence of conservative political cultures rarely went unchallenged. One of the best examples of this early contestation was a political movement known as "Populism." Essentially the mobilization of struggling, angry farmers along class lines rather than racial or ideological ones, Populism reflected a widespread and trans-regional dissatisfaction with the industrializing American economy of the late nineteenth century. Discouraged by economic recessions, cyclical debt, and a lost sense of autonomy, southern and western farmers – as well as some industrial workers and small business owners in other parts of the country – spent more than twenty years during the late 1870s, 1880s, and early 1890s agitating in favor of more, not less, government intervention with the economy. Populism's class-based, biracial potential was particularly threatening to the southern Democratic Party. In response, by the mid-1890s, southern Democrats essentially adopted the new Populist Party's agenda, simultaneously fanning the flames of racial violence in order to re-divide the working class along racial lines.[5]

The strategy worked and the Populist movement quickly died without achieving a lasting or truly biracial coalition. But during its brief time in the political spotlight, this multi-factional movement amplified several of the characteristics that would come to define both the conservative and liberal traditions of the future Sunbelt. For instance, Populists called for federal ownership of railroads, thought inflation was good because it helped alleviate private debt, and wanted farmers to pool their resources and work cooperatively. Future Sunbelt conservatives would not have

---

[5] For more on the populist movement of the late nineteenth century, see Stephen Kantrowitz, *Ben Tillman & The Reconstruction of White Supremacy* (Chapel Hill: University of North Carolina Press, 2000); Michael Kazin, *A Godly Hero: The Life of William Jennings Bryan* (New York: Alfred A. Knopf, 2006); and Robert C. McMath Jr., *American Populism: A Social History, 1877–1898* (New York: Hill & Wang, 1993); Charles Postel, *The Populist Vision* (New York: Oxford University Press, 2007). For more on the character of populist politics throughout American history, see Michael Kazin, *The Populist Persuasion: An American History* (New York: Basic Books, 1995).

agreed with these policies. But Populists were also angry, agitated at the grass roots, did not trust the eastern establishment, and created an image that looked and sounded very much like the same "forgotten Americans" and "Silent Majority" that would define conservative rhetoric against big government during the last half of the twentieth century. Well into the twenty-first century, the term "populist" has endured as a badge of honor for both conservative and liberal politicians seeking to rally grassroots support against various forms of "establishment" power, whether that power was defined as Wall Street or Capitol Hill.[6]

Populism was not the only form of political dissent to influence the future Sunbelt during the late nineteenth and early twentieth centuries. From roughly 1890 to 1920, progressivism – like Populism a generation before – flourished across the region precisely because it was concerned with the economic ills wrought by the rapid pace of industrialization. Yet, progressivism was more national in its appeal and lacked the emotional volatility characteristic of Populism. Its leadership was typically middle or upper-middle class and well educated. Whereas Populists were almost exclusively interested in economics and political action, progressives were also intimately concerned with moral and humanitarian reform. Prohibition, for instance, owed much of its popular support to progressives such as Morris Sheppard, a Democratic senator from Texas. The same is true of laws against the use of child labor and in support of woman suffrage. In several ways, the trajectory of modern liberalism in the twentieth century was profoundly shaped during these years of progressive reform, much of which emanated from political leaders across the future Sunbelt.[7]

---

[6] Ibid.; see also Nancy Beck Young, *Wright Patman: Populism, Liberalism, and the American Dream* (Dallas: Southern Methodist University Press, 2000).

[7] The seminal study of American progressivism remains Robert H. Wiebe, *The Search for Order, 1877–1920* (New York: Hill & Wang, 1967). See also Nell Irvin Painter, *Standing at Armageddon: The United States, 1877–1919* (New York: W.W. Norton & Co., 1987); and Michael McGerr, *A Fierce Discontent: The Rise and Fall of the Progressive Movement in America, 1870–1920* (New York: Oxford University Press, 2005). For more on the influence of progressivism in the South, see William A. Link, *The Paradox of Southern Progressivism,*

Neither Populists nor progressives, however, shaped the future Sunbelt as profoundly as did Franklin Roosevelt's New Deal. Beginning in 1933, the New Deal sought to remedy both the symptoms and causes of the Great Depression through measures designed to bring relief to the unemployed, recovery to sick and dying industries, and reform to the overall economic system. Roosevelt's interventionist platform for relief, recovery, and reform gave millions of Americans hope during a time of profound calamity. Far more than actual results, it was this hope – and the trust that accompanied it – that carried Roosevelt to landslide victories in an unprecedented four consecutive presidential elections between 1932 and 1944.[8]

Nowhere was Roosevelt more popular than in the South. In 1932, FDR carried 88 percent of the vote in Texas, 92 percent of the vote in Georgia, and 98 percent of the vote in South Carolina. His margin of victory was similarly enormous across the rest of the South, and smaller but still overwhelming in the West and Southwest. Results were similar in his three subsequent reelections. Roosevelt's popularity in the South and West owed much to the simple fact that he was a Democrat. This was especially true in the Deep South. With very few exceptions, states of the old

---

1880–1930 (Chapel Hill: University of North Carolina Press, 1992). For more on conservative reactions to progressivism in the South, see John J. Langdale III, *Superfluous Southerners: Cultural Conservatism and the South, 1920–1990* (Columbia: University of Missouri Press, 2012).

[8] For more on the New Deal and U.S. politics during the 1930s and 1940s generally, see Anthony Badger, *The New Deal: The Depression Years, 1933–1940* (New York: The Noonday Press, 1989); Alan Brinkley, *The End of Reform: New Deal Liberalism in Recession and War* (New York: Vintage Books, 1995); Lizabeth Cohen, *Making a New Deal: Industrial Workers in Chicago, 1919–1939* (New York: Cambridge University Press, 1990); David M. Kennedy, *Freedom From Fear: The American People in Depression and War, 1929–1945* (New York: Oxford University Press, 1999). See also Jason Scott Smith, *A Concise History of the New Deal* (New York: Cambridge University Press, 2014); and Nancy Beck Young, *Why We Fight: Congress and the Politics of World War II* (Lawrence: University Press of Kansas, 2013). There have been several effective biographies of Franklin D. Roosevelt, including H. W. Brands, *Traitor to His Class: The Privileged Life and Radical Presidency of Franklin Delano Roosevelt* (New York: Doubleday, 2008); and Jean Edward Smith, *FDR* (New York: Random House, 2007).

Confederacy simply did not vote for Republicans during these years. But partisan loyalty alone does not explain southerners' affinity for an aristocratic career politician from upstate New York. After all, the South's still-powerful conservative establishment largely resented New Deal regulations. Some conservatives even warned that FDR was using the New Deal to slowly ignite a socialist revolution. On the other hand, most other southerners enthusiastically rallied to the New Deal, including the vast majority of struggling farmers and out-of-work fathers who may not have liked the idea of "federal handouts" but liked the idea of starvation even less. It might sound startling to contemporary readers, but the main reason most southerners overwhelmingly supported Roosevelt was that he was willing to use the federal government to help them, not in spite of that fact.[9]

Roosevelt's New Deal influenced the long-term character of Sunbelt politics in several ways. In Texas and surrounding states, the New Deal brought relief to farmers and strategies for future agricultural growth to the parched and windy South Plains of the Dust Bowl.[10] Meanwhile, New Deal programs such as the Agricultural Adjustment Administration (AAA), the Civilian Conservation Corps (CCC), and the Tennessee Valley Authority (TVA) revolutionized the way people in the future Sunbelt related to one another, the land, and their government. In almost every case, this relationship was strengthened. Under Roosevelt, the federal government filled a void left by the temporary failure of the private sector to create jobs and provide stability. New Deal programs regulated crop production; controlled prices; fostered cooperation within naturally competitive industries; and put millions of Americans to work on public projects, building roads, dams, bridges, hiking trails, parks, and schools.[11]

Despite widespread support, such programs were still politically controversial. As the decade wore on, many conservatives across

---

[9] Ibid.
[10] Dochuk, *From Bible Belt to Sunbelt*, 3–26.
[11] For an excellent discussion of New Deal policies on agriculture during the 1930s, see Badger, *The New Deal*, 147–189; Nash, *The Federal Landscape*, 28.

the future Sunbelt denounced the New Deal as another unwelcome and dangerous intrusion of big government. Nevertheless, the funding and supervision provided by the federal government to these and related projects enabled the continued growth and development of the region. Ironically, the New Deal deepened the region's dependence on federal support at the same time that it magnified the political voices openly criticizing that dependence.[12]

As significant as the New Deal was, nothing deepened the future Sunbelt's dependence on the federal government more than World War II. During that war, the federal government reacquired land all across the South and West. It then constructed new military bases on those lands and stimulated once-dormant factories by offering contracts for the mass production of planes, tanks, guns, uniforms, and food rations. It also built new manufacturing plants and prompted the creation of new jobs for hundreds of thousands of Americans. War-related economic stimulus programs also catalyzed the construction of new homes, new highways, and new schools. During the 1930s, FDR identified the South as the nation's top economic problem. During World War II, FDR used the federal government to help transform both the South and the West into a modern, economically thriving Sunbelt.[13]

The impact of wartime intervention was deeply felt all across the future Sunbelt, nowhere more so than in California and Texas. During World War II, the federal government spent $60 billion in the West alone, nearly half of that going to aviation industries in California. Federal defense contracts brought more than a half million new jobs to Southern California, and by the end of the war, Los Angeles had joined Detroit as one of the nation's two mega-hubs for mass industrial manufacturing. Meanwhile, between 1941 and 1945, Texas became the largest military training ground in the world, boasting fifteen army bases and forty military air-fields. During those same years, Texas controlled 41 percent of

---

[12] Ibid.
[13] Nash, *The Federal Landscape,* 42–54; Schulman, *From Cotton Belt to Sunbelt,* 90–111; Randolph B. Campbell, *Gone to Texas: A History of the Lone Star State* (New York: Oxford University Press, 2003), 396–407.

the nation's synthetic rubber industry and boasted a substantial portion of the nation's growing aluminum industry. In 1941, the federal government spent $500 million in Texas on military hardware and supplies. The Lone Star State enjoyed the fruits of these new industries at the same time that it was growing wealthier because of oil, the price of which was skyrocketing thanks in part to wartime demand and federal investment in interstate pipelines. The construction of these pipelines strengthened economic ties among Texas, the federal government, and the already industrialized Northeast.[14]

From Populism and progressivism to the New Deal and World War II, some of the most enduring political developments to shape the future Sunbelt before 1945 were anchored in the politics of contestation, reform, and federal intervention. Federal growth, coupled with massive federal spending, construction, job creation, energy production, and widespread economic relief, deepened the relationship between Washington and the future Sunbelt. At the same time, federal intervention bred both new political loyalties – often thankful for the support – and political hostilities, wary of their region's deepening dependence. Together, these factors helped create the multifaceted Sunbelt of the postwar period.

METROPOLITANIZATION

As it had during the early 1940s, the Sunbelt's economy grew substantially as World War II gave way to a rapidly intensifying Cold War between 1945 and 1960. As the Sunbelt's economy grew, so did its population. Most of that growth was concentrated in young, but quickly developing metropolitan areas and adjacent suburbs. During the first fifteen years following the end of World War II, millions of Americans relocated to emerging Sunbelt metropolises, sometimes from other sections of the country, sometimes from rural areas within other Sunbelt states. Depending on how one defines the Sunbelt's boundaries, the region's population as a whole grew to well over 50 million by 1960. That reflects a

[14] Ibid.

growth rate of at least 100 percent or more in most parts of the region. Between 1945 and 1960, population totals across the United States soared, thanks in large part to the so-called baby boom. But in the Sunbelt, the population grew at a rate nearly three times as fast as that of the rest of the nation and did so primarily because of an influx of new residents relocating to the region in search of jobs.[15]

Nowhere was the Sunbelt's population boom more profoundly experienced than in Southern California's two most prominent cities, Los Angeles and San Diego. Between 1945 and 1960, the city of Los Angeles grew from approximately 1.5 million residents to nearly 2.5 million. During the same years, the population of the sprawling Los Angeles metropolitan area swelled from just more than 2.9 million to nearly 6.75 million. Even more remarkable and reflective of Los Angeles's position in the emerging Sunbelt was the housing status of that population. In 1960, 72 percent of Los Angeles metro area residents lived in a detached home, the highest such percentage among all metro areas in the nation, and about 50 percent more than in New York and other eastern cities. San Diego also grew rapidly during these years. Before World War II, that city's population was 203,341. By 1960, it reached more than 573,000, and its greater metropolitan area boasted a population of more than 1 million.[16]

Los Angeles and San Diego were the epicenters of statewide growth. In 1940, California's total population was just more

---

[15] For a general overview of Sunbelt growth from 1945 to 1980, see Bernard and Rice, *Sunbelt Cities*, 1–26. See also Nickerson and Dochuk, *Sunbelt Rising*, 1–28. For more on suburbanization in the United States generally, see Jackson, *Crabgrass Frontier*; and Kruse and Sugrue, *The New Suburban History*. See also David R. Goldfield, *Cotton Fields and Skyscrapers: Southern City and Region, 1607–1980* (Baton Rouge: Louisiana State University Press, 1982); and Jack Temple Kirby, *Rural Worlds Lost: The American South, 1920–1960* (Baton Rouge: Louisiana State University, 1986).

[16] Bernard and Rice, *Sunbelt Cities*, 8–9, 272; for more on Orange County, California, see Dochuk, *From Bible Belt to Sunbelt*; and McGirr, *Suburban Warriors*. See also Lawrence Culver, *The Frontier of Leisure: Southern California and the Shaping of Modern America* (New York: Oxford University Press, 2010).

than 6.9 million. By 1960, that figure had risen to just less than 16 million. The state's growing population also resulted in growing political influence. In the presidential election of 1940, California had 22 electoral votes. By 1960, it carried 32 electoral votes. By 1970, California was the largest state in the nation, and in 1980, it was worth a whopping 45 electoral votes.[17]

Texas also experienced remarkable population growth between 1945 and 1960. Before World War II, the state's population was less than 6.5 million. By 1960, that figure approached 10 million. Virtually all of this growth was concentrated in metropolitan areas, most notably in the cities of Houston and Dallas. In 1945, the broader Houston metropolitan area boasted a population of just more than a half million people. By 1960, that number had jumped to more than 1.2 million. During the same years, the Dallas–Fort Worth Metroplex saw its population increase from approximately 584,000 to just more than 1.6 million. San Antonio also grew. That city's population more than doubled between the end of World War II and 1960, increasing from 253,854 to 587,718, not including its wider metropolitan and suburban or exurban communities.[18]

Texas and California were not the only states in the emerging Sunbelt with cities boasting remarkable growth. In Arizona, the population of Phoenix ballooned from 65,414 in 1940 to 439,170 in 1960, an increase of more than 670 percent. Including suburbs and other surrounding communities, the actual population of the broader Phoenix metropolitan area in 1960 was more than 633,000. Tucson also grew quite large during these years, as did Albuquerque, New Mexico. But Sunbelt growth was not limited to the Southwest. In the Southeast, cities such as Atlanta, Tampa, Orlando, and Miami made the states of Georgia and Florida hotspots of Sunbelt expansion. From coast to coast, the rapidly emerging Sunbelt – or "southern rim" as Kirkpatrick Sale

[17] Ibid.
[18] Bernard and Rice, *Sunbelt Cities*, 8–9; Campbell, *Gone to Texas*, 402–410.

famously called it in 1975 – gained millions of new residents throughout the 1940s and 1950s.[19]

Why did these Sunbelt states and metropolitan areas grow so rapidly? One major reason for the Sunbelt's rapid growth during these decades was the infusion of federal dollars for national security or defense-related purposes. In January 1961, outgoing President Dwight Eisenhower popularized the term "military-industrial complex" to describe the amorphous partnership between the federal government and the private sector that had emerged out of the joint development of defense and national security industries during and after World War II. The federal government spent more than \$304 billion to wage and win World War II. It continued to spend billions on defense after the war ended. The Sunbelt received a disproportionate amount of that capital investment, thanks in large part to its sunshine, isolation, and vast stretches of undeveloped land. For these and other reasons, the federal government was attracted to what became the Sunbelt. Or, put differently, nowhere was the military-industrial complex that Eisenhower described in 1961 more dominant or influential than in the emerging postwar Sunbelt.[20]

Federal investment – both in terms of dollars and attention – was essential to the Sunbelt's early development. Before federal investment, most of the Sunbelt lacked an established industrial infrastructure. Ironically, this lack of development made it easier for the federal government to build new, technologically innovative facilities that could meet the demands of a rapidly changing and very dangerous world. In this sense, the Sunbelt's advantage over the already industrialized Northeast or Midwest was that it

---

[19] Bernard and Rice, *Sunbelt Cities*, 8–9; Sale, *Power Shift*. For more on Phoenix, see Elizabeth Tandy Shermer, *Sunbelt Capitalism: Phoenix and the Transformation of American Politics* (Philadelphia: University of Pennsylvania Press, 2013).

[20] One of the better recent discussions on the impact of defense spending on Sunbelt economic growth is found in Kari Frederickson, *Cold War Dixie: Militarization and Modernization in the American South* (Athens: University of Georgia Press, 2013). For more on federal spending specifically during World War II, see Gerald D. Nash, *World War II & the West: Reshaping the Economy* (Lincoln: University of Nebraska Press, 1990); and Lotchin, *Fortress California*.

existed as a sort of blank slate, an empty canvas upon which new ideas could more easily be constructed into reality. States such as Texas, New Mexico, Arizona, Nevada, and California were also full of undeveloped desert territory, which allowed federal contractors the freedom to build defense facilities and military bases that were naturally protected by an almost impenetrable isolation. This isolation became particularly useful for aboveground nuclear weapons testing during the 1950s.[21]

Weather was also important. Sunbelt states were (and remain) typically warmer than states in the upper Midwest or the Northeast, making it easier for military bases to productively function year-round. Warm weather was also an advantage in the recruitment of new workers. It also did not hurt the Sunbelt's prospects for development that commercial and civic boosters in cities all across the region aggressively, and often successfully, lobbied Washington for a variety of defense contracts. Within this military-industrial complex, economic power – and eventually political power – was anchored in the dynamic and multifaceted cooperative among private businesses, municipal boosters, and federal contractors.[22]

Other than simply bringing new facilities, new jobs, and new money into the region, what did this military-industrial complex actually look like, and how did it physically reshape the Sunbelt? The latter question cannot be answered without acknowledging an important shift in federal policy. After World War II, and for the first time in American history, the federal government did not initiate a massive demobilization of its armed forces at the conclusion of a major war. At the end of 1945, instead of demobilizing its defenses and re-embracing isolationism, the United States prepared for the eventuality that it could soon be forced into a new and even more dangerous global conflict, this time with the Soviet Union, its former ally. While the federal government

---

[21] Nash, *The Federal Landscape*, 77–83. For more on Southern California specifically, see again, Culver, *The Frontier of Leisure*; and Lotchin, *Fortress California*. For more on the role of corporations and economic individualism on the rise of Sunbelt conservatism, see Phillips-Fein, *Invisible Hands*; and Tandy Shermer, *Sunbelt Capitalism*.

[22] Ibid.

prepared for that possibility by continuing to invest billions of dollars into national security and defense industries across the Sunbelt, it also began to more aggressively encourage private businesses to join that fight.[23]

The Defense Plant Corporation, which had been responsible for the construction and management of most military facilities during the war, was a chief means through which the federal government encouraged that participation. After World War II, the Defense Plant Corporation sold hundreds of federal installations to private businesses, many of them in the Sunbelt. They typically sold those installations at prices far less than market value, thereby attracting thousands of private-sector buyers. Meanwhile, as private capital poured into Sunbelt metropolises, newly created (and well-paying) defense jobs attracted hundreds of thousands of new residents, almost all of whom quickly found that right-to-work laws – which undermined organized labor's power by limiting unions' ability to compel membership – gave private companies another reason to consider the Sunbelt an attractive place to do business. Private companies that either relocated their headquarters to or established branches in the predominantly union-free Sunbelt quickly found that labor was less expensive and more easily controlled than was often the case in older, more industrialized states. Even as late as the 1970s, the percentage of unionized workers in the Sunbelt was less than half that of the national average. The lack of strong labor unions contributed to the Sunbelt's economic vibrancy, at least from management's perspective, and from the perspective of most capital investors, whose interest in regional development had been initially aroused because of federal initiatives.[24]

Federal policies in support of Sunbelt expansion were reinforced when, during the summer of 1950, a war involving the United States broke out on the Korean Peninsula. The Korean War made the ever-expanding military-industrial complex even more central

[23] Ibid.
[24] Ibid.

to the emerging Sunbelt.[25] Not surprisingly, the impact of this engagement was more heavily felt in California than in any other Sunbelt state. Between 1950 and 1963, more than 661,000 new jobs were developed in manufacturing industries in Southern California alone. Nearly 300,000 of those jobs were in the electronics and aerospace industries. Half of those jobs were directly related to national security and defense. By 1953, California was drawing more money from military contracts than any other state in the nation.[26] Companies such as Rockwell International, Northrop, Hughes Aircraft, Autonetics, Ford Aeronutronics, American Electronics, and Lockheed occupied just a handful of the facilities in one section of Los Angeles that became known as Aerospace Valley, an area that historian Gerald D. Nash has noted "contained the highest concentration of high-tech weapons manufacturers in the world."[27] Between 1945 and 1960, the federal government invested $50 billion in Los Angeles, and 17 percent of California's total revenue was earned through defense contracts. The military-industrial complex shaped San Diego during these years as well. By 1960, 75 percent of industrial employees in San Diego worked in defense-contracted aerospace. Meanwhile, more than a third of San Diego's residents depended at least in part, if not entirely, on naval or other federal installations for their income. Thousands of others owned or worked for businesses that depended directly on the patronage of federal employees in and around San Diego.[28]

California's growth during the early postwar years was not limited to its southern extremities. As Los Angeles grew in large part because of aerospace and weapons manufacturing, and San Diego benefited from the pervasive presence of the U.S. Navy, the area that became known as Silicon Valley developed because of high-tech industries that revolutionized communities such as San Jose, Palo Alto, Santa Clara, and other areas south of the San

[25] Bernard and Rice, *Sunbelt Cities*, 16.
[26] McGirr, *Suburban Warriors*, 26.
[27] Nash, *The Federal Landscape*, 87. See also McGirr, *Suburban Warriors*, 27.
[28] Dochuk, *From Bible Belt to Sunbelt*, 170–171; Nash, *The Federal Landscape*, 86.

34 *Cunningham*

Francisco Bay Area. During the 1950s, local institutions including Stanford University increasingly partnered with the federal government to research and develop the technology that would eventually be incorporated into new businesses and state-of-the-art industries. Those developments fueled innovations in computers, electronics, chemicals, pharmaceuticals, weapons, and aviation. For instance, the Stanford Industrial Park, built in 1951, housed such corporations as Hewlett Packard. Silicon Valley would continue to lead America's high-tech research and development for the rest of the twentieth century.[29]

California was certainly not the only Sunbelt state to grow in national prominence because of the emerging military-industrial complex or its related commercial growth. Between 1945 and 1960, military bases, research facilities, and defense industries cast ever-lengthening shadows over the Sunbelt – West Coast, East Coast, and central interior alike. At the same time, however, other industries – some directly related to Cold War defense and some not – also developed across the Sunbelt. These industries further diversified and modernized the region's economy, strengthening its prospects for continued demographic and political growth.

In Texas, for instance, the primary source of long-term economic prosperity (and political power) was oil. Federal demand generated by World War II and later by the Cold War, coupled with the demands of a rapidly modernizing national economy, resulted in soaring profits for dozens of Texas-based oil companies. Between 1945 and 1960, domestic oil production in Texas and its surrounding states increased by 50 percent, whereas crude prices doubled. Natural gas production in Texas also soared to all-time highs. Nowhere was the increased value of oil and gas more powerfully enjoyed than in Houston, which emerged during the decades following World War II as the nation's premier energy producer. By 1980, Houston-based oil companies such as Shell, Texaco, and Gulf were actively trading with partners all over

[29] Gerald D. Nash, *A Brief History of the American West Since 1945* (Orlando, FL: Harcourt Publishers, 2001), 95–107.

the world, especially Saudi Arabia, while the city became one of the largest manufacturing hubs in the United States. By 1980, Houston was responsible for roughly half of all petrochemical manufacturing in the United States, and 25 percent of its refining capacity. Not surprisingly, Houston also led the nation in new housing starts that year. Each of these trends first appeared en masse and quickly accelerated during the first two decades following the end of World War II.[30]

In addition to the thriving oil and gas industries and the related growth in petrochemicals, Texas's postwar economy also grew because of developments in aviation, aluminum, steel, iron, and textiles. The most significant industrial operation in the Dallas–Ft. Worth (DFW) Metroplex was the Consolidated Vultee Aircraft Corporation in Fort Worth. From World War II through 1953, Fort Worth's Convair plant manufactured more than 3,000 airplanes and boasted the largest aviation workforce in the country.[31] Convair (later General Dynamics) and Bell Helicopter supported dozens of defense contracts that enabled them to employ thousands in Fort Worth. Meanwhile, auto manufacturers including General Motors and Ford did the same thing in Dallas. The emergence of Texas Instruments in 1951 also made Dallas a player in the developing world of high tech, though Austin – thanks to the presence of companies such as IBM, Dell, Motorola, and Intel – would eventually be the state's leader in that industry, partnering with, and sometimes competing with, California's Silicon Valley. The 1950s also saw Dallas become a global leader in fashion, thanks in part to the enterprising efforts of the Neiman Marcus Group.[32]

Texas colleges and universities also grew rapidly during the postwar years, as did institutions all across the country and

---

[30] Bernard and Rice, *Sunbelt Cities*, 197, 201; Campbell, *Gone to Texas*, 402–410, 444–447. For more on Texas and the oil industry, see, for example, Kevin Phillips, *American Theocracy: The Peril and Politics of Radical Religion, Oil, and Borrowed Money in the 21st Century* (New York: Viking, 2006); and Bryan Burrough, *The Big Rich: The Rise and Fall of the Greatest Texas Oil Fortunes* (New York: The Penguin Press, 2009).

[31] Bernard and Rice, *Sunbelt Cities*, 165.

[32] Campbell, *Gone to Texas*, 402–410; Nash, *A Brief History of the American West Since 1945*, 105.

region. Much of this growth can be credited to the Servicemen's Readjustment Act of 1944, or the G.I. Bill as it is more commonly known. The G.I. Bill paid for hundreds of thousands of veterans to go to college each year and also provided those same veterans with federally subsidized, low-interest home mortgages. Rising college enrollments and a thriving housing market contributed to the creation of highly skilled, white-collar jobs and a thriving, home-owning, and young suburban middle class. The federal government also awarded major research grants to math, science, and engineering departments at universities all across the Sunbelt. In Texas, such grants were awarded to Rice University in Houston and the University of Texas at Austin, making those institutions among the nation's best. From 1945 to 1960, the federal government provided unprecedented millions in math and science grants to private and public universities all across the Sunbelt, thereby tightening the relationship between the research and development needs of the federal government and the nation's institutions of higher education.[33]

These trends were common all across the Sunbelt. In Phoenix, air force bases and corporations such as Motorola, General Electric, Sperry Rand, Honeywell, and National Semiconductor, together with advances in air conditioning, revitalized the city's and state's retail and residential construction industries. Nearly 300 manufacturing businesses opened in the Phoenix area between 1948 and 1960, and the number of Phoenix-area residents employed in some form of manufacturing tripled. Between 1940 and 1963, aggregate income from manufacturing enterprises in Phoenix increased from less than $5 million to more than $435 million. Phoenix also benefited from a thriving tourism and leisure industry, encouraged by its sunny and dry climate. Luxurious resort hotels and conference centers made Phoenix a hub for business travelers and vacationers throughout the early postwar years. And by 1960, 50 percent of all new houses in

[33] Nash, *A Brief History of the American West Since 1945*, 93–96.

Arizona had air conditioning, a trend made possible in part by federal tax breaks designed to incentivize the use of cold air.[34] More than 1,800 miles to the east, Atlanta saw its economy prosper thanks to wartime and postwar defense industries, most notably aviation contracts awarded to the Bell Aircraft Corporation and Lockheed. General Motors operated a productive plant in Atlanta, and the city was also home to Delta Airlines and Coca-Cola, which distributed an estimated 5 billion drinks to military personnel stationed in all parts of the globe during World War II. Rapid growth between 1945 and 1960 set the stage for Atlanta's emergence during the 1960s as the South's first truly national city. In 1940, 442,294 people lived in the greater Atlanta metro area. By 1960, that number had increased to more than 1 million, with most of the growth coming in surrounding suburbs.[35]

Economic growth also came to the deserts of the Sunbelt Southwest. In 1942, the federal government authorized construction of the Pantex Ordnance Plant just east of Amarillo, Texas. First designed as an assembly plant for conventional munitions, Pantex was transformed during the 1950s into the nation's primary center for the assembly and disassembly of nuclear weapons. The mere existence of nuclear weapons was also tied to federal projects based in the Sunbelt Southwest. Uranium mining brought thousands of jobs and millions of dollars to New Mexico, which also received a $2 billion federal investment for its scientific laboratory in Los Alamos – site of the top-secret and globally transformative Manhattan Project – not to mention the millions that poured into Sandia Laboratories in Albuquerque. By the mid-1950s, New Mexico's state capital was – for the first time in its history – economically dependent on something other than the decaying Santa Fe Railroad. The military-industrial complex,

---

[34] Nash, *The Federal Landscape*, 58–62; Elizabeth Tandy Shermer, "Sunbelt Boosterism: Industrial Recruitment, Economic Development, and Growth Politics in the Developing Sunbelt," in Nickerson and Dochuk, eds., *Sunbelt Rising*, 31–57, 310–311. For more on Phoenix, see also Robert Alan Goldberg, *Barry Goldwater* (New Haven: Yale University Press, 1995).

[35] Bernard and Rice, *Sunbelt Cities*, 32. For more on Atlanta, see Kruse, *White Flight*.

along with the city's growing status as a regional medical and intellectual hub, shaped Albuquerque's economic and population boom during the postwar years.[36] Such trends were similarly evident in Las Vegas, where nearby nuclear weapons testing brought jobs and disposable income, as well as potential fallout. During the 1950s, Las Vegas also enjoyed a golden age of popular growth and attention as one of the premier entertainment capitals of the world. It is worth noting that like most other communities in the arid Southwest, a populated Las Vegas could not have existed without major hydroelectric dams, most of which were federally subsidized and/or managed.[37]

Florida did not have to worry about water in the same way that the arid Southwest did. But like Phoenix and Las Vegas, cities in the Sunshine State also grew quickly during the 1950s, and they did so in large part because of the state's remarkable popularity as an entertainment and tourist destination. In addition to its beaches and beautiful weather, Florida's growth was fueled by a host of modernizing forces, including air conditioning and residential construction, higher education, finance, retail, real estate, and naval and air force bases. For instance, during World War II, the U.S. Army stationed 25,000 men at Tampa's MacDill Field and continued to use the base actively in the decade that followed. Local Tampa shipyards also employed thousands during and after the war, and the federal government invested millions in highway construction, urban renewal, and higher education, even subsidizing the construction of the University of South Florida in 1956.[38] Once defined by its uninhabitable swamps and sprawling playgrounds for the rich, Florida saw its population nearly triple between 1945 and 1960. Not surprisingly, new Floridians living in developing metropolises also wanted new homes. And as was the case in every other state of the emerging

---

[36] Bernard and Rice, *Sunbelt Cities*, 255–256.
[37] Nash, *A Brief History of the American West Since 1945*, 23–25, 111–113. For more on the economic development of Las Vegas, see also Rothman, *Devil's Bargains*, 287–312; and Joseph E. Stevens, *Hoover Dam: An American Adventure* (Norman: University of Oklahoma Press, 1988).
[38] Bernard and Rice, *Sunbelt Cities*, 140–141.

Sunbelt, new homes were made possible in large part because of low-interest mortgages subsidized by the Federal Housing Authority or the G.I. Bill.[39]

Meanwhile, the state government of North Carolina took an exceptionally proactive approach to economic modernization – probably more proactive than that in many other states, even by Sunbelt standards – when it began offering strategic incentives to attract some of the nation's most innovative and technologically advanced new businesses and research firms. In 1959, those efforts resulted in the establishment of the Research Triangle Park. Thanks both to state-enabled corporate investment and lucrative federal contracts, the Research Triangle Park became the East Coast's answer to Silicon Valley. The park was the tangible heart of the cooperative partnership that emerged among the University of North Carolina at Chapel Hill, Duke University in Durham, and North Carolina State in Raleigh, a model that research universities elsewhere in the Sunbelt quickly tried to replicate. Whereas most of North Carolina's industry before 1945 had depended on tobacco farming and blue-collar labor, postwar economic changes exemplified in the Research Triangle infused thousands of highly educated and technically skilled workers into the state's demographic profile, and concurrently fueled housing construction, education, and metropolitan commerce.[40]

Sunbelt growth received yet another boost in 1956 when Congress passed the Federal Highway Act. A $32 billion public works project – the largest such project in American history – the Federal Highway Act used taxpayer dollars to construct thousands of miles of multilane highways all across the region and country. In addition to providing thousands of jobs, highway construction made private automobiles the dominant means of transportation for an expanding middle class that came to own more homes during the 1950s than at any previous time in American history.

---

[39] Ibid., 138–159.
[40] For more on economics and politics in North Carolina, see Link, *Righteous Warrior*. See also Bartley, *The New South, 1945–1980*, 215–216, 443, 447–448; and William A. Link, *North Carolina: Change and Tradition in a Southern State* (Wheeling, IL: Harlan Davidson, 2009).

Again, the best example of this process was in Los Angeles. In 1940, the city's Pasadena Freeway opened as the first such freeway in the American West. By 1960, 250 miles of freeway crisscrossed through Los Angeles County. By 1970, that figure reached 500. These highways promoted suburban development by increasing the area that was accessible to downtown within a half-hour drive. In 1953, 261 square miles were within this range in Los Angeles; by 1962, freeways expanded that area to more than 700 square miles. Suburban growth was also evident in Irving, a suburb of Dallas. In 1950, the population of Irving was just under 3,000. Ten years later, thanks to the convenience of federally subsidized highways, low-interest home mortgages, and a thriving economy, that population figure reached 45,000. In Los Angeles, Dallas, and other parts of the Sunbelt, federal highway subsidies reinforced the middle class's independent mobility, de-incentivized support for mass transit, ghettoized many inner-city communities, and enabled racially motivated white flight across the Sunbelt – all factors that contributed to the region's long-term political culture.[41]

In sum, the metropolitanization of the Sunbelt between 1945 and 1960 was a critical precondition for the region's later emergence as a national political force. In terms of economic modernization, population growth, and industrial development, the years following the end of World War II were very kind to the Sunbelt. Growing Sunbelt metropolises offered thousands of high-paying jobs. Those jobs attracted a flood of new residents, many of whom came to the Sunbelt with preexisting conservative convictions that only deepened within the context of an expanding military-industrial complex. As the military-industrial complex expanded, the Sunbelt flourished. As the Sunbelt flourished, investors grew increasingly committed to preserving a business-friendly atmosphere. Preserving a business-friendly atmosphere, many argued, depended on minimizing government regulations while using

---

[41] William H. Chafe, *The Unfinished Journey: America Since World War II* (New York: Oxford University Press, 2003), 112; Bernard and Rice, *Sunbelt Cities*, 272–273. See also Lassiter, *The Silent Majority*; and James T. Patterson, *Grand Expectations: The United States, 1945–1974* (New York: Oxford University Press, 1996), 10–38, 61–81.

government to promote business growth. As the region began to look increasingly developed and economically secure, many of the Sunbelt's more conservative boosters began to interpret federal intervention not as a helpful agent for facilitating growth, but as a bureaucratic obstacle to overcome and defeat.[42]

But economic growth and metropolitanization within an expanding military-industrial complex is only part of the Sunbelt's postwar story. These years were also characterized by a political climate that was shaped by the pervasive specter of anticommunism.

ANTICOMMUNISM

Historians continue to debate the origins of the Cold War that intensified between the United States and the Soviet Union during and immediately after World War II. But it is beyond dispute that the geopolitical tensions defining that conflict dramatically shaped U.S. policies – both foreign and domestic – during the decade and a half that followed the end of the war.[43]

For most Americans, the Cold War's stakes seemed crucial to their very existence – a battle defined by the struggle between capitalism and socialism, democracy and communism, freedom and tyranny. Such perspectives were not unwarranted. The invention and proliferation of nuclear weapons added a dangerous ingredient to the Cold War's already combustible brew. During the early 1940s, scientists working in the New Mexico desert developed the world's first atomic bomb. In August 1945, the United States became the first nation on earth to use such a weapon against another country – Japan. The United States did not share its new weapons technology with the Soviet Union,

[42] Shermer, "Sunbelt Boosterism," 33, 57.
[43] For more on the Cold War and, specifically, U.S. foreign policy during the Cold War, see John Lewis Gaddis, *The United States and the Origins of the Cold War, 1941–1947* (New York: Columbia University Press, 1972); Justin Hart, *Empire of Ideas: The Origins of Public Diplomacy and the Transformation of U.S. Foreign Policy* (New York: Oxford University Press, 2013); Michael H. Hunt, *Ideology and U.S. Foreign Policy* (New Haven: Yale University Press, 1988); and Patterson, *Grand Expectations*, 105–136.

despite allying with the communist superpower during World War II. After the war, the United States made the protection of its nuclear secrets a top priority. Keeping this information secret proved extremely difficult. During the late 1940s, espionage cases commanded front-page headlines all across the country and the world. Paranoia was pervasive, fear palpable. Such anxieties were not entirely unwarranted. In 1949, thanks in part to stolen intelligence, the Soviet Union successfully tested its own atomic bomb. In 1952, the United States successfully tested the hydrogen bomb – exponentially more potent than the atomic bomb. In 1953, the Soviet Union matched that feat and successfully tested its own hydrogen bomb. In addition, a long civil war in China ended in a communist victory, American soldiers found themselves fighting against communist-backed North Korea's attempted takeover of South Korea, and U.S. foreign policy makers settled on a strategy of containment, committing the nation to resisting communist expansion anywhere in the world. Between 1945 and 1960, Americans lived with the nagging possibility that, at any moment, their country could be thrust into a global conflict, the outcome of which would determine whether they lived in freedom or in slavery – or lived at all.[44]

Accordingly, the Cold War dominated American foreign policy making between 1945 and 1960. It also dominated the nation's social, cultural, economic, and political life. Everything from sex to spirituality, Hollywood to higher education, civil rights to suburbia, and all things in between were affected in some way by the national preoccupation with communism and the connected specter of nuclear annihilation. For instance, historians such as Elaine Tyler May have shown how white, middle-class families managed their Cold War fears by seeking security and stability through the reinforcement of traditional gender roles, marriage, and child rearing, while at the same time retreating to the isolated comforts of modern suburbia. Scholars such as Jason Stevens have further illustrated the ways in which spirituality and, specifically, evangelical Christianity were infused into a cultural

[44] Ibid.

and political discourse contextualized by Cold War anxieties. And countless studies have examined Cold War subtexts in various other forms apparent in popular culture, ranging from Hollywood westerns, science fiction thrillers, and prime-time television to tourism, themed amusement parks, and – perhaps most often – the persistence of racial and ethnic intolerances. Simply put, the Cold War shaped every aspect of American life.[45]

Each of these trends was fully evident in the postwar Sunbelt. When coupled with the Sunbelt's growing population and economic power – and, especially, its deep connections to the military and national defense – it is not surprising, therefore, that several of the country's foremost anticommunist conservatives emerged from this region. Among these was Strom Thurmond of South Carolina. Thurmond became a household name in 1948 when he ran for president under the banner of the States' Rights Democratic Party, a third party most commonly understood as a vehicle for the perpetuation of Jim Crow segregation. Thurmond's party was specifically organized in reactionary opposition to civil rights reforms initiated by President Harry Truman between 1946 and 1948. As the nation's most prominent "Dixiecrat," Thurmond was a symbol of the racially motivated backlash to civil rights that has almost always popularly characterized southern politics. Yet, the

---

[45] Elaine Tyler May, *Homeward Bound, American Families in the Cold War Era* (New York: Basic Books, 1988); Jason W. Stevens, *God-Fearing and Free: A Spiritual History of America's Cold War* (Cambridge, MA: Harvard University Press, 2010). For more on social and cultural ramifications of the Cold War, see, for example, Stephen J. Whitfield, *The Culture of the Cold War* (Baltimore: The Johns Hopkins University Press, 1991). For more on the impact of anticommunism at the state level, see M. J. Heale, *McCarthy's Americans: Red Scare Politics in State and Nation, 1935–1965* (Athens: University of Georgia Press, 1998). For more on the relationship between anticommunism and civil rights, see Jeff Woods, *Black Struggle, Red Scare: Segregation and Anti-Communism in the South, 1948–1968* (Baton Rouge: Louisiana State University Press, 2004). For more on postwar anticommunism broadly, see John Earl Haynes and Harvey Klehr, *Early Cold War Spies: The Espionage Trials That Shaped American Politics* (New York: Cambridge University Press, 2006); Richard Gid Powers, *Not Without Honor: The History of American Anticommunism* (New Haven: Yale University Press, 1995); and Ellen Schrecker, *Many Are the Crimes: McCarthyism in America* (Princeton, NJ: Princeton University Press, 1998).

degree to which Thurmond framed his politics in anticommunist
terms, both in 1948 as well as throughout his long career in state
and national politics, has often been overshadowed and underappreciated. For Thurmond and many other postwar southern
conservatives, the struggle against racial equality was – at least
rhetorically (but often sincerely) – part of a larger struggle against
socialist egalitarianism and big government. For example, as a
presidential candidate in 1948, Thurmond supported Texas
oil companies in their fight against federal control of the oil- and
mineral-rich off-shore tidelands along the Gulf Coast. Routinely
couched in anticommunist or anti-government terms, the tidelands
controversy was a powerful issue in the Sunbelt – and one that
complicates the commonly exclusive racial connotations of the
phrase "states' rights." Later, as a U.S. senator during the late
1950s, Thurmond was typically less willing than most of his southern Democratic colleagues to compromise with liberals on issues
such as economic regulation, taxes, or deficit spending. Thurmond
was also quicker than most southern Democrats to embrace the
John Birch Society, the famously controversial anticommunist
organization founded by Robert Welch in 1958. In 1964, increasingly frustrated by what he understood to be conservative
Democrats' never-ending accommodation of the New Deal and
big government, Thurmond became one of the first and certainly
most prominent southern Democrats to abandon the party of the
old Confederacy to become a Republican. A proponent of limited
government, free enterprise, strong national defense, and virulent
anticommunism, Strom Thurmond was not merely a racist dema-
gogue of the Old South; by the mid-1960s, he was among the
youngest political voices for the emerging Republican Sunbelt.[46]

From the end of World War II to the early 1960s, Strom
Thurmond was unquestionably South Carolina's best-known
politician. He was certainly that state's most prominent example

[46] For more on Strom Thurmond, see Joseph Crespino, "Strom Thurmond's
Sunbelt: Rethinking Regional Politics and the Rise of the Right," in Nickerson
and Dochuk, *Sunbelt Rising*, 58–81. See also Joseph Crespino, *Strom
Thurmond's America* (New York: Hill & Wang, 2012).

of the evolving fusion of segregationism and anticommunism with the postwar Republican Party. In North Carolina, the best example of this fusion was Jesse Helms. Elected to the U.S. Senate in 1972, Helms was politically active throughout the 1950s as a campaign strategist for various regional conservatives running for office at local, state, and national levels. In 1950, for instance, Helms worked for Willis Smith's successful U.S. Senate campaign against the incumbent and far more progressive Frank Porter Graham. Smith's 1950 Senate campaign offers a classic example of conservative efforts to link racial progressivism with socialism and was also noteworthy for the degree to which fears of sexual contact between black men and white women continued to influence southern politics. During the late 1950s, Helms served on the Raleigh City Council, where he established himself as an emerging voice for modern conservatism. From there, Helms launched a career as a political pundit, offering nightly editorials on WRAL-TV in Raleigh. A pioneer in the realm of conservative broadcasting, Helms used his public platform to champion the quintessentially Sunbelt values of limited government, free enterprise, low taxes, and anticommunism. He brazenly supported Republican candidates throughout the 1960s before officially becoming one himself in 1970. Throughout the long postwar period, Helms reflected, in the words of William A. Link, the fusion of "segregationism with anti-Communism and anti-government ideology [that] matured into a full-scale critique of New Deal liberalism." Ever public relations conscious, Helms was another central figure in the South's gravitation toward the new conservative Right and, eventually, its move into the Republican Party.[47]

Anticommunist conservatism was not the exclusive product of politics in the South, however. Arizona's Barry Goldwater did just as much as Thurmond or Helms to advance the anticommunist mantra. But unlike Thurmond or Helms, Goldwater was a lifelong Republican. Goldwater began his long political career

[47] Link, *Righteous Warrior*, 63; see also 32–44. See also George Lewis, *The White South and the Red Menace: Segregationists, Anticommunism, and Massive Resistance, 1945–1965* (Gainesville: University Press of Florida, 2004).

during the Red Scare of the late 1940s and early 1950s, although his political consciousness first blossomed during the Great Depression of the 1930s. During FDR's first two terms as president, Goldwater opposed the New Deal and feared that federal expansion would undermine the preservation of individual liberties. In 1952, after serving briefly on the Phoenix City Council, Goldwater defeated Earnest McFarland to win a seat in the U.S. Senate. McFarland had been the U.S. Senate majority leader, and Goldwater's victory was a stunning upset.[48]

In the Senate, Goldwater emerged as one of the nation's most passionate defenders of free enterprise, the private sector, and muscular defense. Like so many other conservative Republicans, Goldwater also supported Wisconsin Senator Joseph McCarthy's unrestrained war against domestic communist subversion – a national campaign that enjoyed sympathy across much of the Sunbelt. But Goldwater was equally quick to attack what he and other conservatives called "modern Republicanism" – defined as the moderate accommodation of the New Deal that many conservatives feared had come to control the GOP through an elitist "eastern establishment." Along these lines, Goldwater became a leading critic of the Eisenhower administration during the late 1950s. He believed that Eisenhower too often compromised with liberals on issues related to bureaucratic growth, domestic spending, and budget deficits and had, in the process, weakened the Republican Party's ideological core.[49]

Goldwater was also a leading enemy of organized labor. An uncompromising proponent of free enterprise and the private sector, Goldwater used his position in the Senate to deepen ties with Phoenix-area civic and commercial boosters by attacking what he called "monopoly unionism." In 1957 and 1958, he led a high-profile investigation into the Teamsters Union, the United Auto Workers (UAW), and other organizations charged with

[48] Nickerson and Dochuk, *Sunbelt Rising*, 54–55. For more on Goldwater and the rise of modern conservatism in Arizona, see also Rick Perlstein, *Before the Storm: Barry Goldwater and the Unmaking of the American Consensus* (New York: Hill & Wang, 2001).
[49] Ibid.

widespread racketeering. Goldwater's attack on labor unions, and particularly his personal battle against UAW president Walter Reuther, propelled the Arizona Republican to a second term in the Senate. In 1960, Goldwater published the wildly popular *The Conscience of a Conservative*, a treatise that remained influential in conservative Republican circles for the rest of the century. It thrust Goldwater into the conservative spotlight and set the stage for what would be one of the most important presidential campaigns in American history.[50]

Richard Nixon's career also began in the Sunbelt West, Southern California to be precise. Like Goldwater, Nixon made a name for himself as a champion of free enterprise and virulent anticommunism. After serving in the navy during World War II, Nixon won a seat in the U.S. House of Representatives in 1946, defeating the incumbent Democrat Jerry Voorhis whom he attacked as an extreme left-winger. Once in Washington, Nixon quickly landed a seat on the highly influential House Committee on Un-American Activities (HUAC). As a member of this committee, Nixon launched himself into the national spotlight by taking a leading role in HUAC's investigation of Alger Hiss. Hiss was a former New Dealer; an official in the U.S. State Department; and a primary organizer of the United Nations, which many conservatives feared was organized in 1945 as an international front for communist expansion and appeasement. In 1948, Whittaker Chambers, a writer and editor for *Time* magazine, testified before HUAC that he and Hiss had worked together as communist spies during the late 1930s. Hiss adamantly denied the charges. For the next two years, the Hiss investigation was a top national story, one of several sensationalistic spy thrillers to haunt the front pages of American newspapers during the height of the Red Scare. Eventually, Hiss was convicted on two counts of perjury and sentenced to five years in prison.[51]

[50] Ibid.
[51] The most creative and helpful overview of Nixon is found in David Greenberg, *Nixon's Shadow: The History of an Image* (New York: W.W. Norton & Co., 2003). For more on Nixon's early career, see also Stephen E. Ambrose, *Nixon:*

The high-profile nature of the Hiss case enabled Nixon's national political career. In 1950, Nixon won a seat in the U.S. Senate, defeating Helen Gahagan Douglas in one of the most controversial campaigns of the era. As he had done to Jerry Voorhis in 1946, Nixon won largely by aggressively red-baiting Douglas, at one point calling the longtime California progressive and staunch New Dealer a "pink lady." Nixon even went so far as to distribute, on pink paper, a rap sheet of Douglas's "suspicious" support for liberal social programs, which was couched as evidence of her sympathy for left-wingers and, it was implied, communists. It was during this campaign that Nixon's opponents first applied the disparaging nickname "Tricky Dick" – a label that would stick to Nixon throughout his career. Still, it is important to note that Nixon's victory over Douglas was not the sole result of red-baiting. The same is true of his win over Voorhis four years earlier. In both cases, Nixon's opponent ran a sloppy campaign, emphasized issues that most California voters no longer found salient, and lacked the state Democratic Party's unified support. Nevertheless, as a reflection of where Nixon's career was headed, it was his image as a hard-line anticommunist that proved most enduring.[52]

In so many ways, Nixon's early political career serves as a microcosm of the power of anticommunist conservatism in the emerging Sunbelt during the late 1940s and early 1950s. There

---

The Education of a Politician, 1913–1962 (New York: Simon & Schuster, 1987). For more on Nixon during the 1960s, see Stephen E. Ambrose, *Nixon: The Triumph of a Politician, 1962–1972* (New York: Simon & Schuster, 1989). For more on the downfall of Nixon's presidency, see Stephen E. Ambrose, *Nixon: Ruin and Recovery, 1973–1990* (New York: Simon & Schuster, 1991). For more on Nixon and the rise of modern conservatism, see Rick Perlstein, *Nixonland: The Rise of a President and the Fracturing of America* (New York: Scribner, 2009).

[52] Ibid.; some historians question the assertion that Nixon was, above all else, a populist anticommunist. The best source for more on this argument is Irwin Gellman, *The Contender: Richard Nixon: The Congress Years, 1946–1952* (New York: The Free Press, 1999). Gellman argues that Nixon's image as a red-baiter has been overstated, whereas the degree to which candidates such as Voorhis and Douglass were out of step with most California voters has been underemphasized.

is little question that it was this muscular anticommunism that Dwight Eisenhower's campaign found so attractive when it tapped Nixon for its presidential ticket in 1952. But Nixon was far more than a red-baiting anticommunist. In postwar Southern California, Nixon was also a pioneer in the realm of modern conservatism. He was among the first politicians of the postwar era to market conservatism as a populist philosophy. He spoke passionately about free enterprise; the private sector; and the middle class, which he often characterized as "the forgotten man." Later, the "forgotten man" would morph into the famed "Silent Majority," but the sentiment was the same. As a voice for suburban Orange County, Nixon helped make Southern California a hotbed for young conservatives and business leaders who hoped to roll back the regulatory reach of the New Deal. In this sense, Nixon – like Thurmond, Helms, and Goldwater – helped shape the Sunbelt's evolving conservative rhetoric, and ultimately the nation's broader political discourse.[53]

Though voices stretching from the ex-Confederate South to Arizona and Southern California all played an important role in the development of a unique Sunbelt political culture, the region's capital for anticommunist conservatism during the 1950s was Dallas, Texas. From there, oil barons Sid Richardson, Clint Murchison Sr., and H. L. Hunt and others poured millions of dollars into anticommunist political candidates, campaigns, broadcasting, and print media all over the city, state, and region. Based in Dallas, conservative radio personalities Gordon McClendon and Dan Smoot gained national followings by forcefully spewing ultraconservative venom, much of it trending toward the conspiratorial and paranoid. Smoot's fame was primarily the result of H. L. Hunt's investment in an organization known as Facts Forum, a tax-exempt foundation for the advancement of "public education" that, in reality, functioned as a right-wing propaganda machine. Smoot quickly became Facts Forum's most famous radio personality, reaching an estimated 20 million listeners at the height of his popularity in the mid-1950s. Like McClendon and

---

53 Ibid.

Oklahoma radio commentator Billy James Hargis, Smoot was
fiercely patriotic. He referred often to the wisdom of the Founding
Fathers; the sovereign and inerrant nature of the Constitution;
and the slippery slope of socialist liberalism in the United States,
typically conflated with the evils of progressive taxes, deficit
spending, and big government. Facts Forum enjoyed significant
reach during the mid-1950s and even boasted John Wayne as a
member of its national board of directors in 1956.[54]

In 1954, Dallas made another significant political statement
when Bruce Alger became the first Republican in history to win a
congressional seat from Texas's Fifth District. Alger subsequently
served five terms in the U.S. House of Representatives, becoming
one of the Sunbelt's most spirited anticommunist voices. He is
perhaps most famous for spearheading a protest in downtown
Dallas against Lyndon Johnson in 1960, during which he held a
sign that read "LBJ Sold Out to Yankee Socialists." Alger was also
friendly with Edwin Walker, a U.S. Army general most famous for
distributing John Birch Society propaganda to his troops and,
subsequently, being dismissed from the military by President
John F. Kennedy. Walker lived in Dallas during the early 1960s,
made an unsuccessful run for governor in 1962 despite a popular
following in his home city, and narrowly avoided death when Lee
Harvey Oswald failed in an assassination attempt against him in
April 1963.[55] Like Alger, Walker became a symbol of the most
extreme manifestations of anticommunist conservatism, eventually drawing repudiation from national conservatives including
William F. Buckley. But unlike Alger, Walker chose to battle

[54] Sean P. Cunningham, "The Paranoid Style and Its Limits: The Power,
Influence, and Failure of the Postwar Texas Far Right," in David Cullen and
Kyle Wilkison, eds., *The Texas Right: The Radical Roots of Lone Star
Conservatism* (College Station: Texas A&M University Press, 2013). For a
comprehensive study of the Red Scare in Houston, see Don E. Carleton, *Red
Scare!: Right-Wing Hysteria, Fifties Fanaticism, and Their Legacy in Texas*
(Austin: Texas Monthly Press, 1985).
[55] Law enforcement officials did not connect Oswald to the Walker incident until
after Oswald successfully assassinated President Kennedy and also murdered
J.D. Tippit, a Dallas police office, on November 22, 1963. Oswald died on
November 24, 1963 and was never prosecuted for any of these three crimes.

liberalism as a Democrat rather than as a Republican. In Texas as well as much of the rest of the Sunbelt, anticommunist conservatism remained bipartisan during the early postwar years.[56]

But it was Alger, not Walker, whose career representing one of the Sunbelt's most prominent cities better reflects many of the short-term failures – as well as long-term successes – of modern American conservatism. Alger successfully campaigned for public office in Dallas by conflating liberalism with socialism and by labeling "socialist" any number of progressive reforms, including public school desegregation and civil rights. He spoke passionately about being a "Jeffersonian" conservative, marketed himself as a patriotic defender of American liberty, fearfully warned against communist infiltration at home, and used television and radio to depict himself as a churchgoing family man. In fact, much of Alger's political career in Dallas was shaped by efforts to repackage populism through a conservative anticommunist worldview.[57]

Alger also helped organize one of the first truly effective Republican grassroots operations in the Sunbelt. Those efforts proved especially important for John Tower, who in 1961 took advantage of Alger's base in Dallas on his way to becoming the first Texas Republican elected to a seat in the U.S. Senate since Reconstruction. An anticommunist conservative who shared many of Alger's fundamental principles, Tower triumphed in 1961 because he ran as an antiestablishment outsider – as someone who could shake up the monotonous and unproductive grip on state politics held by establishment Democrats. Tower even made inroads among moderates and liberals in 1961, many of whom detested the hammerlock that conservative Democrats maintained on state politics. Though hardly supportive of Tower's conservatism, these liberals were attracted to Tower's message about promoting an authentic two-party culture in Texas.[58]

Alger, unlike Tower, never enjoyed significant bipartisan support, at least not at the statewide level. Over time, Alger's

[56] Cunningham, *Cowboy Conservatism*, 41–51.
[57] Ibid.
[58] Ibid.

strident anticommunism and reactionary anti-liberalism became
less appealing, even by Dallas standards. When Alger was finally
defeated in 1964, it was primarily the result of his being labeled
an extremist – a problem for many Sunbelt conservatives that
year. By the late 1950s and early 1960s, Red Scare anticommunism gave way to a resurgent liberal consensus, seen by most
as more stable and secure. This was true even in Dallas, where
many blamed the 1963 assassination of John F. Kennedy on
the city's ultraconservative and reactionary political climate,
despite overwhelming evidence to the contrary. Following the
assassination, Democrat and former Dallas mayor Earle Cabell
replaced Alger in the U.S. House, and progressive businessman
Erik Jonsson replaced Cabell as the city's mayor, investing time
and money to rebuild the city's public school system and social
services, as well as its national reputation.[59]

Whether it was in Strom Thurmond's South Carolina, Jesse
Helms's North Carolina, Barry Goldwater's Arizona, Richard
Nixon's California, or Bruce Alger's Dallas, anticommunist conservatism was a key force shaping the early postwar Sunbelt's
developing political culture. Anticommunism gave Sunbelt conservatives a context within which they could fuse multiple issues
into a single worldview, no matter how local or unique those
issues may have been. In the Deep South, where race, segregation,
and civil rights dominated the political culture, segregationists
used anticommunism as a means for validating their resistance
to egalitarian reform. Resisting racial equality under the banner
of anticommunism did not always effectively disguise southern
motives, but it did create an ideological bridge to the West, where
race was a less pronounced issue, and where anticommunist rhetoric was frequently used to frame discussions on defense, national
security, taxes, and free enterprise. In the West, conservatives who
may very well have been sympathetic to southern resistance to
civil rights were often able to avoid the polarizing issue of race by
focusing on other issues within the same rubric of anticommunism, local control, and states' rights. Over time, these and other

[59] Ibid.

rhetorical commonalities contributed to the development of a more cohesive brand of color-blind Sunbelt conservatism, impassioned and intensified by the military's strong and growing presence across the region.[60]

The Sunbelt's general hostility toward labor unions provides a relevant example of this emerging rhetorical cohesion. In both the West and the South, conservatives used anticommunism as a weapon in the fight against organized labor. For instance, in 1944, Florida passed the nation's first right-to-work law, making it possible for an employee to receive the benefits of union-negotiated contracts without having to join that union or pay union dues. Two years later, when the national leadership of the highly influential Congress of Industrial Organizations (CIO) launched Operation Dixie in 1946 – an effort to unionize traditional southern industries such as tobacco, milling, and lumber – it faced predictable hostility thanks largely to the perception (promoted by conservatives) that organized labor was a step down the road to socialism and the death of free enterprise. CIO efforts to organize southern workers between 1946 and 1953 failed for many reasons, but politically, the easiest way for conservatives to rally public opinion against Operation Dixie was to couch it in anticommunist terms. In 1947, Congress passed the highly controversial Taft-Hartley Act, which further undermined union power and enabled more states to pass right-to-work provisions similar to those in Florida. By 1960, most Sunbelt states had passed right-to-work laws, and conservatives across the region found that attacking "big labor" or "monopoly unionism" was an easy way to appear "populist" within an anti-communist context.[61]

---

[60] For more on divisions within the Republican Party, including some that erupted across Texas and the South during the late 1940s and early 1950s, see Bowen, *The Roots of Modern Conservatism.*

[61] Bartley, *The New South, 1945–1980,* 27, 39–42, 45–49; Nickerson and Dochuk, *Sunbelt Rising,* 40. For more on labor, the South, and Operation Dixie, see Thomas W. Devine, *Henry Wallace's 1948 Presidential Campaign and the Future of Postwar Liberalism* (Chapel Hill: University of North Carolina Press, 2013); and Robert Rodgers Korstad, *Civil Rights Unionism: Tobacco Workers and the Struggle for Democracy in the Mid-Twentieth-Century South* (Chapel Hill: University of North Carolina Press, 2003). For more on political rhetoric

The economic growth of the postwar Sunbelt shaped the way people in that region thought of themselves politically. Deep ties to the federal government, primarily through the emerging military-industrial complex, fueled economic modernization and population growth, while intensifying preexisting notions of patriotism and nationalist defense. These factors also intensified fears of being controlled by a big, central, and distant federal government. Sunbelt conservatives – both Republicans and Democrats – typically framed their positions on race, religion, economics, defense, and the size of government within the language of anticommunism. In many cases, they did so sincerely. For Republicans, the key was also to change public perceptions that their philosophy catered to wealthy elites, whereas liberalism favored the "common man." By identifying communism as a monolithic and totally evil enemy, anticommunist conservatives – especially Republicans – were able to more easily challenge the prevailing consensus on a wide range of issues. Each of these factors contributed to both the short- and long-term development of the Sunbelt's political culture.

But that transformation was not easy, nor did it take place overnight or go unchallenged. Despite the pervasive and often overwhelming influence of anticommunism on the development of the Sunbelt's postwar political culture, moderates and liberals in and out of the Democratic Party continued to fight for regional influence. Somewhat surprisingly, they were often successful. Despite the ever-present specter of the communist threat, American politics during the 1950s and early 1960s remained in the hands of establishment liberals and pragmatic moderates, most of whom remained loyal to FDR's Democratic Party and its still-powerful New Deal coalition. Essentially, this was a period of liberal consensus. Clearly, conservatives tried to challenge that consensus. But so did African Americans and other racial and ethnic minorities. As the Sunbelt evolved economically and politically during the

related to right-to-work laws in the Sunbelt, see Philip VanderMeer, *Desert Visions and the Making of Phoenix, 1860–2009* (Albuquerque: University of New Mexico Press, 2012). VanderMeer emphasizes a decline in organized labor across the Sunbelt that predates most battles over right-to-work laws.

1950s and early 1960s, it was simultaneously forced to deal with long-standing problems of racial discrimination, prejudice, and disenfranchisement.

The story of Sunbelt politics during the early postwar decades is, in part, a story about convergence, metropolitanization, and anticommunism. It is also a story about civil rights, political contestation, and multifaceted dissent.

2

Race, Rights, and the Liberal Consensus

Anticommunist conservatives were a developing force in American politics during the early postwar decades, especially in the Sunbelt, and especially within the Republican Party. But despite the visibility of that force, it was clear throughout most of the 1950s and early 1960s that the nation's politics remained under the predominant influence of establishment liberals, pragmatic moderates, and others operating within or externally sympathetic to the Democratic Party's New Deal coalition. Having revolutionized the relationship between the federal government and the national economy during the 1930s, New Deal liberals emerged from World War II triumphant, optimistic, and confident. They then fought the early years of the Cold War with a resolute commitment to containing communism abroad, while responsibly preparing the military for the possibility of war. Along the way, the nation's economy grew substantially, with more Americans moving into the middle class than at any time in the nation's history.

Out of this formed a mainstream political culture that many historians have called the liberal consensus. This consensus essentially underscored a widespread acceptance for New Deal programs and goals and created a relatively centrist political culture that gravitated to the moderate middle while marginalizing extremes on both the Left and the Right. Postwar American liberalism was stereotypically rational, technocratic, and patient. By

1960, it also appeared to most as trustworthy and successful. Despite the nascent surge of anticommunism, most Americans, including those living in the Sunbelt, remained confident that their country could and would overcome any and all challenges.[1]

In the decades following World War II, the fiercest of those challenges, at least on the domestic front, was racial discrimination and the related demand for civil rights. Nowhere were these problems more evident than in the states of the old Confederacy, where Jim Crow segregation had persisted almost unabated since the end of the Civil War, and where violence against minorities remained sadly common. But racial discrimination was not just a southern problem. Rather, racism and the need for civil rights reform had grown increasingly apparent across the entirety of the emerging Sunbelt, as it had elsewhere across the country.

Responses to the emerging civil rights movement varied dramatically. From their position of established strength, most postwar liberals believed that in a healthy democracy, civil rights would inevitably result from improved education and economic growth. In other words, establishment liberals and pragmatic moderates argued that as society matured, bigotries would naturally fade. Progress was understood to be an unstoppable force within any democratic political system. Real change, these liberals insisted, would come with patience and faith in the system, not imprudent or aggressive agitation.[2]

---

[1] For more on the idea of a national "liberal consensus," see Godfrey Hodgson, *America in Our Time: From World War II to Nixon* (Princeton: Princeton University Press, 1976). For other examples, see Gareth Davies, *From Opportunity to Entitlement: The Transformation and Decline of Great Society Liberalism* (Lawrence: University Press of Kansas, 1996); Steve Fraser and Gary Gerstle, eds., *The Rise and Fall of the New Deal Order: 1930–1980* (Princeton: Princeton University Press, 1990); Kevin Mattson, *When America Was Great: The Fighting Faith of Postwar Liberalism* (New York: Routledge, 2004); Allen J. Matusow, *The Unraveling of America: A History of Liberalism in the 1960s* (New York: Harper & Row, 1984); Patterson, *Grand Expectations*; and Arthur Schlesinger, *The Vital Center: The Politics of Freedom* (Boston: Houghton Mifflin, 1949).

[2] One of the more provocative treatments on the relationship between Cold War liberalism and civil rights is David L. Chappell, *A Stone of Hope: Prophetic Religion and the Death of Jim Crow* (Chapel Hill: University of North Carolina

For others, including many African Americans in the Sunbelt South, patience was not the answer; it was part of the problem. As establishment liberals and pragmatic moderates rested confidently in their ability to administer democracy at a reasonable pace, others across the Sunbelt began to agitate for immediate reform. Interpreting their nation's espoused commitment to global freedom as hypocritical in the face of racial inequalities at home, African Americans, Hispanics, other racial minorities, college students, and lifelong agitators began to challenge the status quo by demanding federal intervention in places where discrimination had persisted unchecked for far too long. By the early 1960s, widespread local action fused into the semblance of a regional civil rights movement.

Meanwhile, as civil rights reformers pushed the liberal establishment more quickly on racial reform than it was naturally inclined to move, Sunbelt conservatives, especially in the Deep South, passionately resisted. This massive resistance was expressed at the national level through sanctioned political channels, and at the local level through unsanctioned intimidation and violence. Massive resistance to civil rights was a crucial part of the ethos of modern conservatism that flourished across the Sunbelt during the postwar period.

All told, the civil rights movement typified the Sunbelt's multi-faceted and tumultuous political culture for at least twenty years following the end of World War II. Within that political culture, conservatives relied on a discourse of states' rights and anticommunism; establishment liberals and pragmatic moderates contented themselves with unwavering confidence in the democratic system that they administered; and reformers pushed more aggressively than either anticommunist conservatives or the liberal establishment wanted. The result was discontentment and unrest on both the Left and the Right.[3]

Press, 2004). See also Gary Gerstle, "Race and the Myth of the Liberal Consensus." *The Journal of American History*, Vol. 82, No. 2 (September, 1995), pp. 579–586.
[3] For more on the relationship between anticommunism and segregationism in the South, see Woods, *Black Struggle, Red Scare*. For a social and cultural analysis of the United States during the 1950s, see among others Alan Petigny, *The Permissive Society: America, 1941–1965* (New York: Cambridge University Press, 2009). Petigny finds indications of an unraveling consensus throughout the 1950s.

Put simply, it was during the first two decades following World War II – the same years that anticommunist conservatives across the Sunbelt were struggling through the earliest stages of a new political movement on the Republican Right – that progressive reformers and grassroots activists across the Sunbelt chose to demand that their nation live up to its high, moralistic ideals about freedom, democracy, and equality. By challenging the status quo, the postwar civil rights movement threatened to destabilize the liberal consensus and made the Sunbelt the nation's epicenter for local political action.

EISENHOWER'S "MIDDLE WAY"

In many ways, the election of Dwight Eisenhower to the presidency of the United States in 1952 was a powerful reflection of the enduring postwar liberal consensus. Though he was the first Republican to win the presidency since Herbert Hoover in 1928, Eisenhower emerged as a popular choice because of his image as a war hero and consensus builder – an image that was appealing across party lines. During the late 1940s, both the Democratic and Republican Parties courted Eisenhower as a possible presidential nominee. Eisenhower declared himself a Republican well before the 1952 campaign season began, and then he won his party's nomination despite a spirited challenge from Robert Taft, a senator from Ohio dubbed "Mr. Republican" by some, and well known as the embodiment of isolationist, anti-union, conservative opposition to his party's more moderate and internationalist eastern establishment. In fighting off the GOP's conservative Taft wing, Eisenhower reaffirmed his image as a bipartisan moderate. That November, he trounced Adlai Stevenson, the governor of Illinois whose intellect impressed the Democratic Party's upper crust, but whose "egghead" style, as some saw it, failed to connect with most voters.[4] Eisenhower won 55 percent of the popular vote in 1952 and carried the Electoral College 442 to 89. Stevenson did

---

[4] For more on Stevenson, see Mattson, *When America Was Great*, 9–12, 158; see also Bowen, *The Roots of Modern Conservatism*.

not even win his home state of Illinois, but he did carry the Deep South, thereby illustrating the enduring power of that region's Democratic loyalty. Stevenson also won the peripheral states of North Carolina, Kentucky, and West Virginia but lost decisively in California, Texas, and Florida – the emerging power centers of the developing Sunbelt. When Eisenhower ran for reelection four years later, he again defeated Stevenson easily, expanding his popular vote percentage to 57, while adding Louisiana, Kentucky, and West Virginia to his already impressive collection of states carried. Once again, Stevenson's only stronghold was in the loyally Democratic Deep South.[5]

For eight years beginning in January 1953, Dwight Eisenhower presided over a nation anxious because of Cold War tensions, but generally optimistic and confident in the ability of its national government to protect and promote the expansion of the middle class. On the domestic front, Eisenhower governed as a centrist – or the "middle way" as he put it. In speeches, he routinely endorsed the virtues of free enterprise and reduced spending, but on several issues – including Social Security, public housing, the minimum wage, and highway construction – he actually supported growth and expansion. Fueled by Cold War fears, Eisenhower introduced new federal support for research and development for science, technology, engineering, and mathematics departments at universities all across the country. To pay for these new programs, Eisenhower agreed with most liberals and many moderates in supporting an exceptionally progressive income tax policy. As had been the case since the New Deal, marginal tax rates for the wealthiest Americans remained high – topping 90 percent for the highest earners throughout most of the 1950s. As a result, aggregate wealth during the 1950s was more evenly distributed across the population than at any time during the twentieth century. The federal government also invested in highways, home mortgages, and public schools, promoting a standard of living previously

[5] For more on Eisenhower's presidency, see, for example, Stephen Ambrose, *Eisenhower: The President* (New York: Simon & Schuster, 1984); and Jean Edward Smith, *Eisenhower in War and Peace* (New York: Random House, 2012).

unattainable for most Americans, and unthinkable just years earlier for a generation struggling through the Great Depression. Thanks to both federally subsidized, low-interest home mortgages and a rapidly expanding tract housing industry in suburbs like those springing up all over the Sunbelt, more Americans came to own their own homes between 1946 and 1956 than in the previous 170 years of the nation's history combined.[6]

Though partisan bickering never fully disappeared, Eisenhower's relationship with Democrats, and his continuing support for the politics of progress and growth, solidified the essential tenets of Keynesian liberalism, which promoted an active role for the federal government in national economic planning. More than anything, Eisenhower's middle way reassured the growing white suburban middle class that he was not an agent for change. Rather, he was comfortable, stable, and consistent with what they had come to expect from their federal government. As a moderate who largely accepted the New Deal, promoted the status quo, and enjoyed the support of both Republicans and Democrats, Dwight Eisenhower reflected a slightly more conservative continuation of the same liberal consensus that had controlled American politics since the 1930s. For the growing white middle class, many of whom were settling into new jobs and homes in the young, sprawling metropolises of the Sunbelt, this was good news.[7]

That is not to say, however, that Eisenhower's middle way pleased everyone. From the Sunbelt Right, conservatives such as Barry Goldwater criticized Eisenhower for running, as he put it, a "dime store New Deal." Goldwater was among the most vocally unhappy Republicans of the 1950s, challenging White House policy on tax rates and spending. Elsewhere, Phyllis Schlafly, another emerging and influential voice on the Right, was also critical of Eisenhower's brand of "modern Republicanism," which she and other conservatives considered weak and conciliatory, as

---

[6] For more on the role that the federal government played in promoting the growth of the middle class during the postwar decades, see Thomas B. Edsall and Mary D. Edsall, *Chain Reaction: The Impact of Race, Rights, and Taxes on American Politics* (New York: W.W. Norton & Co., 1992).

[7] Ibid.

opposed to the stronger conservative principles of limited government and libertarian individuality that, they argued, had been
virtually compromised out of existence thanks to the New Deal's
expansion of the welfare state. Despite hailing from the Midwest,
Schlafly would emerge during the 1960s as one of the most influential and popular voices for modern Sunbelt conservatism.[8]

Even further to the Right than Goldwater or Schlafly was Robert
Welch – organizer of the highly controversial and fiercely anticommunist John Birch Society. Welch, in attacking the president's
moderate ways on both foreign and domestic fronts, went so far
as to suggest that Eisenhower was "a dedicated, conscious agent of
the Communist conspiracy."[9] Not surprisingly, liberal Democrats
(and many Republicans) denounced Welch's ideas as paranoid
and delusional. As Eisenhower governed from the center for most
of the 1950s, scholars and political pundits uniformly characterized
Welch, the John Birch Society, and others on the conservative
Right as obsessive, extremist, and reckless.[10] Though membership
in the John Birch Society grew during the late 1950s and early
1960s, especially in fiercely patriotic and defense-oriented Sunbelt
states such as California and Texas, the mainstream backlash
against the organization suffocated the political aspirations of
many a conservative. By the mid-1960s, most conservatives, especially in the Republican Party, found it beneficial to distance themselves from the hyper-anticommunist organization in an effort to
appear less reactionary. Popular images associating conservatism
with reactionary paranoia stymied the Republican Party's growth,

[8] The best study of Phyllis Schlafly is easily Critchlow, *Phyllis Schlafly and Grassroots Conservatism*. See also Phyllis Schlafly, *A Choice Not an Echo* (Alton, IL: Pere Marquette Press, 1964).
[9] Quoted in Schoenwald, *A Time for Choosing*, 70–72.
[10] See Daniel Bell, ed. *The New American Right* (Vancouver, BC: Criterion Books, 1955). Bell's book was revised and updated in 1963 as *The Radical Right: The New American Right*, expanded and updated (Garden City, NY: Anchor Books, Doubleday, 1963). A third edition of the book was released in 2001 by Transaction Publishers; Richard Hofstadter, *The Age of Reform* (New York: Vintage Books, 1955); see also Richard Hofstadter, "The Paranoid Style in American Politics," in *The Paranoid Style in American Politics and Other Essays* (Cambridge, MA: Harvard University Press, 1965).

both nationally and in the Sunbelt, during these years. These images also contributed to liberal Democrats' heightened reputation for sanity and dependability.[11]

SUNBELT CIVIL RIGHTS

Whereas most middle and upper-class whites perceived the strength of their nation's rapidly growing economy as a refuge from the scary insecurities of the Cold War, other Americans for whom the liberal consensus had not brought affluence began to mount challenges to the social, economic, and political status quo. The most transformative of these challenges concerned racial equality and civil rights. The struggle for racial equality and civil rights in the United States has a long history, one that predates the 1950s or even World War II. Yet, at the same time, it is also true that the modern civil rights movement picked up considerable steam during the early postwar period and did so most visibly in the Sunbelt, especially in the South. Despite a long history of agitation and dissent, the modern civil rights movement – a multi-ethnic, multi-factional zeitgeist for racial equality and reform – emerged much more visibly onto the national consciousness during the 1950s and 1960s thanks largely to personalities from and events taking place within the rapidly growing Sunbelt.

One of the most significant moments in the acceleration of the postwar civil rights movement was the U.S. Supreme Court's ruling in *Brown v. Board of Education* (1954). In *Brown*, the Court ruled that the doctrine of "separate but equal" – legally established in the 1896 case *Plessy v. Ferguson* – was unconstitutional, specifically so far as segregation in public schools was concerned. *Brown* signaled the end of *de jure* – or legal – segregation in public schools. It also unsettled the racial status quo across the Sunbelt. Yet, as transformative as the *Brown* decision was, it was only one in a long line of Supreme Court decisions to shape the emerging movement. In 1950, for instance, the Supreme Court

---

[11] For more on the John Birch Society, see again Schoenwald, *A Time for Choosing*, 62–99; McGirr, *Suburban Warriors*, 75–78; and Woods, *Black Struggle, Red Scare*, 143–168.

ruled in *Sweatt v. Painter* that the University of Texas at Austin could not maintain a segregated law school. That same year, the Court ruled in *McLaurin v. Oklahoma State Regents* that the University of Oklahoma could not maintain its segregated graduate school. Four years later, and just two weeks before issuing its ruling in *Brown*, the Court ruled in *Hernandez v. Texas* that Mexican Americans – and all other racial minorities – qualified for equal protection through provisions of the 14th Amendment. By the mid-1950s, it was clear that federal courts were establishing precedents favorable to a growing civil rights movement.[12]

Legal action, however, was only a small part of the broader movement for civil rights reform. Geopolitics was also a major force. The struggle against fascist and racist ideologies during World War II created a noticeable surge for civil rights reform in the United States, not just among African Americans but among other racial minorities, as well. Racial strife in places ranging from Mobile, Alabama, to Los Angeles highlighted inequalities that from a global public relations standpoint, created a hypocritical image of the United States that diplomats and policy makers knew would harm efforts to win hearts and minds in the battle to contain communism.[13] These concerns were magnified when the Soviet Union began to use American racial discrimination as a weapon to instill doubt in developing nations as to whether or not the United States could be trusted. Increasingly, politicians in Washington believed that racial injustice at home undermined the credibility of American democracy elsewhere in the world.[14]

---

[12] For more on the politics of desegregation at Texas universities, see Amilcar Shabazz, *Democracy: African Americans and the Struggle for Access and Equity in Higher Education in Texas* (Chapel Hill: University of North Carolina Press, 2004). See also William S. Clayson, *Freedom Is Not Enough: The War on Poverty and the Civil Rights Movement in Texas* (Austin: University of Texas Press, 2010).

[13] For more on the impact of World War II on the developing civil rights movement, see, for instance, Ronald Takaki, *Double Victory: A Multicultural History of American in World War II* (New York: Little, Brown, and Co., 2000).

[14] For more on the geopolitical dimensions of the evolving federal response to civil rights, see Thomas Borstelmann, *The Cold War and the Color Line: American Race Relations in the Global Arena* (Cambridge, MA: Harvard University Press,

If legal action and geopolitics created momentum for the emerging civil rights movement, ongoing violence and injustice across the South gave the struggle a sense of moral urgency. In August 1955, a 14-year-old black male from Chicago named Emmett Till, visiting family in the Mississippi Delta, was kidnapped and brutally murdered simply for whistling at a white woman. His killers were later acquitted by an all-white jury, sparking outrage among blacks all over the country and garnering worldwide criticism of the South's brand of American justice.[15] Months after the Till lynching, Rosa Parks refused to give up her seat on a segregated bus in Montgomery, Alabama. That action led to the highly influential Montgomery bus boycott and the emergence of Martin Luther King Jr. as a leader of the rapidly expanding civil rights movement in the South. Similar boycotts were soon staged in other parts of the South, including Tallahassee, Florida, in 1956 – a protest successful enough to draw the wrath of Sunshine State anticommunists who quickly began to persecute – (they called it an "investigation") – National Association for the Advancement of Colored People (NAACP) officials in the state. Following the success of these and similar boycotts in early 1957, King helped organize the highly influential Southern Christian Leadership Conference (SCLC) in Atlanta, Georgia. Working through the SCLC, King then moved to Atlanta and quickly became the nation's most articulate spokesperson for black civil rights. With King as its most visible leader, the African American civil rights movement began to attract ever more volunteers – local people whose willingness to embrace the movement in the face of direct and immediate threats of violence enabled the widening conscience for equality across the Sunbelt South.[16]

2001); and Mary L. Dudziak, *Cold War Civil Rights: Race and the Image of American Democracy* (Princeton, NJ: Princeton University Press, 2000).

[15] For more on the murder of Emmett Till, see John Dittmer, *Local People: The Struggle for Civil Rights in Mississippi* (Urbana and Chicago: University of Illinois Press, 1994), 55–58; and Stephen J. Whitfield, *A Death in the Delta: The Story of Emmett Till* (New York: The Free Press, 1988).

[16] See again, Dittmer, *Local People*. For a general narrative of the King-centric civil rights movement, see Taylor Branch, *Parting the Waters: American in the King Years, 1954–1963* (New York: Simon & Schuster, 1988). For more on

From Washington, Eisenhower was relatively slow to embrace this budding civil rights movement. For most of his presidency, he was – by most accounts – positioned somewhere between ambivalence and outright opposition. In 1954, Eisenhower publicly expressed his disagreement with the Supreme Court's ruling in *Brown*. Then, in March 1956, more than one hundred congressmen and senators signed the so-called Southern Manifesto, a resolution calling upon both appointed and elected officials in Dixie to use whatever legal means available to defy federal court orders on school integration. Eisenhower's response was meager and ambiguous and did little to undermine southern defiance. Five months later, when Texas Governor Allan Shivers seemed to take the manifesto's call quite seriously by deploying a unit of Texas Rangers to help local whites prevent the integration of Mansfield High School in a suburb outside of Fort Worth, Eisenhower responded by doing nothing. Not wanting to upset Shivers – a conservative Democrat who had gained national notoriety for supporting Eisenhower in 1952 – the president remained quiet when Texas law enforcement joined a mob of more than 300 angry white parents encircling Mansfield High School like a human shield in order to keep black students out. In that case, election-year political concerns in a swing state trumped whatever convictions Eisenhower may have had on the enforceability of federal court orders.[17]

anticommunist investigations of civil rights leaders in Florida, see again Lewis, *The White South and the Red Menace*; see also Woods, *Black Struggle, Red Scare*, 116–123. For more on the civil rights movement generally, see David Chappell, *Inside Agitators: White Southerners in the Civil Rights Movement* (Baltimore, MD: Johns Hopkins University Press, 1996); Hugh Davis Graham, *The Civil Rights Era: Origins and Development of National Policy, 1960–1972* (New York: Oxford University Press, 1990); and Charles Payne, *I've Got the Light of Freedom: The Organizing Tradition and the Mississippi Freedom Struggle* (Berkeley: University of California Press, 1995). For a unique look at black identity using music as a lens for analysis, see Brian Ward, *Just My Soul Responding: Rhythm and Blues, Black Consciousness, and Race Relations* (Berkeley: University of California Press, 1998); see also Brian Ward, *Radio and the Struggle for Civil Rights in the South* (Gainesville: University Press of Florida, 2006).

[17] The most comprehensive treatment of the Mansfield crisis remains Robyn Duff Ladino, *Desegregating Texas Schools: Eisenhower, Shivers, and the Crisis*

As a result of Shivers's action and Eisenhower's inaction, the effort to integrate Mansfield High School failed. In the process, Eisenhower sent a message to other southern governors that the federal government would not intervene in such matters in the future. In essence, Eisenhower's failure to respond at Mansfield was a de facto endorsement of the Southern Manifesto, at least so far as politicians in the South were concerned. For the moderate Eisenhower, the expansion of the middle class through the politics of consensus was one thing, but rocking the boat on civil rights and racial equality was a far more delicate matter.[18]

That is not to say that Eisenhower was always an obstructionist on civil rights. For instance, just months after the episode at Mansfield, Eisenhower introduced what would eventually be the first piece of civil rights legislation passed since the end of Reconstruction – the Civil Rights Act of 1957. In its original form, the act was designed to protect and strengthen minority voting rights, in addition to allowing discrimination-related civil suits. By most accounts, it was a moderate proposal, especially when compared to the transformative civil rights laws that eventually passed during the mid-1960s. But however limited, the mere idea of a civil rights bill was extremely controversial. Over the next several months, Congress waged a bitter fight over the bill.[19]

Eisenhower may have taken the lead in proposing what became the Civil Rights Act of 1957, and he may have even been willing to support a stronger bill than the one eventually signed into law. But without Lyndon Johnson's efforts in the Senate, the Civil Rights Act of 1957 would likely have died before ever reaching the president's desk. Fearing a possible defection of African

at *Mansfield High* (Austin: University of Texas Press, 1996). See also Campbell, *Gone to Texas*, 426–427. For a biographical treatment of Allan Shivers, see Ricky F. Dobbs, *Yellow Dogs and Republicans: Allan Shivers and Texas Two-Party Politics* (College Station: Texas A&M University Press, 2005). For a different perspective on Eisenhower and civil rights – one that paints a more sympathetic image of Eisenhower on the issue of race – see David A. Nichols, *A Matter of Justice: Eisenhower and the Beginning of the Civil Rights Revolution* (New York: Simon & Schuster, 2007).

[18] Ibid.
[19] Nichols, *A Matter of Justice*, 143–168.

American voters to the GOP, Johnson – a Texas Democrat and the majority leader of the U.S. Senate – initially countered the White House's proposal by pushing for a more comprehensive civil rights bill, then subsequently negotiated away some of its more transformative proposals in order to secure votes. Knowing that support for civil rights would alienate conservative voters in his home state, Johnson positioned himself as a national rather than regional Democrat. Johnson had been historically cautious when it came to civil rights. He was often unwilling to commit to one side or the other and was sometimes blatantly oppositional when the political winds dictated resistance. But in 1957, Johnson chose another path. He hoped that by spearheading new legislation on civil rights, he would solidify support among minority voters, while modernizing Sunbelt states such as Texas. Doing so, he hoped, would force the South to move past what he saw as a racist culture that stunted economic growth and modernization. Like many southern liberals, Johnson believed that civil rights progress was essential to the region's growth in a rapidly globalizing and industrializing economy. He also believed that liberalizing the Democratic Party in the South might push conservatives into the GOP, thereby opening new doors for liberals within an expanded and biracial voting base. Not all liberals agreed with this strategy, and some – including eventually Johnson – later concluded that supporting civil rights also meant abandoning the South to the Republican Party for the foreseeable future. Seen later as a prescient forecast of partisan realignment, Johnson's statement should not necessarily be taken at face value. He, like many other Democrats in the South, also understood that expanding the franchise to minority voters in a region where political attitudes were already changing could very well strengthen the party's grip on Dixie, even if it came at the cost of conservative loyalties.[20]

---

[20] For more on Johnson's role in passing the Civil Rights Act of 1957, see Robert A. Caro, *Master of the Senate: The Years of Lyndon Johnson* (New York: Random House, 2002). Caro largely credits Johnson for the passage of this bill, minimizing Eisenhower's role in the process. For a different take, see again Nichols, *A Matter of Justice*, 143–168.

As Johnson struggled to win support for the bill, segregationists ramped up their vocal opposition. Senator Richard Russell of Georgia was perhaps the most influential of these opponents, but the most visible was Strom Thurmond. In late August, Thurmond attempted to filibuster the civil rights legislation, speaking on the Senate floor for more than twenty-four hours – a record for the Senate. Thurmond's filibuster failed, but it nevertheless reflected the intensity of defiance among many of the South's most ardent segregationists. Whether it was in specific response to the Civil Rights Act of 1957 or the widening push for racial equality more broadly, massive resistance was a common impulse among conservative southerners.

Johnson failed to win over most of the Democratic Party's most ardent segregationists. He was far more successful, however, in winning support from those politicians representing states across the broader Sunbelt, especially those from states in the Southwest and peripheral South. Eventually, the Civil Rights Act of 1957 won bipartisan votes from several Sunbelt senators, including both Republican senators from California (William Knowland and Thomas Kuchel) and even Barry Goldwater of Arizona. Also, eventually voting "aye" were both Democratic senators from Texas (Johnson and Ralph Yarborough), Tennessee (Albert Gore Sr. and Estes Kefauver), Oklahoma (Robert Kerr and Mike Monroney), and even one Democratic senator from Florida (George Smathers). Johnson's ability to win Smathers's vote was especially impressive considering that Smathers had come to the Senate by red-baiting his liberal opponent, Claude Pepper, in a famously vicious campaign in 1950 – similar in several ways to Willis Smith's victory over Frank Porter Graham in North Carolina and Nixon's victory over Helen Gahagan Douglas in the famous "pink lady" campaign of that same year. The vote in the House of Representatives reflected a similar split, with several congressmen from the Sunbelt West supporting the bill.[21]

---

[21] Senate Vote #75, HR. 6127. Civil Rights Act of 1957. Passed, August 7, 1957, 85th Congress [http://www.govtrack.us/congress/votes/85-1957/s75]; see also Robert Dallek, *Lone Star Rising: Lyndon Johnson and His Times, 1908–1960* (New York: Oxford University Press, 1991), 517–527.

Finally on September 9, after months of tense negotiation and political gamesmanship, Eisenhower signed the Civil Rights Act of 1957 – the first civil rights bill passed by Congress since Reconstruction. Both Eisenhower and Johnson declared victory, though the final product pleased almost no one. Compromises necessary to win votes had weakened the bill considerably. The bill's failure to accomplish its goals, specifically on the enforcement of enhanced ballot access, led to an ongoing need for civil rights reform at the federal level that would dominate political discussions in the Sunbelt for the next eight years. But in the short term, the bill demonstrated that it was possible to pass civil rights reform without the support of conservatives in the South.[22]

The Civil Rights Act of 1957 was a major moment, and one that gives balance to Eisenhower's otherwise underwhelming record on civil rights. But Eisenhower's legacy on race and civil rights was influenced even more lastingly by his answer to a crisis in Little Rock, Arkansas. On September 4, 1957 – five days prior to final passage of that year's Civil Rights Act – Arkansas Governor Orval Faubus, responding to federal court orders that Little Rock high schools be integrated, ordered his state's National Guard to prevent nine African American students from entering the campus of Little Rock's Central High School. For three weeks, the nation watched as Faubus defied the federal court, while Eisenhower cautiously deliberated over his response.[23]

A year earlier, when faced with a similar situation in Texas, Eisenhower had remained quiet, allowing Allan Shivers to dictate the politics of school desegregation without federal interference. Based on that precedent, Faubus had reason to believe the president would stay out of the crisis at Little Rock. But unlike 1956, 1957 was not an election year, and Eisenhower had far greater freedom to act against the South's political status quo. In a surprise move,

---

[22] HR. 6127. Civil Rights Act of 1957, Dwight D. Eisenhower Presidential Library & Museum [http://www.eisenhower.archives.gov/research/online_docu ments/civil_rights_act/Civil_Rights_Bill.pdf]; Dallek, *Lone Star Rising*, 517–527.
[23] For more on Eisenhower and the Little Rock crisis, see againNichols, *A Matter of Justice*. See also Woods, *Black Struggle, Red Scare*, 68–73.

Eisenhower federalized the Arkansas National Guard and, on September 24, ordered those servicemen to join troops from the Army's 101st Airborne Division in escorting the nine black students into Central High School. Television cameras broadcast images of military personnel, bayonets affixed, marching alongside jeeps down Little Rock streets. Thanks to Eisenhower and the intervention of the U.S. Army, Little Rock's Central High School was integrated for the time being. Less than one year later, however, in another act of massive defiance, Faubus closed all high schools in Little Rock, temporarily preferring no high schools to integrated ones.[24]

Eisenhower's response to the crisis in Little Rock placed him in direct opposition to southerners clinging to segregation through the language of states' rights. Coupling the crisis in Little Rock with the bitter fight on Capitol Hill over the Civil Rights Act of 1957, conservative southerners increasingly recalled nightmarish images of Reconstruction. Resentment against the federal government intensified across the South. There is no question that Eisenhower's legacy on civil rights was transformed by his actions in 1957. But it should not be forgotten that without Eisenhower's lack of response to the Southern Manifesto and the Mansfield crisis of 1956, Faubus would not have felt emboldened to respond as he did in Little Rock in 1957.

Despite Eisenhower's creeping emergence as a supporter for moderate action on civil rights reform or Washington's general reluctance to embrace too many of the movement's goals, the struggle for civil rights and racial equality continued to evolve thanks primarily to organized grassroots action across the Sunbelt. In February 1960, four black students at North Carolina A&T University refused to give up their seats at an all-white lunch counter in a Woolworth's department store in downtown Greensboro. That action sparked several days of sit-in protests. Two months later, in April 1960, the widening sit-in movement led to the formation of the Student Nonviolent Coordinating Committee (SNCC) in Raleigh, North Carolina. Similar sit-ins subsequently

[24] Ibid.

began to pop up all over the Sunbelt. A year later, when a group of self-described "Freedom Riders" attempted to test a federal court decision banning segregation on interstate bus travel – prompting a fury of mass arrests in Mississippi and Alabama, not to mention shocking violence, bloodshed, and further federal intervention – the intensity of mass political action once again pushed the issue of racial discrimination to the forefront of the nation's political consciousness. The Freedom Rides further placed states all across the South at the epicenter of renewed debates on the size of the federal government, the scope of its power, and – among local politicians and economic boosters – the wisdom of massive resistance.[25]

These events – the heart of a well-known and oft-repeated narrative on the early civil rights movement – reflect a critically important form of Sunbelt politics during the first decade and a half following the end of World War II. At least in part, this was a political battle between an established hierarchy – most visible in the massive, segregationist resistance of the Deep South – and grassroots activists no longer content to accept as inevitable the oppressions of Jim Crow. Moderates and liberals in and out of the Sunbelt struggled to mediate that conflict. The ensuing political confrontations at the local, state, and national levels illustrate some of the dynamics at play among those committed to preserving the status quo, those committed to challenging it, and those – such as the liberal intellectuals Arthur Schlesinger and Gunnar Myrdal – who believed that racial progress would come to those who waited patiently.[26]

But this traditional civil rights narrative also obscures different forms of action that were emerging concurrent to the Martin

---

[25] For more on the traditional narrative framing the African American civil rights movement, see again, among many others, Branch, *Parting the Waters*; Dittmer, *Local People*; Graham, *The Civil Rights Era*; and Payne, *I've Got the Light of Freedom*.

[26] See again Chappell, *A Stone of Hope*, 26–43. See also Schlesinger, *The Vital Center*; and Gunnar Myrdal, *An American Dilemma: The Negro Problem and American Democracy* (New York: Harper & Row, 1944). For more on Schlesinger and Myrdal, see again Mattson, *When America Was Great*, 95–99, 114.

Luther King–oriented movement in the South. In North Carolina, for instance, the struggle faced by tobacco workers in their efforts to unionize coincided with a heightened racial consciousness and a demand for civil rights that predated much of what drove the movement in the 1950s.[27] The story of Robert F. Williams also complicates the history of civil rights in North Carolina. In Williams, one finds that many of the elements of what would eventually be called "black power" – typically understood as an armed, militant response to racial oppression – were emerging in places like North Carolina at least as early as the mid-1950s, rather than the mid-1960s as most narratives suggest. At times working through his local NAACP chapter, and at other times working in direct opposition to the NAACP, Williams – whose 1962 book *Negroes with Guns* was later cited by Black Panther Party organizer Huey Newton as a direct inspiration – stood as an example of the multifaceted nature of political resistance to racial inequality bubbling up in Sunbelt states during the postwar decades.[28]

Another example of this multifaceted and growing dissent emerged during the 1950s at the University of Texas (UT) at Austin, where students began to agitate for social justice and racial equality through groups including the Young Men's (and Women's) Christian Association (YMCA and YWCA, respectively), as well as organizations such as UT's Christian Faith-and-Life Community. Through these and similar organizations, students merged a consciousness about racial discrimination with a spiritual quest for authenticity and community engagement. From that merger came a generation of students, at UT and at other universities across the region, ready and willing to be stirred out of political alienation and into what some New Left and countercultural organizations would later emphasize as "participatory democracy."[29]

---

[27] See again Korstad, *Civil Rights Unionism.*
[28] Timothy B. Tyson, *Radio Free Dixie: Robert F. Williams & the Roots of Black Power* (Chapel Hill: University of North Carolina Press, 1999); Robert F. Williams, *Negroes with Guns* (New York: Marzani & Munsell, Inc., 1962).
[29] Doug Rossinow, *The Politics of Authenticity: Liberalism, Christianity, and the New Left in America* (New York: Columbia University Press, 1998).

College students were not alone in agitating for change in Texas. Elsewhere, political organizations such as the Left-leaning American G.I. Forum used incidents like the one involving slain U.S. Army Private Felix Longoria to advocate for greater civil rights for Mexican Americans. In that case, Longoria – killed in action during World War II – unintentionally put South Texas on the national map when, in 1948, his widow tried to have his body buried at a local cemetery, only to be denied on the grounds that the cemetery was for whites only. Using the Longoria case as a springboard for action, the American G.I. Forum, under the leadership of Dr. Hector P. Garcia, raised money and awareness for Mexican Americans fighting discrimination across the Sunbelt. All states, but especially those along the Mexican border, were confronted throughout the 1950s with not simply the emerging African American freedom struggle, but a growing Mexican American movement as well.[30]

Los Angeles was another hotspot for the evolving ethnic consciousness among Mexican Americans and other Hispanics. The most famous incidents in the racial history of mid-century Los Angeles were the "Sleepy Lagoon Case" and concurrent "Zoot Suit Riots" of 1943. Those events involved the arrest of hundreds of young, Mexican American males, some of whom were suspected in the murder of a young man named José Diaz, but most of whom were arrested in a climate of mass hysteria that associated Hispanic youth with criminality based on stereotypes connecting flamboyant clothing with juvenile delinquency. Those events – which included one evening of mass rioting and violence between Mexican American youth and U.S. Navy personnel stationed in the area – rallied progressive reformers to Los Angeles and inspired limited cooperation between other ethnic minorities across Southern California, including coalitions of Jews and Asians. For a time, this multiethnic front succeeded in pushing racial discrimination and civil inequality to the front of Los Angeles's political agenda. But as the 1950s wore on, interethnic

---

[30] Patrick J. Carroll, *Felix Longoria's Wake: Bereavement, Racism, and the Rise of Mexican American Activism* (Austin: University of Texas Press, 2003).

cooperation proved difficult. Local leaders representing different minority groups were unable to maintain a united coalition because of cultural differences as well as disagreements over goals and strategy. Still, during the 1950s and 1960s, California's multiethnic diversity created a racial frontier of sorts, foreshadowing developments that would shape civil rights in the United States for the rest of the century.[31]

Similar struggles shaped civil rights in South Florida. This was certainly true in Miami, where a multiethnic community battled both establishment liberals focused on economic growth and segregationist conservatives focused on maintaining the policies of Jim Crow. Civil rights conflict in Miami during the postwar years often focused on commercial real estate development and residential housing. These issues were central to the politics of growth that characterized much of the Sunbelt's emergence during the late 1940s and 1950s. As was true in Los Angeles, the multiethnic nature of civil rights dissent in Miami inhibited unity and cohesion among different groups. Nevertheless, if the civil rights movement of the Deep South reflects the black–white binary that typically frames most discussions on the postwar fight for racial equality, some experiences in Texas, California, and Florida challenge the applicability of that binary to the movement in other parts of the Sunbelt.[32]

---

[31] For more on civil rights in California, see Mark Brilliant, *The Color of America Has Changed: How Racial Diversity Changed Civil Rights Reform in California, 1941–1978* (New York: Oxford University Press, 2012). For more on the diversity of the early civil rights movement in Los Angeles, see Shana Bernstein, "From the Southwest to the Nation: Interracial Civil Rights Activism in Los Angeles," in Nickerson and Dochuk, *Sunbelt Rising*, 141–163; Becky M. Nicolaides, *My Blue Heaven: Life and Politics in the Working-Class Suburbs of Los Angeles* (Chicago: University of Chicago Press, 2002); and George J. Sanchez, *Becoming Mexican American: Ethnicity, Culture, and Identity in Chicano Los Angeles, 1900–1945* (New York: Oxford University Press, 1993).

[32] For more on the diversity of the early civil rights movement in Miami, see N. D. B. Connally, "Sunbelt Civil Rights: Urban Renewal and the Follies of Desegregation in Greater Miami," in Nickerson and Dochuk, *Sunbelt Rising*, 164–187. For more on the multiethnic complications of race and civil rights reform in Texas, see Brian Behnken, *Fighting Their Own Battles: Mexican*

Historians are still unraveling the complicated story of the postwar American civil rights movement. As part of the Sunbelt's evolving political culture, this movement led to considerable politicization, not just among segregationist conservatives, but also among minorities and progressive whites. As prosperity and multiethnic diversity in western states like California complicated most Americans' understanding of racial discrimination and civil rights, the liberal consensus that had for so long stabilized policy making in Washington began to crumble. Discontent reigned across the nation and across the Sunbelt, South and West alike. It spread among those not benefiting from liberalism's federally subsidized programs for growth and modernity. It spread among those opposed to any change in the political or economic status quo. And it spread against the backdrop of the United States' widely promoted narrative of itself as a bastion of global democracy. The multidimensional struggle for racial equality across the Sunbelt bred not simply massive resistance on the Right; it also bred discontent and political action on the Left, simultaneously rupturing the decades-old alliances between minorities, Sunbelt Democrats, and the national liberal consensus.

COLOR-BLIND CONSERVATISM, PERSISTENT LIBERALISM

Though photographs of fire hoses and police dogs remain among the most enduring images of the southern backlash against civil rights in the late 1950s and early 1960s, the most lastingly influential form of resistance to civil rights was not the violent or brazen actions of the stereotypical southern "redneck." Far more lasting, rather, was an emerging discourse that came to guide both Republican strategy and Sunbelt policies on race for the next several decades. Responding somewhat cooperatively to liberals and moderates in the region, a number of politically savvy and opportunistic Sunbelt conservatives slowly but effectively began to reconceive the struggle against civil rights not as one to preserve white

Americans, African Americans, and the Struggle for Civil Rights in Texas (Chapel Hill: University of North Carolina Press, 2011).

supremacy, but as one for individual rights and economic freedom. This was, in essence, the birth of color-blind conservatism. Over the next several decades, conservatives' ability to oppose government action on civil rights without appearing overtly racist would revolutionize Republican politics in a region long noted for its Democratic dominance. Meanwhile, as many Sunbelt conservatives worked to repackage their hostility to civil rights in less overtly racist terms, progressive reformers began to forge important biracial coalitions, eager to move ahead on issues related to civil rights and economic equality.

The city of Atlanta provides the best example of this multifaceted and evolving political culture. As southern cities like Little Rock were alienating themselves from business investors across the country by embracing reactionary politics, Atlanta – at one time self-promoted as the "City Too Busy to Hate" – thrived as a seemingly model metropolis. During most of the 1950s and early 1960s, local political leaders in Atlanta largely rejected the politics of reactionary conservatism and, instead, promoted a biracial coalition of progressive reformers, establishment liberals, and pragmatic moderates. Among these leaders were Ralph McGill, editor of the highly influential *Atlanta Constitution*; William Hartsfield, the city's longtime mayor, who led a variety of growth initiatives and won his last term as mayor by defeating the staunch segregationist Lester Maddox; and Ivan Allen Jr., who succeeded Hartsfield and continued to promote a brand of city politics that emphasized biracial coalitions for the betterment of economic growth. McGill, Hartsfield, and Allen and other leaders successfully promoted an approach to local politics that helped construct Atlanta's reputation as a bastion of Sunbelt modernity. During these years, the city built massive new highways and developed its downtown business district, while also expanding thanks to federal defense contracts and the growth of local corporations such as Coca-Cola.[33]

---

[33] For more on Atlanta, see Kruse, *White Flight*; and Lassiter, *The Silent Majority*, 44–64. See also Jeff Roche, *Restructured Resistance: The Sibley Commission and the Politics of Desegregation in Georgia* (Athens: University of Georgia Press, 1998).

Atlanta's sterling reputation, along with that of area leaders like McGill, Hartsfield, and Allen, belied, however, another side of the city's politics – one in which many whites were increasingly frustrated by the political role enjoyed by local blacks. For some of these whites, the solution was found in openly racist and sometimes violent organizations on the far Right. But the economic consequences of racial confrontations in other parts of the Sunbelt, such as the one in Arkansas between Faubus and Eisenhower in 1957, strongly suggested the need to find another way. Increasingly, Atlanta's white community found an alternative path by reframing the political discourse on civil rights. Rather than emphasize the biological inferiority of blacks or other racial minorities, these whites emphasized property rights, homeownership, and the evils of big government and high taxes. Rather than insist on public segregation, these whites embraced privacy and isolation. Recognizing that traditional strategies were no longer effective, conservative whites in Atlanta largely abandoned the regressive politics of massive resistance. Instead, they created a political culture in which race was no longer an explicit factor but was, instead, subsumed within a broader ideological framework that fused anticommunism, libertarianism, and moral traditionalism – a fusion that quickly became a hallmark of quintessentially Sunbelt conservatism.[34]

But for all the success that color-blind conservatism would eventually have across the postwar American Sunbelt, it did not immediately result in electoral success stories across the region. In fact, establishment liberals – and even some progressives – continued to do well, not only in the nation as a whole, but in many parts of the Sunbelt. Take Tennessee, for instance. During most of the 1950s and early 1960s, the three most influential public servants in the state of Tennessee were Estes Kefauver, Albert Gore Sr., and Frank Clement – all Democrats with varying levels of progressive sympathies. In 1952, Kefauver, who served as

---

[34] Kruse, *White Flight*. For more on the emergence of a color-blind rhetoric in the Sunbelt South, see also Crespino, *In Search of Another Country*; and Lassiter, *The Silent Majority*.

a U.S. senator from 1949 to 1963, waged a spirited campaign for the Democratic Party's presidential nomination, eventually losing to Adlai Stevenson. He ran again in 1956, again losing to Stevenson, but this time earned the vice-presidential nomination in the process. That same year, he was one of only three senators from the South not to sign the Southern Manifesto. Albert Gore did not sign it either. He served Tennessee in the Senate from 1953 to 1971. Meanwhile, from 1953 to 1959, Frank Clement used the office of governor to establish himself as one of the Democratic Party's most well-respected progressives. As governor, Clement ordered Tennessee's school districts to comply with the *Brown* decision, supported bonds for free textbooks and tax increases for highways and other infrastructural improvements, passed an amendment to the state constitution repealing the poll tax, raised sales taxes, advanced the cause of mental health, and in 1956 delivered one of the most energetic keynote addresses in Democratic National Convention history. Though Tennessee was not always a reliably liberal state, the leadership of Kefauver, Gore, and Clement made it a noticeable exception to whatever stereotypes still lingered so far as the South's penchant of obstructionist segregationism was concerned.[35]

Texas also elected its fair share of liberals during these years, Lyndon Johnson most famously. But Johnson was not alone. In fact, for several decades, the most important figure in Texas's non-conservative political identity was arguably Sam Rayburn, who represented Texas's fourth congressional district from 1913 to 1961. Rayburn was also Speaker of the U.S. House of Representatives on three separate occasions, first from 1940 to 1947, then again from 1949 to 1953, and later from 1955 until his

---

[35] For more on Gore and Tennessee politics during the 1950s, see Kyle Longley, *Albert Gore, Sr.: Tennessee Maverick* (Baton Rouge: Louisiana State University Press, 2004). See also Jack Bass and Walter De Vries, *The Transformation of Southern Politics: Social Change & Political Consequence Since 1945* (Athens: University of Georgia Press, 1995), 284–304. For more on Tennessee and the civil rights movement, see Benjamin Houston, *The Nashville Way: Racial Etiquette and the Struggle for Social Justice in a Southern City* (Athens: University of Georgia Press, 2012).

death in 1961. Highly respected across partisan and ideological lines, Rayburn actively supported most New Deal programs and believed in the power of government to intervene for the betterment of the economy. He supported the construction of interstate highways long before Eisenhower pushed for such expansion, and while debating with congressional colleagues over the value of connecting the South and Southwest with the rest of the country via new road networks such as Route 66, he may have been the first person to use the term "Sunbelt," well before Kevin Phillips did in 1969. Regardless, Rayburn's influence on national politics cannot be understated. It is also worth noting that like Kefauver and Gore in Tennessee and Johnson in Texas, Rayburn also refused to sign the Southern Manifesto in 1956.[36]

During the 1940s and 1950s, both Johnson and Rayburn successfully functioned within the pragmatic boundaries of the liberal consensus. In 1957, they were joined on Capitol Hill by Ralph Yarborough, a progressive reformer who surprised political observers all across the country by winning a seat representing Texas in the U.S. Senate. Yarborough quickly established himself as a reliable and passionate voice for many left-of-center causes, including redistributive economic populism – what he called, putting "the jam on the lower shelf so the little people can reach it."[37] But even before Yarborough established his own progressive bona fides in the Senate, Maury Maverick Jr., the former mayor of San Antonio, spent more than seven years in the U.S. House of Representatives building his own reputation as the Lone Star State's foremost voice for reform. As a congressman, Maverick backed organized labor, was an outspoken proponent of black civil rights, and valiantly resisted much of what he saw as

[36] For more on Lyndon Johnson, Sam Rayburn, and Texas politics during the 1950s, see Patrick Cox, *Ralph W. Yarborough, The People's Senator* (Austin: University of Texas Press, 2001); Chandler Davidson, *Race and Class in Texas Politics* (Princeton: Princeton University Press, 1990); Dallek, *Lone Star Rising*; Dobbs, *Yellow Dogs and Republicans*; and George N. Green, *The Establishment in Texas Politics: The Primitive Years, 1938–1957* (Norman: University of Oklahoma Press, 1979).
[37] Cox, *Ralph W. Yarborough*, 156.

the irresponsible and dangerous persecution of suspected communists in the United States.[38]

The efforts of Johnson, Rayburn, Yarborough, and Maverick
notwithstanding, the Texas Democratic Party remained faction-
alized and predominantly conservative throughout the 1950s and
early 1960s. Texas's Democratic establishment – represented by
men like Allan Shivers and Price Daniel – continued to control
most political offices in the state. But as establishment Democrats
worked to maintain the status quo and liberals worked toward
reform, Texas Republicans began to chip away at conservative
loyalties in the state, highlighting the national Democratic Party's
penchant for big government and high taxes and at the same time
accusing the state's Democratic establishment of not effectively
representing Lone Star State conservatism at the federal level.
Essentially, Texas Republicans determined that the best way to
win elections against conservative Democrats was to frame elections in national terms rather than local ones. Texas Republicans,
like emerging modern conservatives elsewhere in the Sunbelt,
began to see the power of ascribing to all Democratic candidates
culpability in the rapid growth of government, high taxes, and the
perceived ongoing infringement by Washington on local control
and states' rights. It was a risky strategy, and one that certainly
necessitated patience. But in doing so, Texas Republicans began
to successfully articulate a brand of modern conservatism similar
to what was emerging in metropolitan areas like Atlanta. As
Republican pioneers such as John Tower slowly tore down the
walls that separated grassroots conservatives in Texas from the

---

[38] Ibid.; see again Behnken, *Fighting Their Own Battles*; for more on *Smith
v. Allwright*, see Charles L. Zeldon, *The Battle for the Black Ballot: Smith
v. Allwright and the Defeat of the Texas All-White Primary* (Lawrence:
University Press of Kansas, 2004). For more on civil rights in Dallas, see
Michael Phillips, *White Metropolis: Race, Ethnicity, and Religion in Dallas,
1841–2001* (Austin: University of Texas Press, 2006). For examples of reactionary anticommunism related to issues of race in Texas, see Woods, *Black
Struggle, Red Scare*, 63–66. The seminal study of southern politics at mid-
century, and one that discusses Texas's relative racial moderation, is V. O. Key,
Southern Politics in State and Nation (Knoxville: University of Tennessee Press,
1949).

state GOP, they simultaneously boosted the Republican Party's respectability and its prospects for becoming a viable second party in what had always been a one-party state.[39]

Like Texas, California was a critical meeting place for the emerging grassroots Right. But California also boasted a sizable number of moderates, establishment liberals, and progressive reformers. One such reformer was Edmund G. "Pat" Brown. For most of the 1950s, Brown was the state's attorney general, serving under the leadership of moderate Republican governors Earl Warren and Goodwin Knight. He then served as the state's governor from 1959 to 1967, earning a reputation as a responsible liberal. As a policy maker, Brown was perhaps best known as the architect of California's modern system of higher education. In 1962, Brown won the affections of many a California liberal by trouncing Richard Nixon in the state's race for governor.[40]

Californians might have considered Brown more progressive than they did had it not been for reformers such as Jesse Unruh, who often pushed Brown further to the Left than the governor sometimes felt capable of moving. During the late 1950s, Unruh battled on behalf of California progressives by politicizing the grass roots. Then, in 1961, Unruh was elected to the California State Assembly, where he quickly became the state's preeminent voice for progressive reform. Unruh even pioneered civil rights legislation in California that protected minorities from discrimination by local businesses, a bill years ahead of its time.[41]

---

[39] Cunningham, *Cowboy Conservatism*. See also Davidson, *Race and Class in Texas Politics*; Dobbs, *Yellow Dogs and Republicans*; Green, *The Establishment in Texas Politics*; and Roger M. Olien, *From Token to Triumph: The Texas Republicans Since 1920* (Dallas: SMU Press, 1982).

[40] For more on Pat Brown, Jessie Unruh, and California politics during the late 1950s and early 1960s, see Brilliant, *The Color of America Has Changed*; Lou Cannon, *Governor Reagan: His Rise to Power* (New York: Public Affairs, 2003); Donald T. Critchlow, *When Hollywood Was Right: How Movie Stars, Studio Moguls, and Big Business Remade American Politics* (New York: Cambridge University Press, 2013); Matthew Dallek, *The Right Moment: Ronald Reagan's First Victory and the Decisive Turning Point in American Politics* (New York: Oxford University Press, 2000); Dochuk, *From Bible Belt to Sunbelt*; Lotchin, *Fortress California, 1910–1961*; and McGirr, *Suburban Warriors*.

[41] Ibid.

As was true for parts of Texas, Tennessee, and even Georgia, California typified the multifaceted and dynamic political competition that raged across the Sunbelt during the 1950s and early 1960s between conservatives, moderates, and liberals of varying stripes. As the two major parties began to prepare for the presidential election of 1960, the Sunbelt's political leanings seemed anything but certain.

THE ELECTION OF 1960

After eight years under the leadership of Dwight Eisenhower, American voters went to the polls in November 1960 looking for change. On the whole, Americans were not unhappy with Eisenhower. He left office with approval ratings hovering near 60 percent. However, for all the talk of substantive policy changes debated during the campaign that year, the real change voters seemed to be attracted to was more stylistic than substantive. Somewhat tired of Eisenhower's grandfatherly persona, voters gravitated to the youth and apparent vigor of Massachusetts Democrat John F. Kennedy. A pioneer in the realm of political public relations, especially in his use of television, Kennedy captured imaginations when, during his acceptance speech at the Democratic National Convention in Los Angeles, he cast a vision for America's future, looking to the American West – and essentially, to the emerging Sunbelt – as he described an agenda for progress called the "New Frontier."[42]

On many levels, Kennedy was a captivating personality from an almost regal family. Nevertheless, winning the White House, not to mention his party's nomination, proved difficult. Many of the Democratic Party's most revered liberals – including Eleanor Roosevelt and Harry Truman – detested Kennedy's father, Joseph, whose own political ambitions had been derailed two decades earlier as a result of ill-advised and apparently defeatist remarks made while serving as the U.S. ambassador to Great Britain on the eve of World War II. JFK was neither easily nor quickly embraced

---

[42] Slotkin, *Gunfighter Nation*, 1–4.

in the South, where the nomination of a Massachusetts Catholic was hardly a popular choice. In fact, divisions related to Kennedy's nomination in 1960 proved to be a lasting source of tension for Democrats across the South, in Texas especially.[43]

Despite such obstacles, Kennedy won the presidency in November 1960, defeating Richard Nixon by the narrowest popular vote total in American history – just over 112,000 votes. His victory in the Electoral College was similarly slim. Kennedy carried Illinois by less than two-tenths of a single percent, and Texas by a mere two percent.[44] The win in Texas was especially significant considering that Eisenhower had carried Texas – a traditionally loyal Democratic state – in back-to-back contests in 1952 and 1956. Kennedy probably owed his victory in Texas to his running mate, Lyndon Johnson, although the senator from Massachusetts did much of the heavy lifting himself when he spoke before the Greater Houston Ministerial Association that September in an effort to ease concerns that many in the state still had over voting for a Catholic. Kennedy's speech in Houston on the separation of church and state remains one of the most significant and modeled moments in the history of modern American political campaigns.[45]

Kennedy also owed a debt of gratitude to Mexican American activists in Texas who formed "Viva Kennedy" clubs in support of the Democratic ticket. Viva Kennedy was the first statewide political organization for Mexican Americans in Texas and was chaired by Henry B. Gonzalez of San Antonio, who on the same

---

[43] Robert Dallek, *An Unfinished Life: John F. Kennedy, 1917–1963* (New York: Little, Brown, and Co., 2003), 283–284; Laura Jane Gifford, *The Center Cannot Hold, The 1960 Presidential Election and the Rise of Modern Conservatism* (Chicago: Northern Illinois University Press, 2009); for more on the election of 1960, see David Pietrusza, *1960: LBJ vs. JFK vs. Nixon: The Campaign That Forged Three Presidencies* (New York: Union Square Press, 2008); and W. J. Rorabaugh, *The Real Making of the President: Kennedy, Nixon, and the 1960 Election* (Lawrence: University Press of Kansas, 2012). See also Larry Sabato, *The Kennedy Half-Century: The Presidency, Assassination, and Lasting Legacy of John F. Kennedy* (New York: Bloomsbury USA, 2013).
[44] Ibid.
[45] Ibid.

day as Kennedy's victory became the first Mexican American from Texas ever elected to the U.S. House of Representatives. Hispanics flocked to the Kennedy–Johnson ticket in 1960 thanks to Gonzalez, as well as Kennedy's courtship of Hector Garcia's American G. I. Forum. They were also attracted to the Democratic Party's willingness to embrace an array of civil rights issues in its national platform that year, including immigration and migrant worker reform. Kennedy won 91 percent of the Hispanic vote in Texas, and 85 percent of the Hispanic vote nationally. In many ways, the Kennedy–Johnson campaign of 1960 greatly accelerated the political mobilization of Mexican Americans, first in the Sunbelt, and eventually across the entire country.[46]

For this reason, Kennedy performed very well in the heavily Hispanic parts of South Texas. He also did well in most rural counties in the state, with the exception of the northern panhandle. However, Nixon won a majority of the state's most densely populated counties, including Harris (Houston), Tarrant (Fort Worth), and Dallas Counties. In Dallas, Nixon carried 62 percent of the vote – his largest victory in any urban county of comparable size that year. In fact, Nixon's strong showing in Texas in 1960, despite Johnson's presence on the Democratic ticket, underscored the growth that Republicans had achieved in the Lone Star State during the 1950s. It also highlighted the appeal that Republicans increasingly had in the young, thriving metropolitan areas across the growing Sunbelt.

This trend, clearly evident in Texas's most populated metropolitan areas, was similarly demonstrated in several other states that year. For instance, Nixon carried his home state of California and did so largely because of his success in Southern California. The Republican ticket dominated Orange and San Diego Counties and only narrowly lost Los Angeles County, despite losing the vast majority of that

---

[46] For more on the Viva Kennedy movement and Mexican American politicization, see Ignacio M. Garcia, *Viva Kennedy: Mexican Americans in Search of Camelot* (College Station: Texas A&M University Press, 2000); and Arnoldo De Leon, *Ethnicity in the Sunbelt: Mexican Americans in Houston* (College Station: Texas A&M University Press, 2001). For more on the Kennedy presidency, see also Arthur Schlesinger Jr., *A Thousand Days: John F. Kennedy in the White House* (New York: Houghton Mifflin, 1965).

county's large Hispanic vote. Elsewhere in the Sunbelt, Nixon easily carried Arizona, winning almost 60 percent of the vote in Maricopa County (Phoenix). He also carried Florida; Tennessee; Virginia; and Oklahoma, which he won in a considerable landslide. Kennedy, on the other hand, carried Nevada, New Mexico, Georgia, South Carolina, and North Carolina, in addition to Texas. He also carried Louisiana, Arkansas, and Alabama, but not Mississippi, which chose to endorse a slate of unpledged electors rather than Kennedy, and it did so largely in protest of the Democratic Party's decision to formally endorse a civil rights plank in its official platform. All told, Kennedy won 88 electoral votes from Sunbelt states; Nixon won 76.

THE KENNEDY INTERLUDE

John F. Kennedy's brief time in the White House was marked by significant drama, especially on the international front. Cuba was a source of particular angst. Situated less than 100 miles from the Florida coast, Cuba's abrupt transition to communism under the leadership of Fidel Castro greatly worried the United States. Both Eisenhower and Kennedy worked with military leaders and intelligence agencies to develop strategies designed to either neutralize or eliminate the Castro regime. In April 1961, Kennedy green-lit a CIA-backed counterinsurgency effort aimed at overthrowing Castro. That effort ended with the disastrous "Bay of Pigs" episode in which more than 1,400 Cuban insurgents were either killed or captured, thanks in part to U.S. failures to properly administer the invasion or provide it with air cover. Less than two years later, in October 1962, the United States discovered Soviet nuclear missiles in Cuba. The subsequent Cuban Missile Crisis positioned Kennedy and Soviet Premier Nikita Khrushchev on opposite ends of a nuclear chessboard and pushed the planet to the precipice of global annihilation. After much tension and brinkmanship, World War III was averted, and Kennedy – who prided himself in the realm of foreign relations – won his greatest achievement.[47]

---

[47] Don Munton and David A. Welch, *The Cuban Missile Crisis: A Concise History* (New York: Oxford University Press, 2007).

Tensions related to Cuba were also critically important to the developing political culture of Florida. Beginning in earnest in 1960, Florida – the cities of Tampa and Miami in particular – began to receive thousands of Cuban refugees fleeing the oppressions of communism under Castro. Predictably, these refugees typically brought with them intensely anticommunist attitudes. Kennedy's perceived failure at the Bay of Pigs pushed many of these newly arrived Cubans into the world of conservative Republican politics. Although popular nationally, Kennedy's negotiated settlement of the Cuban Missile Crisis did little to quell the discontentment of Cuban anticommunists in Florida, many of whom remained impatient for direct American action against the Castro regime. For the next several decades, the influence of Cuban anticommunism added a distinct and important flavor to the political milieu of the Sunshine State.[48]

Kennedy also unsettled the political status quo in the Sunbelt Southwest by reaching out to other Latin American countries through programs such as his Alliance for Progress, implemented in 1961. In part a plan to strengthen economic cooperation between the United States and developing nations like Mexico, and in part a public relations strategy designed to provide cover for America's widening war against communism in that region, the Alliance for Progress ultimately failed to achieve most of its stated goals for trade and partnership between the United States and Latin America. Nevertheless, the program reemphasized issues such as trade, immigration, and cross-border international investment and labor – all issues that would influence politics in Sunbelt states including Texas, Arizona, and California for decades to come.[49]

Kennedy was also keenly aware of the degree to which racial unrest in the South was harming foreign policy efforts abroad, particularly as the United States sought to influence decolonization movements in Africa and Asia. For most of his presidency,

---

[48] For more on the Cuban influence in Florida politics since World War II, see David R. Colburn, *From Yellow Dog Democrats to Red State Republicans: Florida and Its Politics Since 1940* (Gainesville: University Press of Florida, 2007).

[49] Dallek, *An Unfinished Life*, 340–342.

Kennedy was sympathetic to the civil rights movement but slow to use his executive office to fully support it. Seeking to avoid international embarrassment, Kennedy – along with his brother Robert, who was the nation's attorney general – routinely compromised with segregationist governors in an effort to avoid the type of violence they feared would harm America's image elsewhere in the world. For instance, in the spring of 1961, when Alabama segregationists greeted the Freedom Riders with horrific violence, Kennedy intervened to protect the civil rights protesters from further bloodshed, but not arrest. Kennedy also tried to negotiate his way through desegregation crises at the University of Mississippi in 1962 and the University of Alabama in 1963.[50]

As confrontations like these became increasingly frequent, Kennedy gradually took a more resolved approach in support of the movement. Following a confrontation at the University of Alabama in which he federalized the state's National Guard to protect two black students seeking enrollment against the symbolic defiance of Governor George Wallace, Kennedy delivered the most important speech of his presidency on the issue of civil rights. During that speech, he called racial discrimination a "moral issue" and announced his support for a comprehensive civil rights bill aimed at accomplishing the movement's wider goals for reform and equality. This proposal, which eventually became the monumentally important Civil Rights Act of 1964, did not get very far in Congress while Kennedy remained in office. Nevertheless, it was Kennedy's shift toward the movement in the summer of 1963 that Americans would later recall when they assessed his legacy on civil rights. Less than three months after Kennedy's speech, Martin Luther King Jr. delivered his famous "I Have a Dream" speech during the March on Washington, further connecting – at least in the public's mind – the Kennedy White House with the oft-perceived peak of the civil rights movement.[51]

---

[50] Branch, *Parting the Waters*, 633–672; Dallek, *An Unfinished Life*, 383–388, 514–518, 597–603. For more on Kennedy, civil rights, and foreign relations, see again Dudziak, *Cold War Civil Rights*, 162–202.
[51] Dudziak, *Cold War Civil Rights*, 180–182.

As Kennedy came to embrace the civil rights movement, his popularity in the South declined. Racial equality had not been a major issue during the election of 1960. Kennedy's moderate approach during the first two years of his presidency did little to upset the balance of Democratic support he enjoyed in the South. But his shift toward the movement in 1963 infuriated segregationist Democrats and threatened to cost Kennedy several key states in his reelection campaign of 1964. Wanting to lay the early groundwork for that campaign, Kennedy embarked on a grand swing through Florida and Texas. On November 15, 1963, he visited his family's home-away-from-home in Palm Beach, Florida. Over the next several days, Kennedy made campaign appearances in Cape Canaveral, Tampa, and Miami. On November 21, he flew to Texas, campaigning in both Houston and San Antonio, before flying to Fort Worth. On the morning of November 22, Kennedy delivered a speech to the Fort Worth Chamber of Commerce before flying to Dallas, where he joined Texas Governor John Connally and a host of other state and local officials in a motorcade through downtown Dallas. At approximately 12:30 PM, Kennedy was assassinated while riding in that motorcade. Two hours later, Lyndon Johnson was sworn in at Dallas's Love Field while aboard Air Force One, becoming the thirty-sixth president of the United States, and the first of several to hail from a Sunbelt state.[52]

Between 1945 and 1963, the Sunbelt expanded economically and diversified politically. Establishment liberals and pragmatic

[52] The Kennedy assassination has been the subject of immense popular writing and scholarship, too abundant to cite comprehensively. For concise detail on the assassination and the politics leading up to it, see Steven M. Gillon, *The Kennedy Assassination – 24 Hours After: Lyndon B. Johnson's Pivotal First Day as President* (New York: Basic Books, 2009). See also Alice L. George, *The Assassination of John F. Kennedy: Political Trauma and American Memory* (New York: Routledge, 2013); Bill Minutaglio and Steven L. Davis, *Dallas 1963* (New York: Twelve, Hatchet Book Group, 2013); James Piereson, *Camelot and the Cultural Revolution: How the Assassination of John F. Kennedy Shattered American Liberalism* (New York: Encounter Books, 2007); and Gerald Posner, *Case Closed: Lee Harvey Oswald and the Assassination of JFK* (New York: Anchor Books, Doubleday, 1993).

moderates maintained their grip on power, but they did not do so without a fight. From the Right, conservatives decried the Democratic Party's embrace of interventionist government while also accusing the GOP's moderate eastern establishment of enabling the same thing. Meanwhile, African American and Hispanic activists across the grassroots Sunbelt joined both elected and unelected progressive whites in challenging the racial status quo of their region, building a civil rights movement that eventually captured the attention of political leaders all across the country. Fought on predominantly Sunbelt battlegrounds, the civil rights movement destabilized the region's political status quo, sparked divisions in both major parties, and catapulted the issue of race directly to the forefront of the nation's consciousness. The civil rights movement also forced southern conservatives to rethink their strategies for resisting social and racial change. Doing so would pay significant political dividends in the coming years, especially as many of those conservatives abandoned the party of the old Confederacy in favor of a renewed GOP.

For Lyndon Johnson, there were more battles yet to be waged and won. In 1964, sensing that momentum was still clearly on his side, the new president promoted the most ambitious program for economic, social, and political reform since the New Deal. He called his program the Great Society and promised that, if successful, his plan would mark the fulfillment of all that FDR – his political hero – had hoped to achieve, but had not been able to finish. Unfortunately for Johnson, a major war in Southeast Asia, coupled with intensified discontentment, protest, and anger at home over a wide range of issues, worked in almost constant opposition to those goals. Meanwhile, as conservatives watched the liberal consensus evaporate under the weight of this tumult, they seized the opportunity to grab the political momentum and accelerated the process of reshaping the Sunbelt into the modern Republican Right's undisputed home.

3

Wars against Liberalism

If politics during the first two decades of the postwar era were characterized by an embattled but resilient liberal consensus, then the mid-to-late 1960s were characterized by the unraveling of that consensus and the related fracturing of the New Deal coalition. In 1968, despite Lyndon Johnson's best efforts, the postwar liberal consensus that had largely framed American politics since the days of FDR finally imploded. When it did, the nation's political floodgates were breached by waves of ideological polarization, grassroots agitation, and divisive intraparty factionalism. In 1963, nearly half of American voters identified themselves as "liberal." By decade's end, that number had been reduced to barely 33 percent.[1] For most of these voters, liberalism simply did not stand for the same things at decade's end that it had fewer than ten years before. Circumstances had changed. More than anything, liberalism no longer seemed as competent or triumphant. An unpopular war in Vietnam, coupled with the perceived failure of Johnson's most ambitious domestic programs, not to mention the ongoing struggle for racial equality that continued to rage nationwide, all worked against liberalism's forward march. As the liberal consensus evaporated, a new brand of conservatism, birthed predominantly in the metropolitan Sunbelt,

---

[1] Steven F. Hayward, *The Age of Reagan: The Fall of the Old Liberal Order* (Roseville, CA: Prima Publishing, 2001), 233.

began to ascend in ways that many would have thought impossible just a few years earlier.[2]

The Democratic Party's struggles were clearest in the Sunbelt, especially in the South. During the mid-to-late 1960s, Democrats divided into increasingly polarized camps, thanks to disagreement on issues including civil rights, entitlement spending, foreign policy, and – broadly speaking – the role of the federal government in citizens' lives. Southern whites were among the first to leave the party of Jefferson, Jackson, and Roosevelt. Although not all southern whites left the Democratic Party during these years, by 1968 it was clear enough that the New Deal coalition that had functioned as the party's electoral safety net since the 1930s had been irreparably compromised.

The Republican Party was the chief beneficiary of these troubles. As the Democratic Party struggled across the Sunbelt, the extreme anticommunist paranoia that had popularly defined conservatism during much of the 1950s was replaced by a far more strategically evolved, charismatic, and appealing political worldview – one designed in large part as an answer to the questions that many middle-class whites in the Sunbelt began to ask more frequently as national stability seemed to fade. In different ways, and with varying degrees of success, Sunbelt conservatives such as Barry Goldwater and Ronald Reagan – along with a slew of activists working behind the scenes – began to repackage the central tenets of postwar anticommunism, and they did so at a time when voters seemed poised to try something new. This process was by no means easy. But by leading the charge, these conservatives accelerated the Sunbelt's transformation into the undisputed capital of the Republican Right. They also put Sunbelt conservatism on

---

[2] For more on Johnson, the Great Society, and American liberalism during the 1960s, see Mitchell B. Lerner, ed., *A Companion to Lyndon B. Johnson* (West Sussex, UK: Wiley-Blackwell Publishing, 2012); see also Davies, *From Opportunity to Entitlement*; Matusow, *The Unraveling of America*; Bruce J. Schulman, *Lyndon B. Johnson and American Liberalism: A Brief History with Documents*, 2nd ed. (New York: Bedford/St. Martin's, 2006); and Randall B. Woods, *LBJ: Architect of American Ambition* (New York: The Free Press, 2006).

an ascendant trajectory toward national power and, eventually, the White House.

But the rise of modern conservatism was hardly the New Deal coalition's only problem during the mid-to-late 1960s. Rather, as it struggled to maintain the allegiance of middle-class whites across the Sunbelt, Lyndon Johnson's party was simultaneously strained by the agitated and boisterous discontent of its increasingly radicalized left wing. As Johnson and other consensus-building liberals tried to use their democratically mandated power to construct a more orderly and just world, impatient and increasingly cynical activists challenged the political status quo, demanding more reform in less time, while questioning the essential goodness of the liberal establishment itself. All told, by the time LBJ finished his first and only full term in the White House, the liberal consensus upon which his career had depended was overwhelmed by a Democratic crack-up.

THE GREAT SOCIETY, CIVIL RIGHTS, AND THE GOLDWATER INSURGENCY

Johnson's presidency began much more hopefully than it ended. On January 8, 1964, during his first State of the Union address, the new president invoked the spirit of his slain predecessor and declared "unconditional war on poverty in America."[3] Less than five months later, during a commencement speech at the University of Michigan, Johnson went a step further and shared a vision for an even more comprehensive federal initiative – one that would both encompass and expand the heart and soul of the recently launched War on Poverty. He called that vision the "Great Society." According to Johnson, the Great Society's goal would be to maximize individual opportunity, reduce dependency, and make the American Dream more accessible to all citizens regardless

---

[3] Lyndon B. Johnson, "Annual Message to the Congress on the State of the Union," January 8, 1964, Speech Transcript, Lyndon B. Johnson Presidential Library & Museum [http://www.lbjlib.utexas.edu/johnson/archives.hom/speeches.hom/640108.asp].

of race, color, creed, or national origin. It was a bold and expansive initiative.[4]

For the next eleven months, Johnson worked feverishly to make his Great Society a reality. Among other things, he and the Democratic-controlled Congress passed laws related to environmental protection, transportation and highways, the beautification of public space, welfare relief, and federal support for the arts. To grease the legislative tracks on Capitol Hill, Johnson manipulated the nation's grief over Kennedy's death and the related notion that passing such laws would in some way fulfill JFK's unfinished legacy. In later years, Johnson would recall these efforts as a strategy designed to "take the dead man's program and turn it into a martyr's cause."[5]

Most notable in this regard was the Civil Rights Act of 1964. Passed in August after months of contentious debate, the Civil Rights Act of 1964 represented a culmination of sorts to the earliest phase of the modern African American civil rights movement. Among its other accomplishments, the bill included provisions for the desegregation of public space and the enforceability of fair hiring practices. Conservative Sunbelt Republicans Barry Goldwater of Arizona and John Tower of Texas opposed the legislation. So did all conservative southern Democrats, including Senator Robert Byrd of West Virginia. Byrd filibustered against the bill for more than fourteen hours. Senators Richard Russell of Georgia and Strom Thurmond of South Carolina were also, not surprisingly, intractably opposed. Thurmond went so far as to call it the "worst civil rights package ever presented to the Congress," dramatically comparing it to the efforts of Reconstruction-era Radicals. Russell denounced the bill as a federal attempt to mandate the "amalgamation of the races." He, like almost all

[4] See again Davies, *From Opportunity to Entitlement*; Matusow, *The Unraveling of America*; Lerner, *A Companion to Lyndon B. Johnson*; Schulman, *Lyndon B. Johnson and American Liberalism*; and Woods, *LBJ*.

[5] Quoted in Doris Kearns, *Lyndon Johnson and the American Dream* (New York: Harper & Row, 1976), 178; see also Maurice Isserman and Michael Kazin, *American Divided: The Civil War of the 1960s* (New York: Oxford University Press, 2000), 105–107.

his fellow conservatives, questioned the bill's constitutionality, while reaffirming a commitment to states' rights and local government. Most southern whites – elected and unelected alike – lined up in opposition to the bill. Even Tennessee's Albert Gore Sr. – who had voted in favor of the moderate Civil Rights Act of 1957 – voted nay in 1964.[6]

The efforts of staunchly segregationist southern conservatives including Byrd, Russell, and Thurmond is not surprising. Neither is Goldwater's opposition, nor Tower's. But an examination of the votes cast by elected officials representing the wider Sunbelt reveals a much more diverse collection of opinions. It is true that most senators representing Sunbelt states voted against the Civil Rights Act of 1964. But not all of them did. The bill won the support of Arizona Democrat Carl Hayden, as well as both senators from California, Thomas Kuchel (a Republican) and Clair Engle (a Democrat). Additionally, both Republican senators from Colorado voted for the bill, as did Democrats Clinton Anderson of New Mexico, Alan Bible and Howard Cannon of Nevada, Mike Monroney and Robert Kerr of Oklahoma, and Ralph Yarborough of Texas. In the House of Representatives, the bill won votes from all three of Arizona's representatives and all but five of California's thirty-seven. Also, notably voting "aye" in the House were Claude Pepper of Florida and Jack Brooks, Jake Pickle, and Henry Gonzalez of Texas – all liberal Democrats.[7]

Like virtually all of the battles waged over the Great Society, the struggle to pass the Civil Rights Act of 1964 came with

[6] For more on Thurmond, Russell, and other southern politicians who spoke out against the Civil Rights Act of 1964, see Robert Dallek, *Flawed Giant: Lyndon Johnson and His Times, 1961–1973* (New York: Oxford University Press, 1998), 112–121; for voting details on the Civil Rights Act of 1964 in the Senate, see Senate Vote #409, HR. 7152. Civil Rights Act of 1964. Passed, June 19, 1964, 88th Congress [http://www.govtrack.us/congress/votes/88-1964/s409]; for more on the Civil Rights Act of 1964, see Taylor Branch, *Pillar of Fire: America in the King Years, 1963–1965* (New York: Simon & Schuster, 1998).
[7] House Vote #182, HR. 7152. Civil Rights Act of 1964, Adoption of a Resolution (H. Res. 789) Providing for House Approval of the Bill as Amended by the Senate. Passed, July 2, 1964, 88th Congress [http://www.govtrack.us/congress/votes/88-1964/h182].

significant political consequences. For Johnson, the most obvious
consequence was his alienation from conservatives in the Deep
South. But for the most part, the Civil Rights Act of 1964 was
widely supported by both the public at large and congressional
Republicans outside the Sunbelt. GOP support for the bill came
thanks in large part to Johnson's relationship with Senate Minority
Leader Everett Dirksen of Illinois. At the same time, and despite
widespread perceptions to the contrary, the Great Society also
resonated with most Americans in 1964. Its goals reflected the
technocratic optimism of the embattled but still reigning liberal
consensus. Buttressed by liberalism's inherent confidence in the
ability of government to solve almost any problem, Johnson used
the Great Society to expand the size and power of government at
a time when the American people still believed in and trusted
government. Polls taken in 1964, for example, showed that nearly
three out of every four Americans trusted the federal government
and American political institutions as a whole. As Johnson promoted the Great Society, he raised hopes for a better world. Taken
together, Johnson's Great Society, its related War on Poverty, and
the Civil Rights Act of 1964, represented an apex for the postwar
liberal consensus.[8]

The Great Society also confirmed most conservatives' worst
fears about the ever-expanding regulatory reach of a bloated
welfare state. In reacting to those fears, conservatives across the
Sunbelt fought to seize control of the Republican Party. Doing
so would demand an attack both against Johnson as well as the
moderate, eastern establishment within their own Republican
ranks. In need of a leader for this fight, conservative activists
looked to the state of Arizona where, in 1964, they convinced a
deeply divided Republican Party to nominate Barry Goldwater for
president of the United States. As it turned out, Goldwater's 1964
campaign for the presidency was possibly the most important

---

[8] Seymour Martin Lipset and William Schneider, "The Decline of Confidence in
American Institutions," *Political Science Quarterly*, Vol. 98, No. 3 (Fall 1983),
pp. 379–402. For more on massive resistance and conservatism in the Deep
South, see Crespino, *In Search of Another Country*.

event in the history of modern American conservatism, and certainly one of the most important moments in the political history of the postwar Sunbelt.

Goldwater's nomination was a major triumph for grassroots conservatives – one many years in the making. It was also a triumph unintentionally enabled by establishment liberalism's long-standing power in Washington. After several years of liberal consensus – years in which Democrats and moderate Republicans sustained a relatively harmonious cooperation on Capitol Hill – conservatives found themselves almost entirely relegated to the margins of national political power. As conservatives lost their voice in Washington, grassroots organizers – out of necessity – began to fill that void in places all across the country, but especially across the Sunbelt, where the foundational tenets of modern conservatism had already been established within the region's political culture. From this desperate need for new leaders sprang organizations such as the John Birch Society (JBS). However, because of its reactionary and paranoid brand of anticommunism, JBS proved incapable of leading a wider conservative movement, let alone one predicated on a desire to win more elections. Instead, other organizations and different leaders were needed.[9]

One of those organizations was the highly influential Young Americans for Freedom (YAF), born in 1960. Like JBS, YAF was fiercely anticommunist. But unlike JBS, it was dedicated to evangelizing conservative principles more than it was to simply ridding American society of all things left wing. Also like JBS – and like most other conservative organizations in the early 1960s – YAF enthusiastically identified Goldwater as its hero.[10] Primarily a college student organization, YAF's principle founder was William F. Buckley Jr. In 1951, Buckley rose to fame thanks to

---

[9] McGirr, *Suburban Warriors*, 113; Schoenwald, *A Time for Choosing*, 62–99.

[10] Gregory L. Schneider, *Cadres for Conservatism: Young Americans for Freedom and the Rise of the Contemporary Right* (New York: New York University Press, 1998); and Andrew, *The Other Side of the Sixties*. Schneider points out that YAF chapters in the West were particularly libertarian, even going so far as to endorse the legalization of some drugs, while eventually opposing the Vietnam War. Such sentiment led to massive divisions within the organization.

the publication of his provocative book *God and Man at Yale*, which alleged that faculty at Yale were indoctrinating students with liberal ideas, even going so far as to criticize several professors by name. Using that success as a springboard, Buckley then created the highly influential political magazine *National Review*. Thanks in large part to Buckley's leadership, *National Review* tripled its readership during the early 1960s and became an influential voice on the growing conservative Right.[11]

The Conscience of a Conservative, Goldwater's own book, proved even more influential than *National Review*, at least in the short term. Published in 1960 and ghostwritten by Buckley's brother-in-law Brent Bozell, *Conscience* quickly became a fundamental text for most conservatives. Remarkable for a quasiphilosophical work of political nonfiction, the book sold 85,000 copies during its first month on shelves and made the *New York Times* best seller list within three months. Sales eventually topped three million. Pat Buchanan later called the book "the New Testament of conservatism." Over the next several years, *Conscience* was read and discussed in conservative reading clubs and at YAF meetings on college campuses and in suburban living rooms all over the country. For several years, conservatives would reference Goldwater's book in search of guidance on almost every political issue.[12]

The Conscience of a Conservative was not exclusively Goldwater's brainchild, nor Bozell's. Clarence Manion, another conservative activist and eventual Goldwater campaign organizer, had actually commissioned it. A former dean of Notre Dame Law School turned conservative talk radio host, Manion first tried to win the GOP's presidential nomination for Goldwater in 1960. That effort failed. But in terms of the Republican Party's evolving strategy, Manion was a visionary. He resolutely believed that conservatism's future depended on Republican growth in

[11] George H. Nash, *The Conservative Intellectual Movement in America Since 1945* (New York: Basic Books, 1976), 235–286.
[12] Quoted in Goldberg, *Barry Goldwater*, 139–145; Perlstein, *Before the Storm*, 61–68; Barry Goldwater, *The Conscience of a Conservative* (Shepardsville, KY: Victory Publishing, 1960).

the South, and he worked tirelessly to that end. One of his most important contacts in that region was Strom Thurmond. A Democrat until 1964, Thurmond – like most other conservative southern Democrats – felt increasingly alienated from his party because of developments in the civil rights movement. Thanks in part to Manion, Thurmond became one of the first of many southern conservatives to leave the party of Dixie in favor of the GOP. Manion was also among the first to use broadcast media to promote conservative ideas. His weekly radio show, the *Manion Forum of Opinion*, reached thousands of listeners during the 1950s and 1960s and was heavily bankrolled by Texas oil tycoons H. L. and Bunker Hunt.[13]

Another important insurgent working behind the scenes to advance Goldwater's career was F. Clifton White. A native New Yorker, White – like most conservatives – was frustrated by the hammerlock that moderate Republicans held on his party. In 1961, he emerged as a mobilizing force behind what would eventually be called the Draft Goldwater Committee, an organization dedicated to winning Goldwater the GOP's presidential nomination in 1964. White eventually left this organization for Citizens for Goldwater–Miller, a group tasked with generating conservative enthusiasm and increasing voter turnout during the general election. Either way, whether through the Draft Goldwater Committee or Citizens for Goldwater–Miller, White was a major force behind the merger of several early 1960s conservative influences, including most importantly those bubbling up at the grass roots in places across the metropolitan Sunbelt.[14]

Dallas, Texas, was one of those places and Peter O'Donnell another of those insurgents. In 1963, O'Donnell – chairman of

[13] Dan T. Carter, *The Politics of Rage: George Wallace, the Origins of the New Conservatism, and the Transformation of American Politics* (Baton Rouge: Louisiana State University Press, 1995), 336; Goldberg, *Goldwater*, 139–145; Perlstein, *Before the Storm*, 11, 61–68, 476.

[14] McGirr, *Suburban Warriors*, 138; Perlstein, *Before the Storm*, 193–194, 214–217, 480–482. "Miller" refers to Goldwater's running mate in 1964, William E. Miller – a conservative congressman from New York.

the Texas Republican Party and local Dallas political strategist –
became chairman of the National Draft Goldwater Committee.
O'Donnell's influence in Texas Republican politics had already
captured the attention of ambitious conservatives all across the
Sunbelt well before he took a position of leadership within the
Goldwater campaign. Among his other credentials, O'Donnell
was the mastermind behind Bruce Alger's improbable ten-year
congressional career. Alger, however, was hardly O'Donnell's
only political success story of the early 1960s. In 1960, for instance,
O'Donnell was almost singularly responsible for Richard Nixon's
overwhelming success in Dallas against JFK. And in 1961,
O'Donnell was the creative force behind John Tower's stunning
victory over establishment Democrat William Blakely in that year's
special election to fill Lyndon Johnson's vacated U.S. Senate seat.[15]

Above all his other goals, O'Donnell was committed to building
the Republican Party in Texas. In the early 1960s, he believed
that Goldwater's brand of ideologically resolute conservatism
was the key to accomplishing that goal. In later years, he backed
off that position, believing that moderation was more important
to winning elections, a conviction undoubtedly formed in the wake
of Goldwater's failure. But in 1963 and 1964, O'Donnell operated
under the belief that for Republicans to win in Texas, they had to
reframe the national political discourse along ideological lines and
then present themselves as the only true champions of authentic
conservatism. O'Donnell was convinced that most Americans were
inherently conservative; they just didn't know it yet.[16]

Texans oil barons H. L. Hunt and Sid Richardson also supported the Goldwater insurgency. Not surprisingly, their contributions typically came in the form of money. Money served not
simply the immediate needs of Goldwater's national campaign;
it also provided crucial funding for conservative efforts at the
grass roots. Those efforts ranged from event staging to leaflet

---

[15] For more on Tower, see John R. Knaggs, *Two Party Texas: The John Tower
Era, 1961–1984* (Austin: Eakin Press, 1986).

[16] Cunningham, *Cowboy Conservatism*, 45; Goldberg, *Goldwater*, 168–177;
Perlstein, *Before the Storm*, 191–194, 214–228.

publication to all variety of miscellaneous political tools in between. Meanwhile, J. Evetts Haley – a Texas rancher, former professor, failed gubernatorial candidate, and author – contributed to the campaign by writing *A Texan Looks at Lyndon*, a controversial book released in early 1964 in which Goldwater's opponent was vilified as the personification of all that was corrupt and wrong with American politics. Goldwater enjoyed pockets of enthusiastic support among grassroots conservatives in Texas, but it was the direct action and financial contributions of men like Hunt, Richardson, and Haley that really made the movement in Texas move.[17]

In terms of overall campaign contributions, however, Texas took a backseat to Arizona – Phoenix specifically. Two of the most influential personalities within the Goldwater campaign were Denison Kitchel and Stephen Shadegg, both of Phoenix. Kitchel met Goldwater in the 1930s when he moved to Phoenix after graduating from Harvard Law School. A successful local attorney in 1952, Kitchel ran Goldwater's surprisingly successful Senate campaign against Earnest McFarland. From 1957 to 1963, he served as general counsel to the Arizona Republican Party. In 1958, he essentially wrote the Arizona Republican Party's entire platform. It was a natural choice, therefore, when Goldwater tabbed Kitchel to manage his national campaign for the presidency in 1964.[18] Working next to Kitchel in the Goldwater campaign was Stephen Shadegg. In 1964, Shadegg served as a regional campaign director after having worked on Goldwater's Senate campaigns in 1952 and 1958. He also served as chairman of the Arizona Republican Party from 1960 to 1963. During that same time, he ghostwrote a nationally syndicated newspaper column under Barry Goldwater's byline. Together, Kitchel and Shadegg formed the core of Goldwater's famed "Arizona Mafia." The Arizona Mafia was the strategic brains behind Goldwater's increasingly organized, but still grassroots-oriented campaign.[19]

---

[17] Cunningham, *Cowboy Conservatism*, 58–61; for a more comprehensive treatment of the links between Texas oil money and conservative politics, see Burrough, *The Big Rich*.

[18] Goldberg, *Goldwater*, 92–99, 125–131, 142; Perlstein, *Before the Storm*, 255, 314.

[19] Ibid.; for more on Phoenix, see Shermer, *Sunbelt Capitalism*.

While funding and leadership poured in from Texas and Arizona, some of the most dramatic grassroots action on behalf of the Goldwater insurgency was staged in Southern California – Orange County to be specific. Populous, suburban, and neatly situated between Los Angeles and San Diego Counties, Orange County witnessed exceptional growth and development in the years after World War II. It attracted thousands of new residents, most of them coming from Texas, Oklahoma, or various parts of the Midwest. These migrants typically came to Southern California in search of jobs and new opportunities, but they carried with them deeply rooted and quite traditional ideas about individual merit, evangelical Protestantism, and national security. Such ideas flourished in California's defense-oriented and anticommunist southern counties.[20]

Conservative migrants to Southern California also quickly discovered that neither the state Democratic nor Republican Parties were working very hard to represent their values. They were especially disheartened by their marginalization within the California Republican Party, which was dominated by a moderate wing deeply connected to the GOP's eastern establishment. Failing to have their voices heard in either Washington or Sacramento, a growing number of grassroots conservatives organized through local JBS chapters; neighborhood reading clubs; and even the Orange County School of Anti-Communism, founded by Fred Schwarz in 1961. Schwarz was a lay pastor from Australia and architect of the Christian Anti-Communist Crusade, a global ministry designed to educate youth on the spiritual perils of the Left. In 1960, Schwarz moved the headquarters of the Christian Anti-Communist Crusade to California, where he quickly found a receptive audience. He organized his new school for anticommunism in Orange County the next year and garnered a great deal of attention from local media in the process, much of it positive.[21]

---

[20] McGirr, *Suburban Warriors*, 21–31. For more on migrations into Southern California and the infusion of evangelical Protestantism, see also Dochuk, *From Bible Belt to Sunbelt*.

[21] McGirr, *Suburban Warriors*, 50–62.

Momentum continued to build in Southern California through 1962, 1963, and 1964. Local business leaders including amusement park owner Walter Knott openly supported the movement, giving it an added sense of credibility in the process. Despite losing to Republican moderates in battle after battle, conservatives continued to advance their cause within the state GOP. Then, in March 1964, conservatives sent shockwaves through state and national politics when they seized a commanding 60 to 39 majority in the California Republican Assembly – an unofficial political body responsible for identifying and supporting GOP candidates for state and local offices all across California. Moderate Republicans and liberal Democrats – both locally and nationally – panicked, decrying the takeover as evidence of right-wing radicalism's insurgent power in Southern California. Less than three months later, those fears seemed realized when Goldwater won the California Republican primary, defeating New York Governor Nelson Rockefeller, the choice of California moderates. Goldwater owed his victory in the California primary largely to the overwhelming turnout in San Diego, Orange, and Los Angeles Counties, in addition to the organizing efforts of Joe Shell, a conservative state assemblyman from Los Angeles who first gained prominence in 1962 when he challenged Richard Nixon for the state GOP's gubernatorial nomination, a fight that typified the state party's divide between moderates and conservatives.[22]

It was Goldwater's victory in the 1964 California primary that eventually propelled him to the Republican nomination, which he accepted in August at the party's national convention in San Francisco. But far more than simply the efforts of grassroots conservatives in Orange County, the Goldwater insurgency succeeded in winning their candidate the GOP nomination because of the hard work of strategists, operatives, and foot soldiers all across the Sunbelt and beyond. These men and women – some of them very wealthy and powerful – believed in Goldwater's conservative message about limited government, reduced spending, low taxes, and

[22] Ibid., 101–126, 138–139; see also Critchlow, *When Hollywood Was Right*, 155–159.

states' rights. Goldwater's message was undoubtedly and powerfully conservative – stark in its diametric opposition to Johnson's vision for the Great Society. In evangelizing this message, Goldwater rallied the conservative faithful. Unfortunately for those faithful in 1964, Goldwater failed to rally anyone else.

THE ELECTION OF 1964

Goldwater's nomination represented a triumph for the postwar conservative Right, as well as for the Republican Party's long-term political aspirations and the Sunbelt's status as an emerging regional power. But by almost any other measurement, Goldwater's campaign against Lyndon Johnson was an unmitigated disaster. In one of the nastiest campaigns of the twentieth century, Johnson was swept into office on November 3 by the greatest popular landslide in American history. He defeated Goldwater with 61 percent of the electorate, which translated into a margin of nearly 16 million votes. In the Electoral College, Johnson won 486 to 52. Goldwater carried only six states: Arizona, Louisiana, Mississippi, Alabama, Georgia, and South Carolina. In Arizona, he won by 1 percent of the vote. In the Deep South, he won more handily, most dramatically in Mississippi, which delivered the Republican an astounding 87 percent of the vote, a figure all the more remarkable considering that Goldwater was the first Republican to carry the state of Mississippi since Ulysses S. Grant in 1872.

Elsewhere across the Sunbelt, Goldwater floundered. In California, he lost by nearly 20 percentage points and won only five counties – most notably (and not surprisingly) Orange and San Diego Counties. In Texas, Goldwater lost by 27 points, though this had much more to do with the fact that Johnson was from Texas and had assumed the presidency after John F. Kennedy's assassination in Dallas. These two factors created the dual force of a candidate running in his home state, which also happened to be a state seeking atonement for whatever role it may have played in a national tragedy. Widely considered the capital of the Far Right, even Dallas shied away from all things extremist in 1964, ousting its ultraconservative congressman,

Bruce Alger.[23] Goldwater was similarly rejected in other parts of the Sunbelt. He lost Florida, though the Sunshine State was much more hotly contested than either Texas or California. Goldwater actually carried a majority of Florida's counties but lost the popular vote by less than 3 percent. Elsewhere across the Sunbelt, Johnson won relatively easy victories in Virginia, North Carolina, Tennessee, Arkansas, Oklahoma, New Mexico, and Nevada.

Goldwater's victory in his home state of Arizona makes sense, but why did Goldwater do so well in the Deep South, which was traditionally the most solidly Democratic region in the nation? The question almost answers itself. Goldwater won the Deep South because of race, or, more specifically, Goldwater won the Deep South because of his opposition to the Civil Rights Act of 1964. In opposing that act, Goldwater argued that mandating racial equality – although perhaps well intentioned – was an unconstitutional violation of states' rights. That was essentially the same argument that most southern conservatives were making. Also, contributing to Goldwater's popularity in the Deep South was that many conservatives in that region felt betrayed by Lyndon Johnson, a Texan who they believed was abusing his executive power to force racial equality onto Dixie. In several editorials broadcast on WRAL-TV in Raleigh, Jesse Helms lamented the role that liberals like Johnson were playing in what Helms saw as an unnecessary destabilization of otherwise fine relations between whites and blacks in the South. For Helms and other conservative southern Democrats in 1964, civil rights was *the* issue.[24]

Conservative southerners like Helms may not have understood the true nature of black–white relations in their region, but they were at least accurate in viewing Johnson as an agent for change. Civil rights was at the forefront of Johnson's agenda; it had been since the moment he took office.[25] Johnson's insistence on passing

[23] Cunningham, *Cowboy Conservatism*, 49–50.
[24] Link, *Righteous Warrior*, 74–75.
[25] Gillon, *The Kennedy Assassination – 24 Hours After*, 181–192. Johnson met with advisors on the night of the assassination and decided during those meetings that civil rights would a priority.

civil rights reform alienated many of his former colleagues in the Senate and exacerbated divisions within the Democratic Party. Few white southerners found convincing Johnson's case for memorializing the martyred Kennedy with new race laws. Eventually, voters who were turned off by Goldwater's opposition to civil rights immediately gravitated to Johnson, whereas voters like Helms and others in the South who admired Goldwater's opposition defected to the GOP.

The racial dimensions of the election of 1964 shaped many long-term perceptions about the rise of modern conservatism and the growth of the Republican Party, especially in the Sunbelt. Because Goldwater was successful in the Deep South largely because of that region's white backlash against civil rights, and because Goldwater was and continues to be identified by historians as one of the preeminent founders of modern conservatism, certain dots are easily connected. Very quickly, modern conservatism, especially as it grew in the Sunbelt after 1964, was interpreted as racially motivated. On a certain level, it is hard to argue against this logic. If the Deep South was once solidly Democratic and then became Republican beginning in 1964, it would stand to reason that those who abandoned the party of secession in favor of the GOP did so in the hopes of preserving the status quo of racial inequality. However, this analysis lacks nuance at the same time that it lacks broader regional and national perspectives built over longer periods of time. It fails to distinguish between the political cultures of the Deep South as opposed to the peripheral South, and it fails to consider the multifaceted class dimensions within the South. It also fails to consider the full spectrum of other social, cultural, and economic issues at play during the 1960s and beyond.[26]

---

[26] For more on the racial dynamics at play in the South's growing attraction to the Republican Party, see Gerard Alexander, "The Myth of the Racist Republicans." *Claremont Institute for the Study of Statesmanship and Political Philosophy: Claremont Review of Books* (Spring 2004). See also Timothy N. Thurber, *Republicans and Race: The GOP's Frayed Relationship with African Americans, 1945–1974* (Lawrence: University Press of Kansas, 2013).

Was the South's conversion to the Republican Party about nothing more than its commitment to white supremacy? If so, does that implicate the entirety of Sunbelt conservatism as complementarily regressive on race? Was the Republican Party already the party of white backlash by 1964? The developing narrative of conservatism's contested ascendancy in the Sunbelt suggests a more complicated answer.

Beyond the question of race and the origins of modern conservatism, the Goldwater campaign of 1964 was important for at least three additional reasons. First, it rallied millions of previously un-mobilized grassroots conservatives into active identification with the Republican Party and did so most powerfully and abundantly in Sunbelt states. In doing so, the campaign produced and seasoned a new generation of conservative foot soldiers. Many of these men and women would continue to fight on behalf of conservative candidates for the rest of the century. Second, in mobilizing these conservatives into the GOP, the Goldwater campaign significantly weakened the eastern establishment's grip on Republican Party politics. By weakening that grip, pro-Goldwater activists launched an ideological and geographical war for the heart of the party. That war pitted consensus moderates such as Rockefeller against a slew of up-and-coming candidates representing the conservative Sunbelt Right. Among these candidates was Ronald Reagan. Reagan, a former Hollywood actor, president of the Screen Actors Guild, and virulent anticommunist, first gained national political prominence when he delivered a rousing speech on Goldwater's behalf, televised one week before the general election in October 1964. It was this speech that conservative activists had in mind when they decided to run Reagan for the governorship of California in 1966.[27]

Finally, though ultimately unsuccessful in its effort to win the White House in 1964, the Goldwater campaign provided Sunbelt conservatives with an invaluable opportunity to showcase their

[27] Ronald Reagan, "A Time for Choosing," October 27, 1964, Speech Transcript, Ronald Reagan Presidential Library & Museum [http://www.reagan.utexas.edu/archives/reference/timechoosing.html].

philosophy on a national stage. In the process of losing an election, these conservatives learned several new campaign tricks, especially in the art of campaign advertising and the importance of perception management. Conservatives would grow far more public relations savvy in the coming years and would blaze new trails in the realm of political campaign advertising and overall strategy. Sunbelt conservatives may have failed to convince the nation of the wisdom of their political philosophy in 1964, but they would have other chances. All told, the Goldwater campaign of 1964 was a critically important step in the growth and maturation of the political philosophy that would soon become almost synonymous – at least in popular imagination – with the Sunbelt's overarching political culture.[28]

THE END OF CONSENSUS

In early 1965, with a clear mandate in his back pocket, Johnson accelerated the Great Society's already hectic legislative pace. Over the next several months, he and the still overwhelmingly Democratic Congress passed hundreds of laws creating new federal programs including Medicare, Medicaid, the National Endowment for the Arts, the National Endowment for the Humanities, and the Corporation for Public Broadcasting. He also allocated hundreds of millions of dollars to infrastructural enhancements related to public transportation and housing, especially for urban areas. For Johnson, whose political hero had always been Franklin Roosevelt, the Great Society was the

---

[28] The Goldwater movement and campaign of 1964 has received significant attention by scholars, especially in recent years. However, the best treatments remain Goldberg, *Barry Goldwater*; McGirr, *Suburban Warriors*; and Perlstein, *Before the Storm*. See also David Farber and Jeff Roche, eds., *The Conservative Sixties* (New York: Peter Lang, 2003); Laura Jane Gifford and Daniel K. Williams, eds., *The Right Side of the Sixties: Reexamining Conservatism's Decade of Transformation* (New York: Palgrave Macmillan, 2012); and Robert Mann, *Daisy Petals and Mushroom Clouds: LBJ, Goldwater, and the Ad That Changed American Politics* (Baton Rouge: Louisiana State University Press, 2011).

fulfillment of all that the New Deal was designed to accomplish but had not been able to complete.[29]

For all its legislative success, the Great Society proved politically expensive. Among other things, it greatly intensified debates over the nature of liberalism and the proper role of government in American lives. For Johnson, the Great Society's overarching goal was to foster individual achievement by providing opportunities to those whose chances for social mobility seemed impossible or at least severely restricted. Like Roosevelt, Johnson abhorred the notion of dependency. As was essentially true of mainstream American liberalism through the mid-1960s, Johnson hoped that by creating an environment in which individuals could more easily access education and job training, efficient government action could break the cyclical patterns of poverty that seemed to plague certain populations. Liberals like Johnson believed that the fundamental structure of American society was not broken, neither did it need to be fixed; it simply needed to be expanded. The Great Society's job, therefore, was to create new opportunities for those citizens who, because of their willingness to work, deserved a chance at a better life.

In advancing these ideas, the Great Society represented the apex of postwar American liberalism. By giving conservatism something concrete to complain about, the Great Society also, ironically, represented the beginning of postwar liberalism's sudden demise. Conservative antipathy toward the Great Society was not surprising. This was, after all, the heart of Goldwater's message in 1964. But, presumptively abandoned for dead in the wake of Goldwater's failure in 1964, conservatism's growing appeal to voters as the decade wore on caught many observers by surprise. Perception management was critical to that success. Rather than relying on a strategy of convincing a skeptical public of their ideology's veracity, conservatives during the late 1960s instead repackaged conservatism through a lens of accessible practicality, at the same time conflating liberalism with all strands

[29] For more on Johnson, civil rights, and the Great Society, see again Dallek, *Flawed Giant*; and Isserman and Kazin, *America Divided*.

of left-of-center political thought and extremism. By articulately vilifying the Great Society, its related War on Poverty, and the civil rights movement as un-American (and costly) experiments in collectivism and social engineering, conservatives could point to specific examples of government programs that did not work and/or seemed nonsensical. This approach helped conservatives connect with average (mainly white) voters when that connection might otherwise have been lost because of esoteric ramblings about ideology and philosophy. Becoming more populist and mainstream while charging liberalism with elitist radicalism was a risky but deft strategy that quickly began to pay dividends.

This was certainly true of Ronald Reagan's approach to campaign politics; he said as much, and more, during his famous, nationally broadcast campaign speech for Goldwater on October 27, 1964. In questioning Johnson's vision for the Great Society, as well as his and other liberals' commitment to defeating global communism, Reagan's speech captured the imagination of many influential California conservatives. By the time Reagan finished his speech that night, many conservatives had already abandoned their hopes for a Goldwater presidency. They were eager, however, to embrace the possibility of a Reagan governorship.[30]

Meanwhile, as conservatives began to plan Reagan's future, the rest of California waged a spirited fight against what many on the Right perceived to be a government-mandated experiment in social engineering and forced equality. On the same day that Lyndon Johnson won the state of California by twenty percentage points, California voters also overwhelmingly approved the controversial Proposition 14, a measure that reasserted the right of homeowners to sell or not sell their property to individuals at their own discretion. Essentially, Proposition 14 nullified most of California's antidiscrimination real estate laws. In part the result of a campaign that shared many of its resources with Goldwater,

[30] Ronald Reagan, "A Time for Choosing," October 27, 1964, Speech Transcript, Ronald Reagan Presidential Library & Museum [http://www.reagan.utexas.edu/archives/reference/timechoosing.html]. For more on Reagan's emergence as a Republican gubernatorial candidate, see Dallek, *The Right Moment*.

California conservatives won the fight for Proposition 14 by a margin twice as large Johnson's margin against Goldwater in the state.[31]

Despite also winning a surprising number of votes from California liberals committed to the protection of individual rights, the fight for Proposition 14 nevertheless typified a clear manifestation of the Sunbelt's emerging conservative backlash against Great Society liberalism. Protecting individual rights had long been a hallmark of American liberalism; expanding individual opportunity was the Great Society's core essence. But during the mid-1960s, conservatives in California – as they were also arguing in Atlanta and other places across the Sunbelt – appropriated the discourse of individual rights, reframing those rights in juxtaposition to what they argued was liberalism's drift toward collectivism and social engineering. As many liberals increasingly called for the expansion of opportunity, conservatives increasingly framed their opponents as advocates of entitlement and did so while embracing the traditionally liberal language of individuality. Goldwater may not have convinced many California voters that he would make a good president, but the vast majority of those voters, along with a surprising number of self-described liberals in Northern California, were at least convinced that one of Goldwater's causes – the protection of individual property rights – was worth supporting.[32]

Proposition 14 was only the beginning of conservatism's ascendancy at ballot boxes across California. In August 1965, that surge was imbued with an added sense of moral urgency and palpable fear when the Watts section of Los Angeles erupted in riotous violence, just months after police had narrowly prevented a similar riot in the same area, the result of a "turf war" between local

---

[31] For more on Proposition 14, see Daniel Martinez HoSang, "Racial Liberalism and the Rise of the Sunbelt West: The Defeat of Fair Housing on the 1964 California Ballot," in Nickerson and Dochuk, *Sunbelt Rising*, 188–213; see also Brilliant, *The Color of America Has Changed*, 190–213. Brilliant discusses Republican opposition to Proposition 14, a subject also addressed in detail in Critchlow, *When Hollywood Was Right*, 157, 181–182.

[32] Ibid.; Kruse, *White Flight*.

Mexican Americans and area blacks. Police were less effective the second time around. Making matters worse, Pat Brown, California's Democratic governor, was out of the country when the riot broke out, leaving to subordinates the almost impossible task of restoring order to the largely black section of the state's most populous city. Reagan and other conservatives immediately pounced on Brown and the state's liberal establishment, analogizing incompetence with complicity as the riots dragged on for several days and the death, injury, and arrest totals mounted. The Watts riots gave conservatives a visible example of liberalism's culpability in a growing climate of unrest, lawlessness, and entitlement – all adjectives used to describe the situation in Watts, despite evidence suggesting that much of the unrest was actually an explosive response to enduring inequalities, not simply a disorganized spree of criminality. Reagan was especially effective in his ability to connect Watts with the ongoing student unrest at the University of California, Berkeley, where students had been organizing in favor of free speech and racial equality since the previous summer. Clearly visible in California, but common elsewhere in the Sunbelt during the widely tumultuous 1960s, the public's growing associations of lawlessness and protest with liberalism unquestionably aided Sunbelt conservatives in their quest to move out of the political margins and into the political mainstream.[33]

If Barry Goldwater's failed presidential campaign of 1964 was not the most important event in the history of modern conservatism, Ronald Reagan's victorious campaign for the governorship of California in 1966 perhaps was. Of course, the latter would not have happened without the former. Regardless, California's decision to oust an incumbent liberal in favor of a conservative such as Reagan was a monumental statement about the growing power and resilience of the Sunbelt Right. Pat Brown, who had

---

[33] Dallek, *The Right Moment*, 128–149, Perlstein, *Nixonland*, 71. For more on the association between perceptions of crime and liberalism, see Michael W. Flamm, *Law and Order: Street Crime, Civil Unrest, and the Crisis of Liberalism in the 1960s* (New York: Columbia University Press, 2005).

easily defeated Richard Nixon to win reelection in 1962, became politically vulnerable in the wake of Proposition 14's success, ongoing student unrest at Berkeley, and riotous bloodshed in Watts. His popularity on the decline, Brown struggled to repel a spirited challenge from Los Angeles mayor and fellow Democrat Sam Yorty, who ran as a law-and-order populist in the state's 1966 Democratic primary. Brown survived the primary but was then handily defeated by Reagan in the general election. It was not close; Reagan won by nearly 1 million votes and carried fifty-five of the state's fifty-eight counties.[34]

Reagan's campaign largely succeeded where Goldwater's had failed. He successfully avoided the extremist label and did so by framing his conservatism in very practical and immediate examples, such as those offered by Watts and Berkeley. Reagan also surprised reporters with his affability, a trait absent from Goldwater's repertoire. He even benefited from Brown's efforts through television ads to paint Reagan as a radical, efforts that came across to most voters as desperate and meanspirited. In short, Reagan did not scare voters the way Goldwater had. In becoming the freshest face of Sunbelt conservatism, Reagan inaugurated an eight-year career in the governor's office of the nation's largest state. He was also beginning a path that would eventually take him to the White House.[35]

Reagan was not the only Sunbelt Republican to do well in 1966. In the November midterms, Republicans picked up forty-seven seats in the U.S. House of Representatives, one of those coming from a newly created district in Texas representing much of Houston's growing suburban and oil-rich middle and upper classes. That district, Texas's Seventh, made George Bush its new congressman, thus setting in motion the career of another future president. Republicans also picked up one seat in Arizona,

[34] Dallek, *The Right Moment*, 150–172, 238.
[35] For a comprehensive examination of Reagan's victory in 1966, see Cannon, *Governor Reagan*; Critchlow, *When Hollywood Was Right*; and Dallek, *The Right Moment*.

Ronald Reagan celebrates his victory in the 1966 California gubernatorial election with his wife, Nancy, and supporters. (Courtesy of the Ronald Reagan Presidential Library.)

Arkansas, Colorado, Florida, Georgia (two, net one), North Carolina, Oklahoma, and Tennessee; two in Virginia; and three in California. Florida also made political waves by electing Claude Kirk, a Republican who ran as a champion of the state's growing suburban middle class. Kirk was the first Republican to win the governor's office in Florida since Reconstruction, a distinction shared that year by Winthrop Rockefeller, a moderate Republican who won the governorship of Arkansas. Meanwhile in the Senate, Republicans picked up only three new seats, but one of those was a notable win in Tennessee by Howard Baker, a conservative who easily defeated the state's former governor and liberal hero Frank Clement. Baker would remain in the Senate for the next

George Bush celebrates his victory in the 1966 Texas congressional election (District 7) with his wife, Barbara, and supporters. (Courtesy of the George Bush Presidential Library.)

twenty-one years before becoming chief of staff to President Ronald Reagan.[36]

The other noteworthy Republican success that year was John Tower's surprising reelection in Texas. Tower's election to the Senate in 1961 had been largely viewed as a fluke by pundits who credited liberals' unwillingness to support their party's conservative establishment as a momentary anomaly in what would

[36] Election returns and other statistics related to recent U.S. politics can be accessed through J. Clark Archer, Steven Lavin, and Kenneth C. Martis, *Atlas of American Politics, 1960–2000* (Washington, DC: CQ Press, 2001); see also Bass and De Vries, *The Transformation of Southern Politics*, 89–106, 118–121.

116   *Cunningham*

otherwise be conservative Democrats' ongoing dominance of state politics. In 1966, Tower proved those pundits wrong by defeating another establishment Democrat, Waggoner Carr. Tower's successful campaign against Carr cemented his status as the father of the modern Texas Republican Party. On election night, Tower and his supporters gathered to celebrate a surprisingly comfortable victory. Their cheers at the announcement of Tower's victory only barely exceeded their cheers for Reagan, whose victory would ultimately prove almost as important as Tower's to the future of Republican Texas.[37]

Restyled in the wake of Goldwater's loss in 1964, conservative arguments against Great Society liberalism gained traction over the next two years, thereby contributing to the election of Sunbelt Republicans including Reagan, Baker, Bush, and Tower in 1966. These and other conservative Sunbelt Republicans capitalized on a growing sentiment that Great Society liberalism, although perhaps well intentioned, wasted valuable tax dollars on programs that did not work. This argument was especially effective in the Sunbelt, where the broadly defined ethos of individualism and self-help was already popular. Within this widening argument, the commitment to states' rights and local government, which in the South had almost always been deeply connected to the politics of race, seemed increasingly relevant across the broader Sunbelt because of the region's heightened sensitivity to federally mandated action at the local level. The Republican Party capitalized on such developments, attracting an increasing number of white-collar, middle-class, college-educated voters who were competing for jobs in an increasingly postindustrial, technology driven, and nonunionized Sunbelt economy. These voters would eventually become the heart and soul of the new Sunbelt Right.[38]

Also critical to this growing animosity against government was that, for arguably the first time since Reconstruction, federal action was not being employed for the uplift of those same white,

[37] For more on Tower and the elections of 1966 in Texas, see Cunningham, *Cowboy Conservatism*, 73–79.
[38] Critchlow, *The Conservative Ascendancy*, 281, 286.

middle-class voters increasingly attracted to the GOP. During the years of liberal consensus, and especially since World War II, whites – especially those in the Sunbelt – had largely accepted federal intervention because it came in the form of defense jobs, new highways, and low-interest mortgages – all programs designed to help them. As Johnson fought to expand those policies to those for whom the affluent 1950s had not been so affluent, conservatives subordinated the politics of race under more broadly ideological and intentionally color-blind discussions about the role of government and the fairness of tax policies that took from the "hard working" to subsidize the "undeserving." At its core, there was nothing terribly innovative about this argument. However, repackaged for a new generation during the mid-1960s, such ideas surged in popularity, thereby contributing to the growing conservative backlash against Johnson and the Great Society.[39]

The Right's attacks against Johnson and his Great Society resonated with many voters. But Great Society liberalism was also falling apart because of criticism coming from Johnson's Left.[40] In selling his Great Society, Johnson helped spark a revolution of rising expectations among many progressive reformers and civil rights activists – former supporters whose impatience with the slow progress of change would quickly whittle away at Johnson's standing within the Democratic Party. When some of those expectations for progress and reform went unmet, many progressive activists began to call for more radical solutions to enduring problems such as racial discrimination, poverty, and disfranchisement. One major source of discontentment on the Left was the growing sentiment that liberals were simply not ambitious enough in their declared war against poverty. This sentiment became more pronounced as Great Society programs increasingly struggled through the process of implementation. Such problems often revolved around disagreements between local administrators and federal bureaucrats or between local

---

[39] These and other arguments can be found in Edsall and Edsall, *Chain Reaction*.
[40] For more on the Left in the 1960s and beyond, see Michael Kazin, *American Dreamers: How the Left Changed a Nation* (New York: Vintage, 2012).

administrators and grassroots activists. Such problems also typically centered on questions of how to properly serve those citizens
living in the midst of crime and squalor. In Houston, for instance,
Wallace B. Poteat, reverend of the Ecumenical Fellowship United
Church of Christ, led a grassroots fight against the city's federally
appointed antipoverty board, which included George Bush and
several other conservative business leaders, many of whom had
been appointed to the board as a political favor, despite having
expressed opposition to the very existence of federal antipoverty
programs in the first place. In fighting this board, Poteat's main
argument was that for federal antipoverty programs to work at
the neighborhood level, they needed input from those living in the
targeted neighborhoods. The federal War on Poverty, in other
words, was excessively paternalistic; it needed local input from
the ground level. As was true of similar contests in other cities
across the region and nation, Poteat's agitation in Houston eventually forced both the federal government and its municipal board
to reorganize to better represent Houston's impoverished citizens.
Such capitulation, however, only went so far. In Houston, as in
other cities where antipoverty programs struggled through the
process of implementation, efficiency and effectiveness often fell
victim to political squabbling, thereby undermining both the program's goals and the loyalties of those citizens for whom such
programs were designed.[41]

[41] Wesley G. Phelps, "Ideological Diversity and the Implementation of the War
    on Poverty in Houston" in Annelise Orleck and Lisa Gayle Hazirjian,
    eds. *The War on Poverty: A New Grassroots History, 1964–1980* (Athens:
    University of Georgia Press, 2011), 87–109. For more on the War on Poverty,
    see Robert Bauman, *Race and the War on Poverty: From Watts to East L.A.*
    (Norman: University of Oklahoma Press, 2008); David C. Carter, *The Music
    Has Gone Out of the Movement: Civil Rights and the Johnson Administration,
    1965–1968* (Chapel Hill: University of North Carolina Press, 2009);
    Marisa Chappell, *The War on Welfare: Family, Poverty, and Politics in
    Modern America* (Philadelphia: University of Pennsylvania Press, 2009);
    Clayson, *Freedom Is Not Enough;* and Kent Germany, *New Orleans after the
    Promises: Poverty, Citizenship, and the Search for the Great Society* (Athens:
    University of Georgia Press, 2007).

So while conservatives rallied public opposition to the Great Society on the ground that it was a wasteful experiment in social engineering, activists on the Left increasingly challenged Johnson for not going far enough to empower the underprivileged in the fight to better their own communities. Over the next several years, progressives on the Left pushed the Democratic Party away from its traditional focus on expanding individual opportunities through existing systems and toward a more reform-minded and entitlement-driven brand of activist liberalism. These challenges further hastened the decline of the quickly weakening New Deal coalition.

Another major source of irritation among those on Johnson's Left was the ongoing political disfranchisement of minorities that plagued most of the South until Congress finally passed the Voting Rights Act of 1965. Passing a bill on voting rights had not seemed feasible in the immediate aftermath of the tumultuous battle over the Civil Rights Act of 1964. It had cost Johnson and other liberals on Capitol Hill significant time and energy to secure enough votes on that first act; it seemed unlikely that there would be any momentum left for a separate bill on voting rights less than one year later. But circumstances in the ongoing civil rights movement, especially those in Mississippi during the summer of 1964, unexpectedly gave liberals the political capital needed to push forward with a new agenda for political equality and ballot access in 1965. Against the predictable wishes of the Deep South's most ardent segregationists, Johnson supported a voting rights bill that, among other advancements, gave the Justice Department jurisdiction in local elections where less than half of eligible voters were registered. It also eliminated most of the South's classic tools for disfranchisement, such as literacy tests and poll taxes.[42]

The Voting Rights Act of 1965 had a profound impact on the Sunbelt's long-term political culture, especially in the Deep South.

---

[42] The best overview of the Voting Rights Act of 1965 and its aftermath remains Steven F. Lawson, *In Pursuit of Power: Southern Blacks & Electoral Politics, 1965–1982* (New York: Columbia University Press, 1987). For more on the impact of anticommunism on resistance to voting rights in the South, see Woods, *Black Struggle, Red Scare*, 199–225.

For the first time since the immediate aftermath of the Civil War, African Americans registered to vote en masse. As a result, conservative Democrats immediately faced challenges in primary elections from moderates and liberals who were far more amenable to Johnson's goals for societal transformation, civil rights, and racial peace. These challenges did not result in the immediate defection of conservatives into the Republican Party, but they did accelerate the process. Over the next two decades, southern conservatives increasingly identified with the Sunbelt's wing of the Republican Party – resolutely Right but ostensibly color blind – while the region's Democratic Party became more freely cooperative with national liberals. Ironically, however, the creation of a more representative Democratic Party in the South did not help Johnson or other opportunity-focused liberals; rather, it opened the door for an increasingly vocal grassroots Left to gain influence within the national party. Again, Johnson, the New Deal coalition, and the liberal consensus – long dominant from its status as the political mainstream – increasingly struggled to hold their ground against attacks from both the Left and the Right.[43]

As crucial as the political debates surrounding the Great Society were to the unraveling of the liberal consensus, few issues destabilized American political culture during the 1960s more than the war in Vietnam. Opposition to the war fused with discontentment over the federal government's management of the Great Society to almost completely erode Johnson's political standing. In 1967 and 1968, peace activists abandoned Johnson and the liberal Democratic establishment, splintering that party into a multitude of factions. The Left's most damaging accusation was that Johnson, perhaps even in cahoots with corporations benefiting financially from the war, was robbing the Great Society in order to pay for an unjust and unnecessary invasion of Southeast Asia. Johnson, of course, rejected such charges and even shared the Left's lament that Vietnam was robbing the Great Society of funds. But the Democratic Party continued to fracture on this issue, nonetheless. For antiwar activists in the 1960s, Johnson's resume of liberal

[43] Ibid.

successes was not enough to overcome his newfound reputation as a warmonger. Antiwar activism emerged at flagship institutions across the Sunbelt, including most prominently at the University of California, Berkeley, the University of Texas at Austin, and the University of Florida in Gainesville. At these and other universities, students came to question not simply American intervention in Vietnam, but also the liberal consensus and its long-standing policy of containment.[44]

Even African Americans openly abandoned Johnson because of the war in Vietnam and what they perceived to be his related failure to keep the promises of his Great Society. Frustrated that new civil and voting rights laws had not resulted in more immediate changes at the local level, blacks in and out of the Sunbelt began turning to different voices and strategies in their fight for racial equality. Part of this story includes the rise of Black Power and the growth of related organizations such as the Black Panther Party, organized in Oakland, California, in 1966. Attractive to many disaffected African Americans, the militant images associated with Black Power alienated many moderate whites and some liberals, including many in the Sunbelt who had previously been happy to support a movement popularly associated with nonviolence and passive resistance. Black Power, however, frightened both voters and politicians, thereby unintentionally aiding the conservative backlash across the Sunbelt. The Democratic Party also suffered within this context because conservative Republicans became increasingly adroit at appealing to working-class sensibilities by not simply associating liberalism with black militancy, but also with spoiled, unpatriotic, "draft-dodging" students who were unwilling to fight for their country. Agitators on both the Left and the Right were quick to point out that the war in Vietnam was being disproportionately fought by the sons of the less privileged, though their motivations for doing so were

---

[44] For more on student activism and the Left, see Rossinow, *The Politics of Authenticity*; for more on the class dynamics of the Vietnam War, see Christian Appy, *Working-Class War: American Combat Soldiers and Vietnam* (Chapel Hill: University of North Carolina Press, 1993).

quite different. Regardless, these dueling political attacks worked against the liberal consensus's ability to endure.[45]

As antiwar activism and dissent on both his Left and Right flanks undermined Johnson's national standing, the explosive birth of identity politics further destabilized whatever remnants of the liberal consensus still remained. Essentially a consciousness of activism rooted in an individual's primary identification within a particular societal subgroup, identity politics largely rejected the essential goodness of American democracy, choosing instead to highlight both the virtues of multiculturalism and the need for greater diversity. In Texas, for instance, Hispanics mobilized through organizations like MAYO (Mexican American Youth Organization) and La Raza Unida, which began running slates of political candidates in local and state races. Stylistically more militant and less willing to partner with established liberal leaders, these organizations often drew the ire of older Mexican Americans such as San Antonio's liberal congressman Henry Gonzalez. Gonzalez viewed such militancy as counterproductive to the Democratic Party's overall goals for steadily achieving social and political equality through the established structures of American liberalism.[46] The objections of men like Gonzalez notwithstanding, Chicano activism and "Brown Power" rallied youth in Southern California, as they did in Arizona and other places across the Sunbelt Southwest. Inspired by the times, American Indians also organized during the late 1960s, as did women, environmentalists, homosexuals, the disabled, the incarcerated, and the elderly. These were national movements, but each maintained an organized and active voice throughout the Sunbelt.[47]

[45] Appy, *Working-Class War*; Rossinow, *The Politics of Authenticity*. For more on the working class's developing identification with the Right, see Jefferson Cowie, *Stayin' Alive: The 1970s and the Last Days of the Working Class* (New York: The New Press, 2010). For more on the growth of Black Power, see Peniel E. Joseph, *Waiting 'til the Midnight Hour: A Narrative History of Black Power in America* (New York: Owl Books, 2006).

[46] Cunningham, *Cowboy Conservatism*, 109–113.

[47] For more on the birth of identity politics, see Terry Anderson, *The Movement and the Sixties: Protest in America from Greensboro to Wounded Knee* (New York: Oxford University Press, 1996). The social, cultural, and political

The fracturing of the civil rights movement and the growth of identity politics diversified the political Left at the same time that it gave the conservative Right a collection of easy targets against which to mirror its own brand of patriotic populism. Black Power militants, antiwar activists, and countercultural hippies all emerged as favorite targets for aspiring Sunbelt conservatives who used images of the radical Left to support their warnings against the dangers of unchecked liberal expansion. Conservatives also highlighted the Left's criticism of American institutions as evidence of their "socialism" and disloyalty. Joe Pool, a conservative Democratic congressman from Dallas, even tried to have so-called peaceniks prosecuted under various treason and sedition statutes. Increasingly image conscious, Sunbelt conservatives often identified the members of the New Left by their appearance and behavior – specifically their long hair, eccentric and immodest attire, sexual promiscuity, "filth," and conspicuous drug use. These conservatives used such images as evidence of the disintegration of traditional family values, even before that term was widely utilized in a political context. Such images were particularly salient in places where the Sunbelt was popularly thought of as synonymous with the Bible Belt.[48]

Sunbelt conservatives did not simply oppose the methods and arguments of the antiwar Left and emerging counterculture; they also actively supported the war in Vietnam and often urged Johnson to let the military do more to win a quick and decisive victory. In some ways, the Vietnam War actually stabilized Johnson's popularity in the otherwise libertarian Sunbelt. Texas, for instance, became a hotbed for pro-war activism during the

upheavals of the 1960s have also been well documented. For studies that touch on these and other themes, see, among many others, Daniel M. Cobb, *Native Activism in Cold War America: The Struggle for Sovereignty* (Lawrence: University Press of Kansas, 2008); Sara Evans, *Personal Politics: The Roots of Women's Liberation in the Civil Rights Movement & the New Left* (New York: Alfred A. Knopf, 1979); Flamm, *Law and Order*; Isserman and Kazin, *America Divided*; and Mark Lytle, *America's Uncivil Wars: The Sixties Era from Elvis to the Fall of Richard Nixon* (New York: Oxford University Press, 2006).

[48] Cunningham, *Cowboy Conservatism*, 79.

late 1960s, attracting visits from Ronald Reagan and William F. Buckley, among other conservatives. These conservatives came to the Lone Star State on several occasions to deliver speeches that criticized the antiwar Left and challenged Johnson to wage his war against communism more aggressively. Moderate Texas Democrats such as Congressman George Mahon of Lubbock, whose support for the Great Society had been relatively lukewarm, remained loyal to LBJ specifically because of his support for the war. Hawkish attitudes were also enhanced in Sunbelt states like Texas because of the defense contracts that provided jobs and fueled economic growth because of Vietnam-related demand. Some in the Sunbelt also supported the war simply because they did not want to appear weak. Johnson himself spoke often about not wanting to be the first American president to lose a war. In private conversations with his advisors, he even equated his unwillingness to surrender Vietnam to communism as a modern-day reenactment of the Alamo, couching his resolve in terms suggesting that it was in his blood as a Texan to never give up, even in the face of seemingly insurmountable odds.[49]

Ultimately, the war in Vietnam divided the United States at a time when it was already susceptible to division because of the civil rights movement and the Great Society. These divisions were clearly present in the Sunbelt, and it was during these years of increasing ideological polarization that conservative Republicans began to more visibly gain popular support across the region. As progress on civil rights slowed and a diverse array of new movements began to gain steam, moderates and establishment liberals buckled under the weight of discontentment surging on both their right and left. Conservative Democrats became increasingly unwilling to share their party with "agitators," whereas progressives and New Left radicals began to question the fundamental goodness of the American society in which they had, for

---

[49] Ibid., 79–83; Dallek, *Flawed Giant*, 100. See also Sandra Scanlon, *The Pro-War Movement: Domestic Support for the Vietnam War and the Making of Modern American Conservatism* (Amherst: University of Massachusetts Press, 2013).

so many years, placed their confidence and faith. Conservative Republicans, meanwhile, seized the opportunity to welcome disaffected Democrats on the Right into their tent, while generalizing the Left as one, monolithically un-American collection of "liberals."

And then came the election of 1968.

4

Southern, Suburban, and Sunbelt Strategies

On January 30, 1968, a combined force of North Vietnamese and Viet Cong insurgents caught American troops in South Vietnam by surprise when they launched a massive and coordinated assault that became known as the Tet Offensive. Over the next several weeks, American forces rallied to repel the offensive and win a decisive military victory. That victory notwithstanding, the Tet Offensive was a fatal political defeat for Lyndon Johnson, whose administration had been promising for months that its communist opponents in Southeast Asia were crumbling and that the war in Vietnam would soon be won. The newly presented evidence of Tet suggesting otherwise, the Democratic Party's already fading political consensus quickly evaporated.[1]

These divisions became clearer on March 12 when Senator Eugene McCarthy of Minnesota, an antiwar candidate, came stunningly close to defeating Johnson in the Democratic Party's New Hampshire primary. Four days later, Robert F. Kennedy – Johnson's

---

[1] For more on the Tet Offensive and Johnson's policies in Vietnam, see George C. Herring, *America's Longest War: The United States and Vietnam, 1950–1975* (New York: McGraw-Hill, 1996); and Dallek, *Flawed Giant*, 463. See also Ron Milam, *Not a Gentleman's War: An Inside View of Junior Officers in the Vietnam War* (Chapel Hill: University of North Carolina Press, 2009). For more on the political impact of Vietnam, see Andrew L. Johns, *Vietnam's Second Front: Domestic Politics, the Republican Party, and the War* (Lexington: University Press of Kentucky, 2010).

most hated and feared political foe – announced his candidacy for the Democratic Party's presidential nomination. Unwilling to face the possible humiliation of failing to win renomination, Johnson shocked the country two weeks later when he announced that he would not seek a second term as president. Then, on April 4 – just four days after Johnson's announcement – Martin Luther King Jr. was assassinated in Memphis, Tennessee, while visiting that city in support of striking sanitation workers. Race riots subsequently erupted in several cities, including Washington, D.C.; Chicago; and Kansas City. Kennedy almost single-handedly helped mitigate the eruption of further riots as a result of an impromptu speech given in Indianapolis on the night of King's death. Over the next two months, RFK – essentially seizing a mythical torch surrendered by his assassinated brother five years earlier – emerged as the candidate of choice for many of the nation's most impoverished and politically disaffected citizens, especially recently enfranchised minorities. For many on the Left, Kennedy was their greatest hope for a truly progressive shift in national politics.[2]

But progressive hopes for an RFK presidency vanished on June 5 when Kennedy was assassinated at the Ambassador Hotel in Los Angeles, just minutes after publicly celebrating his victory in the California Democratic Primary. Two months later, a wounded and divided Democratic Party convened in Chicago for its national convention. Chaos and violence ensued. Antiwar protesters descended on the Windy City where they were met by the billy club–wielding officers of the Chicago Police Department. Those bloody confrontations were broadcast via television to an incredulous nation – one that was rapidly losing patience with social and political instability.[3]

Since 1963, Americans had endured multiple assassinations; an escalating and unpopular war in Vietnam; and widespread social, political, and economic unrest, much of it in the form of street

---

[2] For more on the final months of the Johnson presidency, see again Dallek, *Flawed Giant*.
[3] For more on the 1968 Democratic National Convention, see David Farber, *Chicago '68* (Chicago: University of Chicago Press, 1988). See also Flamm, *Law and Order*, 154–161.

protests and race riots. For many, the 1968 Democratic National Convention in Chicago was the last straw. The convention finally ended with the nomination of Johnson's vice president, Hubert H. Humphrey of Minnesota, but the campaign for the White House had only just begun.

So had the era of Richard Nixon.

NIXON

Three weeks prior to the Democratic Party's implosion at its national convention in Chicago, the Republican Party held its own convention in Miami Beach, Florida. With the debatable exception of San Francisco in 1956 and 1964, Miami was the first Sunbelt city to host the GOP's most important nominating meeting. At the end of that convention, Republicans nominated Richard Nixon as their candidate for president of the United States. Nixon won the nomination rather handily, though not all Republicans were happy to fall in line. Earlier that year, George Romney of Michigan had been a favorite for the Republican nomination, but he dropped out of the campaign during the primaries, embarrassed by comments he had made suggesting that his previous support for Johnson and the war in Vietnam was the result of "brainwashing." Then, in April, Nelson Rockefeller jumped into the race and essentially claimed what he could of Romney's support from the eastern establishment. Ronald Reagan also ran a limited and mostly undeclared campaign. He eventually carried 182 delegates at the convention – hardly enough to challenge for the nomination, but enough to make a statement about the growing strength of Sunbelt conservatism, and enough to garner some unfulfilled support for a vice-presidential nod, especially from the Texas delegation. Still, although by no means a unanimous convention, the GOP left Miami appearing quite stable, especially when compared to the chaotic divisions that ruptured the Democratic Party during its meeting in Chicago later that month.[4]

---

[4] For a journalistic overview of the election of 1968, see Theodore H. White, *The Making of the President, 1968* (New York: Atheneum Publishers, 1969).

Nixon's nomination would have shocked political observers just a few years earlier. When Nixon failed in his bid to become the governor of California in 1962, losing rather decisively to Pat Brown, many considered his career over. Nixon even said as much the day following that loss during what he termed his "last press conference," bitterly telling reporters that they would not "have Nixon to kick around" anymore. For the next several years, Nixon worked as a private attorney in New York City, achieving a lifelong ambition to become a prominent East Coast lawyer. Nixon's political career, beginning in Los Angeles during the Red Scare and continuing throughout the 1950s as Eisenhower's vice president, had been characterized to a large extent by his ability to project an antiestablishment populism, specifically an anti-eastern one. But this belied Nixon's persistent desire to be accepted by that establishment. Throughout his early political career, Nixon utilized images of the "forgotten man" as a means for positioning himself within the mainstream of what was becoming a suburban and Sunbelt-oriented middle class. Privately, however, Nixon would have preferred inclusion in the Ivy League circles of power that controlled American life from the East Coast. For most of his life, such inclusion had been elusive. Rather than openly pine for inclusion, Nixon resentfully channeled his insecurities into what was an unnatural, but politically effective, populist style. Regardless, conservative Republicans had long vacillated on whether or not Nixon was truly one of them. Much of that distrust centered on their disdain for the so-called Compact of Fifth Avenue – a compromise between Nixon and Rockefeller related to the GOP's national platform in 1960, in which Nixon agreed to endorse a number of domestic policy initiatives, as well as a stronger plank on civil rights, in exchange for Rockefeller's endorsement of the Nixon ticket. Conservatives had considered this a "sell out" and never fully trusted Nixon again.[5]

Having faded into what most assumed was political oblivion after his 1962 loss in California, Nixon played a patient game from

[5] Pietrusza, *1960: LBJ vs. JFK vs. Nixon*, 215–221. See also Rorabaugh, *The Real Making of the President*, 106–112.

his new seat as a private citizen in New York City. He supported but did not fully invest in Goldwater's conservative movement in 1964, then he reemerged in 1966 as a sort of attention-grabbing campaign weapon for various Republican candidates running for office during the midterms that year. In the process, Nixon accumulated political favors, which proved vital in 1968 as he was seeking the GOP's nomination. At the convention in Miami, Nixon won a decisive victory, appearing more conservative than Rockefeller and more moderate, experienced, and electable than the still-too-new Reagan, who at the time had been governor of California for less than two years. In accepting his party's nomination, Nixon positioned himself as both a statesman – ready to bring an "honorable end" to the war in Vietnam, and a disciplinarian – ready to reestablish civility and order to an unraveling society. As a national figure, Nixon ran as the responsible and reasonable solution for a nation spiraling out of control. Adopting the message of one campaign sign, Nixon promised to bring the country "together again."

But this was only one side of Nixon's campaign persona. There was another side – one not always captured during his speeches, but one that was nevertheless plainly apparent in his campaign commercials and in the efforts of his political subordinates and those operating at the grass roots in battleground states all across the nation, especially in the Sunbelt. This was a much tougher Nixon; this was a Nixon of law and order.

One of Nixon's most effective law-and-order subordinates was Ben Carpenter, a cattle-ranching, multimillionaire business leader from Dallas, Texas. In March 1968, Carpenter used the annual meeting of the Texas and Southwest Cattle Raisers Association to deliver a blistering critique of Great Society liberalism and its complicity in the downfall of American stability. He blamed liberals for promoting "moral relativism," which pacified "alcoholics," "pacifists," "homosexuals," and other "deviates," thereby contributing to lawlessness and societal decay. Carpenter's words resonated with Texas business leaders, not to mention the state's growing base of middle-class, suburban whites – many of whom were fleeing cities like Dallas for the comforts of suburbs like Las

Colinas, which Carpenter himself had financed and developed. Four months after his speech to the Texas and Southwest Cattle Raisers Association, Carpenter became chairman of the newly formed Texas Democrats for Nixon committee. To many in Texas, the connections between the failures of liberalism and the need for law and order seemed clear.[6]

Attention to crime and the call for law and order dominated the election of 1968, even more so than the issue of Vietnam. Southern conservatives such as South Carolina's Strom Thurmond, who by this time had become the South's leading Republican and whose support for Nixon at the GOP convention had been crucial to Nixon's success there, joined a chorus of conservatives across the Sunbelt drawing connections between rampant crime, escalating street violence, and the trajectory of entitlement-driven liberalism. In the South, where fears of an uncontrolled black population were as old as the region itself, the call for law and order resonated with both the growing Republican population and the traditional Democratic establishment. Across the wider Sunbelt, the emphasis on law and order reflected a culture that prioritized openness, comfort, and security – values intimately connected to the region's preference for suburban expansion rather than urban renewal.[7]

The growth of prisons in the Sunbelt underscores this cultural and political emphasis. During the late 1960s and continuing through the rest of the century, the Sunbelt's attention to law and order facilitated the exponential growth of prisons. It also inspired the politically appealing argument that those prisons should be privatized and also fostered a heightened support for gun-ownership rights. The Sunbelt's obsession with criminal justice also contributed to rising arrest rates and, eventually, the mass incarceration of alleged delinquents, especially African Americans and "illegal" Hispanics.[8] Suburban, middle-class whites across

[6] Cunningham, *Cowboy Conservatism*, 68–69, 83.
[7] For interpretation of the intersections between Vietnam and the law-and-order phenomenon through the lens of popular culture, see Slotkin, *Gunfighter Nation*, 613–620.
[8] Volker Janssen, "Sunbelt Lock-Up: Where Suburbs Met the Super-Max," in Nickerson and Dochuk, *Sunbelt Rising*, 217–239.

the prosperous postwar Sunbelt were determined to preserve the fruits of their new affluence. That determination made conservatives' promises to protect families from the criminal violence of quickly ghettoizing inner cities all the more politically incisive. In campaign ads and during public appearances, the debate over whether criminal justice could best be advanced through the construction of more prisons or the funding of better schools epitomized the much larger ideological debate that was emerging between Sunbelt conservatism and entitlement-driven liberalism.[9]

"Law and Order" was only the most visible theme of Nixon's masterfully constructed and much broader national campaign. Throughout 1968, a new breed of media handlers and campaign strategists carefully controlled Nixon's image. These men included H. R. Haldeman, a longtime Nixon associate from California, former ad executive, and eventual White House Chief of Staff; John Ehrlichman, whom Haldeman had befriended while the two were students at UCLA; Henry Bellmon, a Sunbelt Republican from Oklahoma who served as the campaign's national manager before leaving that post to run for a seat in the U.S. Senate, a race he surprisingly won against the multi-term Democrat Mike Monroney; and Harry Treleaven, a rising ad executive whose first political job had been as a strategist for George Bush's first successful congressional campaign in Houston two years earlier. These and other strategists labored to create a "new Nixon." In 1960, Nixon's televised campaign ads had almost exclusively featured the then vice president engaged in a one-way conversation directly with the camera. In 1968, Nixon's ads were bloody and scary, featuring images of cities in flames, riotous looting, overwhelmed police, and hippie student "radicals" protesting on the streets, thereby instigating – it appeared – much of the nation's instability.[10]

[9] For more on advertising in the 1968 presidential campaign, see Kathleen Hall Jamieson, *Packaging the Presidency: A History and Criticism of Presidential Campaign Advertising* (New York: Oxford University Press, 1984), 221–275.
[10] For more on Nixon and the 1968 presidential campaign, see Joe McGinnis, *The Selling of the President: The Classic Account of the Packaging of a Candidate*

In some ways, Nixon's campaign strategy was derivative of that of both Johnson and Goldwater in 1964. In critiquing Johnson and Great Society liberalism in 1964, Goldwater had warned Americans that moral relativism was undermining notions of civic responsibility and respect for authority. Nixon's campaign message emphasized a similar idea. But like Johnson, Nixon's ads were innovatively frightening and suggested that voters approach the election as though their "whole world depended on it." Goldwater's approach had not worked in 1964, but the circumstantial changes of the intervening four years, when mixed with the apocalyptic overtones borrowed from Johnson, provided Nixon with a much more fruitful context in which to communicate images of lawlessness, disorder, and sociopolitical decay. As it had for Johnson in 1964, Nixon's use of scare tactics worked well in 1968.[11]

Meanwhile, Nixon refused to debate Humphrey, choosing instead to appear in a series of town hall meetings, all of which were carefully staged for television audiences. By the time the general campaign kicked into high gear after Labor Day early that September, Nixon held a commanding lead, thanks to both the Democratic Party's implosion and his skillfully crafted image as both a moderate statesman and a voice for the marginalized and "forgotten American" whose interests, he and other conservatives argued, had been subordinated by liberals more interested in appeasing the radical New Left.[12]

WALLACE

Nixon's law-and-order strategy would be considered more pioneering to the history of Sunbelt politics were it not for the fact that George Wallace was an even more dramatic mouthpiece for the backlash-oriented fear associated with the growing sentiment against both liberalism and the region's concurrent obsession with

(New York: Penguin Books, 1988); Perlstein, *Nixonland*; and White, *The Making of the President, 1968.*

[11] Ibid.

[12] Ibid.

crime. In 1968, Wallace – then the former governor of Alabama – ran one of the most successful and influential third-party presidential campaigns in American history. Having risen to Alabama's highest office on the sails of racial backlash – famously declaring in his 1963 inaugural address that his would be an administration committed to "segregation now, segregation tomorrow, and segregation forever" – Wallace was the most visible and media-conscious conservative southern Democrat to consistently steal headlines during the mid-1960s.[13]

Like Nixon, Wallace's political career was rooted in an almost obsessive preoccupation with perception management. Just months into his governorship, Wallace symbolically promised to defiantly "stand in the schoolhouse door" to prevent the federally mandated integration of the University of Alabama in Tuscaloosa. Keeping the promise until just after television cameras had captured his moment of resolve, Wallace used the incident to project himself as both a defender of southern values and a warrior in the battle against federal tyranny. Like much of Wallace's political career, the event in Tuscaloosa had been staged for political benefit. A former populist-progressive in the 1950s, Wallace's political ambitions in the 1960s demanded an almost constant attention to political gamesmanship through the politics of race. As governor, he used state government to advance public education, transportation, and health care, but he spent far more time using his office to illegally graft money from private contractors into his campaign war chest while emphasizing the imperativeness of southern resistance to civil rights. Some of the most memorable and influential moments in the history of the southern civil rights movement – including the bombing of the Sixteenth Street Baptist Church in Birmingham in 1963 and the police riot at the Edmund Pettis Bridge in which state troopers used tear gas to thwart a peaceful march to Selma in support of voting rights in 1965 – happened under Wallace's watch. As a populist Democrat, Wallace very effectively equated civil rights protest with unruly, divisive, and

---

[13] The definitive work on Wallace remains Carter, *The Politics of Rage*.

un-American agitation, while connecting that agitation with lawlessness, disorder, and entitlement-driven liberalism.[14]

Wallace spoke less overtly about race after the Voting Rights
Act of 1965 enfranchised thousands of blacks in Alabama and
the South. Instead of harping on segregation, Wallace more
directly emphasized the dangers of Great Society liberalism, federal encroachment, and escalating crime. For Wallace, this was a
rhetoric of code words designed to appeal to both the same rural,
working-class southerners who had been attracted to his position
against civil rights because of race and a wider audience of blue-
collar Americans outside the South. His message intersected with
those of many conservative Sunbelt Republicans, but it was not
exactly the same, as Wallace's lack of support in the Sunbelt
West suggested. Wallace's message was tailored far more for the
racially motivated and predominantly rural working class than
was the message coming from most Sunbelt Republicans – most of
whom, like Nixon, were from the West – who preferred connecting to the region's more educated and suburban middle class. For
Wallace, the use of code words was an effective way of continuing
to manipulate the divisive politics of race in the South, but not all
conservatives in the Sunbelt agreed with this strategy.[15]

In 1967, Wallace launched a third-party campaign for the presidency. His first goal was to get onto the ballot in all fifty states. The
first and most critical state the Wallace team identified for that effort
was California. Having primarily risen to prominence as a defender
of states' rights on behalf of the ex-Confederacy, Wallace knew
he needed to expand his following beyond Dixie. In California, he
enjoyed a limited but enthusiastic following among members of the
hyper-anticommunist John Birch Society, but JBS affiliation was
hardly a political asset by this time, at least not in the court of public
opinion.[16] In order to widen his following and moderate his image,
Wallace tapped William Shearer to run his campaign in California.

---

[14] Ibid.; see also Woods, *Black Struggle Red Scare*, 220–234.
[15] Ibid.; see also Critchlow, *The Conservative Ascendancy*, 85–86.
[16] Carter, *The Politics of Rage*, 343. Wallace relied on JBS organization support in
several states during the 1968 campaign.

Shearer was a California Republican strategist whose greatest political achievement to date had been his leadership in the fight for
Proposition 14, the conservative property rights law stunningly
passed in California in 1964. In 1967 and 1968, Shearer tried to
transform Wallace's image in California as a race-baiter into that of a
conservative more in Reagan's mold – an effective and modern leader
who was also ideologically strong. Those efforts were successful
enough to get Wallace onto the ballot in California, but were not
convincing enough to make the Alabama ex-governor a major influence on the state's growing conservative movement, which continued
to favor Reagan, the Republican Party, and free-market libertarianism – all things Wallace was not. From late 1967 to early 1968, the
Wallace campaign focused much of its attention on California and
Texas – Los Angeles and Houston especially – as potential bases for a
wider national campaign. Marginally successful in those efforts,
Wallace raised funds and solidified the framework for his campaign
but failed to make either state a truly fruitful home base.[17]

Whether or not Wallace's insurgency in 1968 was a success
remains open to interpretation. Whereas Nixon's campaign
largely succeeded by targeting the Sunbelt's growing middle
class – white, suburban, and college educated – Wallace's campaign drew on the ire of the more racially motivated and rural
working class. At the same time, Wallace's message was received
with remarkable enthusiasm in several northern cities, where
blue-collar workers were being decimated by postindustrial economic change, corporate outsourcing, and the relocation of businesses to the sunny and anti-union Sunbelt. Some analysts would
later identify these Wallace voters as the core of the new Reagan
Democrats, thereby reinforcing the perceived connections
between Wallace, racial backlash, and modern conservatism.[18]

Regardless of whether or not his constituency evolved into
the conservative GOP's future base, Wallace's greatest and most

[17] Ibid., 307–314.
[18] For more on the cultural conservatism of the national working class, see Cowie,
Stayin' Alive. See also Randy D. McBee, *"Don't Shoot the Easy Rider": The
Motorcyclist, the Rise of the Biker, and the Making of a Political Tradition,
United States, 1940s–1990s* (Chapel Hill: University of North Carolina Press,
forthcoming).

lasting tactical achievement was his ability to inflame social conservatives by focusing not on liberalism's economic policies, but
its alleged moral relativism and the concurrent disintegration
of American culture. Emphasizing cultural politics ahead of
economics, Wallace told supporters in 1968 that they (and their
values) had been disrespected and ignored by politicians in both
parties, and that he alone was the antiestablishment voice they
had longed to elect. Vitriol aside, Wallace's campaign manager
Tom Turnipseed later admitted that the antiestablishment impulse
of the Wallace movement in 1968 was its racially motivated opposition to the civil rights movement. Put another way, Wallace
supporters in 1968 were driven by the politics of race and social
conservatism, stylized by an antiestablishment southern populism powerfully and emotionally recast against the backdrop of
national chaos and decay. It lacked the libertarian element that
informed so much of the Sunbelt's growing Republican Right
and was, therefore, far less effective in its appeal to GOP voters.
Nevertheless, Wallace's emotional style influenced both Nixon's
competing campaign in 1968, as well as broader conservative
campaign strategies for the next several decades.[19]

THE ELECTION OF 1968

In early September, Nixon began the general campaign with a
sizable lead over Humphrey, who in national polls was running
a distant third, trailing even Wallace. The Democratic National
Convention in Chicago, coupled with the nation's generally dis-
contented condition, put Humphrey – essentially representing the
incumbent Johnson administration – at a great disadvantage.
Faced with almost certain defeat, Humphrey made a critical strategic decision to disavow his previous support for the war in Vietnam.
In doing so, Humphrey alienated Johnson, not to mention his

---

[19] For more on the legacy and style of conservative politics in 1968, see again
Carter, *The Politics of Rage*; and Perlstein, *Nixonland*. For more on Nixon's
evolving image, see Greenberg, *Nixon's Shadow*; see also Daniel Frick,
Reinventing Richard Nixon: A Cultural History of an American Obsession
(Lawrence: University Press of Kansas, 2008).

typically conservative and now only semi-loyal Democratic campaign managers across the South. In Texas, for instance, John
Connally – the state's governor and LBJ's longtime political
ally – refused to be photographed with Humphrey at one campaign fund-raiser in Houston, even though Connally was, at the
time, Humphrey's campaign manager in the state. Instead,
Humphrey rubbed elbows and took photographs with the state's
most vocal liberal, Senator Ralph Yarborough. Conveniently
(or not), Yarborough was also Connally's most-hated political
enemy at the time.[20]

Humphrey's decision to prioritize the antiwar Left of his party
undermined his standing across most of the hawkish Sunbelt,
but it gave him a much-needed boost across the rest of the nation.
As September moved into October, Nixon's lead began to slip.
Meanwhile, Nixon feared that Wallace might steal enough conservative support in the South to prevent any single candidate
from winning enough electoral votes to claim the election. Under
such a scenario, the deadlocked race would be sent to the
Democratic-controlled House of Representatives, which would
then execute its responsibility of selecting the next commander in
chief. Nixon knew he had no hope of winning in such a scenario.
Splitting the electorate was indeed Wallace's goal, whereas
Humphrey's beleaguered campaign simply hoped to rally for at
least one last time the same New Deal coalition that had served
Democrats so well since 1932.

At the end of the day, Nixon won the presidency by a razor-thin
margin, taking just 43.4 percent of the popular vote, compared to
Humphrey's 42.7 – a margin of less than 1 percent. In the Electoral
College, Nixon won 301 votes, Humphrey took 191 and Wallace
46. Wallace won the same Deep South states carried by Goldwater,
with the exception of South Carolina, where Nixon defeated
Wallace and Humphrey with just 38 percent of the overall vote,
and Arkansas, which Goldwater had lost but Wallace actually
won. Not surprisingly, Wallace carried Alabama and Mississippi

[20] Cunningham, *Cowboy Conservatism*, 87.

in landslides, winning 65 percent and 63 percent of the vote in those states, respectively.

However, the Wallace backlash was far less effective in other parts of the Sunbelt. Nixon carried Florida rather handily – at least by 1968 standards – whereas Wallace finished a distant third, twelve points off the pace. Humphrey finished second in Florida but won only two of the state's counties – Alachua (home of the liberal-leaning University of Florida) and Dade (Miami). Wallace did extremely well in the less populated and more culturally southern Florida panhandle, whereas Nixon narrowly controlled the state's most populated and suburban central corridor, stretching from Tampa to Orlando along what is now Interstate 4.[21] Nixon also carried North Carolina and Tennessee, though Wallace outpaced Humphrey in both of those states. Importantly, although he did not carry Georgia, Nixon also did well – and even won – in DeKalb and Cobb Counties, both places filled with suburban, middle-class voters on the outskirts of Atlanta. Nixon's success in these counties, despite losing the rest of the state to Wallace, further underscored his strength among suburban, middle-class whites.

Wallace was far less appealing to voters in the Sunbelt West. In California, he garnered less than 7 percent of the vote, whereas Nixon narrowly defeated Humphrey, winning 47 percent of the state's popular vote and a majority of its counties. Credit for Nixon's win in California went to Orange and San Diego Counties, where the Republican dominated as expected. Nixon also won Los Angeles County, though only narrowly. In Arizona, the Republican again dominated, winning nearly 60 percent of the state's overall vote and carrying all but three of its counties. In Maricopa County (Phoenix), Nixon outpaced his Democratic opponent two to one and bested Goldwater's 1964 showing by a whopping 20,000 votes. Meanwhile, Wallace carried only 9 percent of the vote in Maricopa County, same as he did in the state overall. Nixon also carried Utah, Colorado, and New

---

[21] For more on Florida, see Colburn, *From Yellow Dog Democrats to Red State Republicans*.

Mexico – winning more than 50 percent of the vote in each of those states, whereas Wallace won less than 10 percent. Nixon also carried Nevada and Oklahoma, where Wallace won 13 percent and 20 percent of the vote, respectively.

The most interesting outcome of any Sunbelt state was generated in Texas, which Humphrey actually carried by less than 2 percent. Democrats maintained their hold on Texas in 1968, winning the vast majority of the state's 254 counties. Nixon controlled most rural counties in West Texas but did most of his damage in the heavily urban and suburban counties of Dallas and Harris (Houston). Wallace's support in Texas was held to less than 20 percent – his weakest showing in any state of the old Confederacy. That support was almost exclusively isolated to small, rural counties along the Louisiana border. Humphrey also benefited in Texas from the strength of Democrat Preston Smith's resolutely law-and-order campaign for governor, a race Smith won by defeating Paul Eggers, a Nixon-backed Republican.[22]

Post-election analysis suggested that without Wallace, Nixon would have carried Texas as well as the Sunbelt South. This conventional wisdom has long reinforced the connections between Nixon, the Republican Party, and the politics of race – connections that really began in earnest with Goldwater's campaign of 1964. Most evidence supports the idea that Wallace took votes away from Nixon; although in Texas, polls leading up to the election suggested a surprisingly strong correlation between Humphrey's growing support and Wallace's fade to the back of the pack. Although it seems reasonable to conclude that Nixon, who shared Wallace's strategic emphasis on law and order, would have benefited in the Sunbelt from a two-way matchup against the liberal Humphrey, it is not entirely clear that Texas – where loyalty to Johnson and the Democratic Party remained relatively strong – would have gone for the Republican were it not for the Alabama conservative's third-party insurgency.

Post-election analysis is further complicated by the outcome of congressional races in 1968. Despite Nixon's win, Republicans

[22] Cunningham, *Cowboy Conservatism*, 88–90.

Lyndon Johnson and Richard Nixon confer at the White House on the morning of Nixon's inauguration, January 20, 1969. (LBJ Library photo by Frank Wolfe.)

picked up only five seats (net) in the U.S. House, though New Mexico, North Carolina, and Oklahoma provided two new GOP seats each, and Virginia provided one. Republicans also picked up five seats in the Senate, including Florida – where Edward Gurney won a seat vacated by the retiring George Smathers, and Arizona – where Barry Goldwater reclaimed his old spot in the Senate, winning the seat vacated by retiring Democrat Carl Hayden. All told, Nixon's narrow victory over two Democrats – one liberal and one conservative running as an Independent – provided little in the way of coattails for the GOP, which remained a clear minority in both houses of Congress.

Regardless, the election of 1968 was an important acceleration point in the history of the Republican Sunbelt, modern conservatism, and the demise of the liberal consensus and its New Deal coalition. Outside of Texas, the Democratic Party failed in the South for the second consecutive election. It also failed in the rest of the country, with the exceptions of Washington, Minnesota, Michigan, and most of the Northeast. Outside of those liberal holdouts, the idea that government could and would solve the nation's clearly growing problems had lost considerable credibility in the years between 1964 and 1968. The political trend most popularly ascendant as the 1960s began its transition into the 1970s was no longer liberalism, but conservatism – one that emphasized law and order, social traditions, and libertarian individuality, while appealing to the racially moderate and economically oriented sensibilities of a growing suburban middle class. This brand of conservatism also fomented a heightened cynicism toward federal power – an attitude seemingly legitimized by Johnson's failure to eradicate poverty or end the war in Vietnam as he had so hopefully promised four years earlier.[23]

A SOUTHERN OR SUBURBAN STRATEGY?

One of the lasting questions about the election of 1968 – specifically regarding the way Nixon's campaign operated against the backdrop of Wallace's conservative third-party insurgency – concerns the degree to which race actually shaped both the election's outcome as well as the long-term growth of a conservative Republican Party in the Sunbelt, especially in the South. In fact, the relationship between American politics in the postwar Sunbelt – and specifically the relationship between race and conservatism – remained a frequently debated and passionately divisive topic of political conversation well into the twenty-first century. To a point, the connections between the South, conservative Republicans, and race are logical and essentially self-evident.

[23] For a statistical analysis of the 1968 campaign, see Byron E. Shafer and Richard Johnston, *The End of Southern Exceptionalism: Class, Race, and Partisan Change in the Postwar South* (Cambridge, MA: Harvard University Press, 2006), 165–171.

If Goldwater succeeded among southern conservatives in 1964 simply because of race, and both Wallace and Nixon then successfully continued that trend in 1968 by exploiting different strands of the same white backlash, then it would stand to reason that the heart and soul of the postwar conservative ascendancy was its South-centric reactionary opposition to racial egalitarianism and civil rights. In other words, if both Nixon and Wallace simply picked up in 1968 where Goldwater had left off in 1964, then racism is the motivational genesis of modern conservatism – stretching as a continuum from Goldwater to Nixon to Wallace and then, eventually, to Reagan and beyond.[24]

With specific regards to 1968, there is little question that Nixon's campaign attempted to capitalize on the white South's growing disenchantment with the Democratic Party, much of which was clearly the result of its opposition to race and civil rights. It is also clear that a significant overlap existed between Goldwater's southern constituency in 1964 and Wallace's in 1968, and that some southern conservatives – Strom Thurmond, most notably – left the Democratic Party to become Republicans because of Goldwater. But it is less clear that Nixon's Southern Strategy was designed to attract precisely these same constituencies.

In fact, evidence suggests that Nixon's ideas about the South were different from either Goldwater's or Wallace's. As early as 1966, it is clear that Nixon considered the South a priority so far as his presidential aspirations were concerned. That spring, Nixon

---

[24] The correlations between race and the conservative Republican South have been documented and discussed at length in recent years. Most of the scholarship already cited in this and previous chapters at least touches on Nixon's Southern Strategy and the impact that he and Wallace had on fomenting partisan realignment in the South. For instance, see Earl Black and Merle Black, *The Rise of Southern Republicans* (Cambridge, MA: Harvard University Press, 2002); Farber and Roche, *The Conservative Sixties*; Kari Frederickson, *The Dixiecrat Revolt and the End of the Solid South, 1932–1968* (Chapel Hill: University of North Carolina Press, 2000); Robert Mason, *Richard Nixon and the Quest for a New Majority* (Chapel Hill: University of North Carolina Press, 2004); and Thurber, *Republicans and Race*. Whether or not Wallace served as a gateway to Reagan, however, remains in question. On this, see again Shafer and Johnston, *The End of Southern Exceptionalism*.

attended a fund-raiser in South Carolina with Strom Thurmond.
During his visit, Thurmond introduced Nixon to one of his top
aides, Harry Dent. Nixon and Dent spent several minutes discussing Republican growth in the South, with specific attention to
Goldwater's success in the Deep South in 1964. During that
conversation, Nixon told Dent that his approach in 1968 would
be different from what Goldwater's had been in 1964, arguing
that Goldwater had been far too distracted by the most volatile
and reactionary aspects of the southern backlash. According to
Nixon, Goldwater had won the "wrong states." In Nixon's view,
GOP growth in the South – not to mention his own prospects
for success in that region – depended not on a limited, short-term
appeal to the white, racial backlash of the largely rural Deep
South, but rather on a more lasting conversion of middle-class
voters – white, suburban, and educated – living in the sprawling
metropolises of the emerging and much broader Sunbelt. These
were people living in places such as Atlanta, Tampa, and Dallas,
not the Mississippi Delta or the Alabama "Black Belt." According
to Nixon, focusing too much attention on the more racially motivated Deep South was a political dead end. Over the next two
years, Nixon and Dent – along with other campaign strategists –
worked, instead, to create a "suburban strategy" in which an
insecure white middle class would be encouraged to defect to the
GOP not simply because of its resolute, though more moderate
opposition to federally enforced racial equality, but because of its
opposition to liberalism more generally, as well as because of its
concurrent support for the politics of limited government, free-
market capitalism, and ostensibly color-blind racial harmony.[25]

Between 1966 and 1968, Nixon prepared to implement this
strategy, frequently speaking at Republican fund-raisers and local
campaign rallies throughout the South. During those appearances, he typically expressed sympathy with the white South's
overarching resistance to federal encroachment, though he always
prefaced those sympathies with statements about his prior support

[25] Carter, *The Politics of Rage*, 326. Credit for the term "suburban strategy," in
this case, goes to Lassiter, *The Silent Majority*.

for the *Brown* decision of 1954, the Civil Rights Act of 1964, and the Voting Rights Act of 1965. Distinguishing himself from Goldwater's (and Wallace's) perceived extremism, Nixon made these statements in order to bridge the gap between the moderate, color-blind conservatives of the white, suburban middle class, and the more volatile and less electorally appealing "redneck" voters to whom Wallace was directing most of his energy. Nixon's emphasis on law and order certainly capitalized on the South's heightened sensitivity and opposition to civil rights, but it also struck a chord in other parts of the country, where race was a present, though slightly less powerful or salient issue. Nixon's brilliance in 1968 was not that he manipulated southern white fears about race, but that he capitalized on the more moderate manifestations of those fears and did so most effectively in the peripheral South, the broader Sunbelt, and the rest of the nation. In this way, Nixon helped lay the groundwork for a much more viable strategy for long-term Republican growth across the region. Yes, Nixon used a Southern Strategy in 1968 that took advantage of racial bigotries. But it was a more moderate, suburban-oriented strategy distinct from Wallace's or even Goldwater's in important ways.[26] As Matthew Lassiter has so articulately argued, Nixon's Southern Strategy was typically much closer to being a suburban strategy than it was to being a derivation of George Wallace.[27]

Nixon's version of the Southern Strategy did not simply reflect his insights into the importance of middle-class politics; it also reflected his sensitivity to political developments originating not during operative-led strategy sessions, but from grassroots activists working across the Sunbelt on a variety of issues ranging from homeownership and property rights to taxes, public schools, and busing. This is an important point. The election of 1968, in conjunction with the much broader political culture of the late 1960s, profoundly and lastingly transformed the fundamental

---

[26] Carter, *The Politics of Rage*, 324–328; Critchlow, *The Conservative Ascendancy*, 85–86.

[27] For more on the dynamics between massive resistance and color-blind conservatism in the Deep South, see Crespino, *In Search of Another Country*. See also again Lassiter, *The Silent Majority*; and Kruse, *White Flight*.

character of Sunbelt politics. Moreover, the political culture of the Sunbelt during the late 1960s transformed the fundamental character of American politics for the rest of the century. The dawn of Nixon's presidency witnessed an acceleration in the social, cultural, and political modernization of the Sunbelt. That acceleration emphasized the need for conservatives – and especially ambitious southern Republicans – to reject the vilest dimensions of the old Confederacy's racist political heritage, a heritage seen by most across the country as outmoded, at best. By 1970, it was no longer politically viable to lead a regional movement, let alone a national one, by exploiting the basest of racial prejudices. As the Sunbelt modernized socially, culturally, and economically, the region's growing middle class became a far greater force for political change than had historically been the case. This middle class was by no means universally open minded when it came to race or civil rights, but neither did it see any benefit in promoting Jim Crow or overt white supremacy. This shift away from the old political culture of segregation and toward a new political culture that deemphasized race altogether, instead promoting ideas about the free market, federal spending, taxes, and a variety of other conservative issues, changed the Republican Party's image in the South and contributed to partisan realignment. In this process, growing metropolises like Dallas, Houston, and Atlanta – far closer in nature to cities in the Sunbelt West like Phoenix or San Diego than they were to the still-predominately rural Deep South – assumed far greater influence on the long-term trajectory of southern politics than those cities had enjoyed in the past.[28]

Another city that deserves attention along these lines is Charlotte, North Carolina. By 1970, Charlotte – much like Atlanta – had built a reputation as a thriving metropolis characteristic of the postwar Sunbelt. For years, municipal officials, Chamber of Commerce leaders, and white middle-class business owners across the city publicly eschewed the divisive politics of segregation in favor of a more forward-thinking, progress-oriented, and color-blind sensibility of moderation and compromise. The city's economic

[28] Ibid.

development was especially important to Charlotte's Chamber of Commerce, which in the process of attracting new investors, routinely prioritized stability and moderation as the city's political backbone. As in Atlanta, much of what some called the "Charlotte Way" was a precarious facade, masking the persistence of ongoing racial tensions in order to encourage and support economic growth. For these and related reasons, Charlotte was a community ready-made for Nixon's suburban strategy. In 1968, Nixon carried Mecklenberg County, of which Charlotte was the county seat, by nearly twice as many votes as Humphrey, and nearly three times as many as Wallace. It was by far his best showing in all of North Carolina that year.[29]

Less than one year later, a school desegregation crisis set off a political firestorm that intensified the salience of Nixon's suburban-oriented message. In 1969, a federal district court ordered the Charlotte-Mecklenberg school district to resolve what the court considered the unsatisfactory racial imbalance between the city's inner and urban schools – almost completely African American – and its outer, more suburban ones – almost entirely white. After much political wrangling, the city's board of education proposed a modest plan to relocate by bus a limited number of white junior high and high school students into the mostly black schools. It also rejected suggestions to include elementary school students in that plan. Unresolved, the issue eventually made its way to the U.S. Supreme Court, which, in the case of *Swann v. Charlotte-Mecklenberg* (1971), issued a mixed opinion that, on the one hand, found busing to be a constitutionally legal means for achieving racial balance in public schools, but on the other hand limited the degree to which districts could seek a more mathematically representative balance. *Swann* also made the enforcement of busing a temporary action, able to be undone at whatever point later courts would deem Charlotte to no longer be in violation of federal desegregation laws.[30]

---

[29] Lassiter, *The Silent Majority*, 121–147.
[30] Ibid., 148–174; see also Bartley, *The New South, 1945–1980*, 409–410. See also again Graham, *The Civil Rights Era*.

Swann established a critically important legal precedent in the history of civil rights and public schools, but so far as its impact on the evolving nature of Sunbelt political culture, its major importance was in the mobilization of conservative grassroots activists in 1969 and 1970. Angered that a federal court would "punish" them and their children simply for being successful enough to live in an affluent neighborhood, Charlotte whites organized the Concerned Parents Association (CPA) to argue that their rights to freedom of assembly and freedom of choice were being violated. These CPA activists insisted that they were not motivated by race, but that they and their children had the right to attend neighborhood schools, regardless of the racial makeup of those schools. CPA protestors said they supported integration and the rights of African Americans to receive a quality and equal education. For the CPA, race was not the issue – at least not according to its public statements. For the CPA, the issue was freedom of choice and the right to provide for their children. These arguments resonated with middle-class whites. Rejecting charges that what CPA activists really wanted was to avoid putting their kids into contact with blacks, white parents employed a rhetoric of individuality, libertarian choice, and color-blind access to local schools. For white middle-class parents in Charlotte – as for middle-class parents in Houston, which was experiencing a similar upheaval over busing – along with homeowners in Atlanta and suburban whites all across the Sunbelt, the regressive language of white supremacy that had long guided the southern Democratic Party was being replaced by a much less divisive and more racially moderate rhetoric. Color-blindness, regardless of how insincere such sentiment may actually have been, was a central characteristic of modern Republican conservatism's broad, rhetorical appeal.[31]

---

[31] Ibid., 225–250. The city of Houston experienced a similar crisis over busing and school desegregation during the same years that Charlotte was fighting over its schools. That story is told in Cunningham, *Cowboy Conservatism*, 116–120. For more on Houston and the long-term politics of school desegregation, see also William Henry Kellar, *Make Haste Slowly: Moderates, Conservatives, and*

The mobilization of suburban parents in Charlotte, Houston, and other Sunbelt cities both reflected and informed Nixon's opinion on the future of Republican growth across the region. In California, Ronald Reagan curried favor with suburban parents by opposing new busing measures, at the same time successfully attracting more Hispanic voters into his conservative tent by supporting bilingual education programs in public schools.[32] The mobilization of suburban parents across the Sunbelt also reinforced Nixon's suburban strategy as the right play, while suggesting that the more overtly racial politics being advised by strategists including Kevin Phillips – who saw the GOP's future in the ashes of Wallace's backlash – was the wrong play.[33]

Running for reelection in 1972, Nixon told a crowd in Atlanta that his was not a Southern Strategy, but an American strategy. Describing a brand of racially moderate, color-blind conservatism rooted in economic growth and national defense, Nixon told his Atlanta audience that such ideas represented "what the South believes in and ... what America believes in. We seek what I call a 'new American Majority.'" For Nixon, the suburban strategy he used in 1968, and would use again in 1972, was the basis not for the "southernization of American politics" as some have suggested, but rather the Americanization – or suburbanization – of southern politics.[34]

School Desegregation in Houston (College Station: Texas A&M University Press, 1999).

[32] For more on Reagan, busing, bilingual education, and California politics, see Brilliant, *The Color of America Has Changed*, 227–256. Brilliant refers to Reagan's political balance in this chapter as part of a "Southwest Strategy."

[33] Phillips, *The Emerging Republican Majority*. Phillips popularized the term "Sunbelt" but emphasized the GOP's need to steal Wallace voters, not suburban or more metropolitan ones.

[34] Lassiter, *The Silent Majority*, 312–313. Lassiter uses the phrase "Suburbanization of Southern Politics," and it is to him that I credit this idea, though he also cites John Egerton, *The Americanization of Dixie: The Southernization of America* (New York: Harper's Magazine Press, 1974). Lassiter's argument is largely a response to Dan Carter, who used the phrase "Southernization of American Politics" in Carter, *The Politics of Rage*, 324–370. Bruce Schulman presents an argument similar to Carter's in Schulman, *The Seventies*; see also Peter Applebome, *Dixie Rising: How the South Is Shaping American Values, Politics, and Culture* (New York: Times Books, 1996). Glenn Feldman, ed.,

Curiously enough, however, Kevin Phillips's vision for a more Wallace-oriented Southern Strategy was not entirely ignored. Two years after winning the presidency on the strength of a suburban strategy, and two years before he would win reelection while proclaiming the birth of a new American majority, Nixon aggressively courted Wallace voters on behalf of other candidates in the midterm elections of 1970. Those elections represent the only full-scale implementation of an overtly racial and reactionary Southern Strategy during Nixon's presidency. For Nixon and the Republican Party, the result was an overwhelming failure.

EMERGENCE OF THE "NEW DEMOCRATS"

Despite indications in Charlotte that the key to GOP success in the South was a racially moderate suburban strategy, the quickly developing controversy over busing in 1969 and 1970 prompted Nixon to deviate from that plan, sensing that the time was right to see if the South's race-baiting, segregationist culture still had life. Seeking a Republican surge in both houses of Congress, Nixon went to political war in the South in 1970, backing segregationist ex-Democrats over their more moderate opponents in Republican primaries and general elections all over the region. As a result, Nixon unintentionally (and only temporarily) stunted Republican growth in the Sunbelt and paved the way for the emergence of a new breed of moderate southern Democrats.[35]

In Virginia, for instance, Nixon backed longtime segregationist Senator Harry Byrd Jr.'s reelection campaign, which Byrd waged as an Independent. Nixon hoped Byrd would win reelection and convert to the Republican Party, and he pressured the state's moderate Republican governor, Linwood Holton, to back Byrd. A racial progressive, Holton refused. The Virginia Republican

Painting Dixie Red: When, Where, Why, and How the South Became Republican (Gainesville: University Press of Florida, 2011).

[35] For a broad look at the emergence of New South Democrats in 1970, see Randy Sanders, *Mighty Peculiar Elections: The New South Gubernatorial Campaigns of 1970 and the Changing Politics of Race* (Gainesville: University of Florida Press, 2002).

Party also refused to endorse Byrd and ran Ray Garland, a racial moderate, to oppose both Byrd and the Democratic opponent. Holton – elected in 1969 as the first Republican governor of Virginia since Reconstruction – had hoped to build a moderate Republican majority in Virginia in the mold of Nixon's color-blind, suburban strategy of 1968. But Nixon's support for Byrd undermined the GOP's growth in Virginia, at least in the short term. In refusing to support Byrd, Holton lost standing among Republican conservatives in the state, and Byrd was reelected. Though a lifelong conservative, Byrd served in the U.S. Senate until 1983 without formally becoming a Republican. Meanwhile, Holton's hopes for a moderate Republican majority in Virginia were quickly replaced by increased partisan polarization.[36]

In South Carolina, Nixon recruited Albert Watson, a Republican congressman, ex-Democrat, and open segregationist to run for governor. The Democratic Party nominated John West, the state's lieutenant governor, whose campaign emphasized faith, Christian charity, and a brand of color-blind racial moderation appealing to the growing metropolitan suburbs. As it did in other parts of the South, the fight for South Carolina's governor's office centered on the issue of busing. With Nixon and Strom Thurmond's backing, Watson tried to exploit segregationist animosity toward federal authority, explicitly fanning the flames of racism through speeches and advertising. Watson's Southern Strategy did not work; West won the election, carrying most of Nixon's 1968 suburban voters in the process. Watson's Southern Strategy also had the costly impact of reigniting the anti-extremist fears previously associated with Goldwater. West's moderate campaign promoted the South Carolina GOP as the party of radical reaction, and the state's voters responded to Watson as most Americans had to Goldwater in 1964. Considering that South Carolina had voted for Goldwater then, those voters' repudiation of a segregationist Republican in 1970 indicated a significant shift in that state's political culture. West also impressively managed to portray Watson as an instigator

---

[36] Bartley, *The New South, 1945–1980*, 399; Bass and De Vries, *The Transformation of Southern Politics*, 354–368; Lassiter, *The Silent Majority*, 261–266.

of disorder and unrest, thereby using Nixon's own law-and-order strategy against the state's still-fledgling GOP. In every way, it was a clear defeat for Nixon and the Southern Strategy.[37]

The Southern Strategy also failed in Florida, where the incumbent Republican and previously moderate Claude Kirk was defeated by centrist Democrat Reuben Askew. At Nixon's suggestion, Kirk moved sharply to the segregationist Right in 1970, hoping to capitalize on a Wallace-style backlash to busing crises in different parts of the state. Again, the Southern Strategy failed, whereas a Democrat successfully co-opted Nixon's suburban strategy. Floridians elected Askew, as well as the moderate Democrat Lawton Chiles, who claimed a seat in the U.S. Senate thanks to the same suburban repudiation of Kirk's newfound reactionary racism. As governor, Askew promoted tax policies that favored middle-class, suburban whites, and he embraced busing as a regrettable but necessary step in the process of healing the divisive wounds that remained from the state's segregationist past.[38] Nixon's Southern Strategy proved equally ineffective in Arkansas, where Dale Bumpers defeated the former governor and still segregationist Orval Faubus in the state's Democratic primary, before defeating the state's incumbent governor, Republican Winthrop Rockefeller. Nixon's lone success story in 1970 came in Tennessee, where Bill Brock unseated Albert Gore Sr. for a seat in the U.S. Senate, thanks in large part to White House backing.[39]

Nixon's most costly defeat came in Alabama, which actually proved to be an exception to the rule of Southern Strategy failure in 1970. That year, cashing in on a variety of back-channel favors as well as tapping into numerous slush funds, the White House quietly but substantially financed the gubernatorial reelection campaign of Albert Brewer, a relative moderate by Alabama standards. In the state's Democratic primary, Brewer faced the

[37] Bass and Vries, *The Transformation of Southern Politics*, 262–263; Lassiter, *The Silent Majority*, 251–261.
[38] For more on Florida politics, see again Colburn, *From Yellow Dog Democrats to Red State Republicans*.
[39] Black and Black, *The Rise of Southern Republicans*, 93–102; Lassiter, *The Silent Majority*, 266–272.

daunting challenge of running against George Wallace, who was seeking to reclaim the stage from which he had launched his previous campaigns for national office, and from where he intended to challenge Nixon in 1972. Responding primarily to the busing crisis, Wallace constructed his quest to reclaim Alabama's highest office around both a critique of Nixon and an openly racist appeal to white supremacy. Nixon feared a potential matchup against Wallace in 1972 and hoped that by backing Brewer, he could end Wallace's presidential aspirations, while destroying the segregationist South's last non-Republican option at the national level. In response, Wallace ran what was arguably the most disgustingly racist campaign of his life, doctoring photos of Brewer meeting with Muhammad Ali and other perceived "black militants," in addition to promoting images of a little white girl surrounded by small black boys with a caption that read, "WAKE UP ALABAMA! IS THIS THE IMAGE YOU WANT? BLACKS VOW TO TAKE OVER ALABAMA." Sadly, the tactics worked and Wallace defeated both Brewer and his Republican opponent in the general election.[40]

Of all the South's political contests in 1970, however, none had a more lasting impact on national politics than Jimmy Carter's election as governor of Georgia. A peanut farmer and former navy officer from the rural South Georgia community of Plains, Carter began his political career in 1962 as a state senator. Then, in 1966, he narrowly lost to arch-segregationist Lester Maddox in the Democratic Party's gubernatorial primary. Four years later, he waged a much more effectively organized campaign, defeating Carl Sanders – a racial moderate with widespread support among suburban, middle-class whites – in the Democratic primary. Had Georgia followed the trend of several other southern states that year, Sanders would have defeated Carter because of his support in the growing, metropolitan counties surrounding Atlanta and elsewhere. But Carter, thanks in large part to the efforts of his political advisors Jody Powell and Hamilton Jordan, effectively undercut Sanders's support by attacking the moderate

[40] Carter, *The Politics of Rage*, 383–389.

as a liberal elitist, while appealing to both Maddox and Wallace supporters with thinly veiled references to the evils of federally mandated busing. Carter's manipulation of segregationist voters was far more subtle than either Maddox's or Wallace's, and upon defeating his Republican opponent in the general election, Carter reached out to state minorities, declaring that the era of racial discrimination in Georgia was over. He then symbolically hung a portrait of Martin Luther King Jr. in the state capitol building. Carter's move to the center angered the Maddox conservatives who had supported him, but it enabled him to establish an image in keeping with other "New South" governors such as Bumpers, Askew, and Holton.[41]

Carter was not the only future president to run for office in a Sunbelt state in 1970, nor was political action the exclusive product of electoral contests in Dixie. In California, Ronald Reagan easily won reelection to a second term as governor, defeating Jesse Unruh, the state's most prominent progressive officeholder, after Unruh had defeated Sam Yorty in the Democratic primary. Still the mayor of Los Angeles, Yorty established himself as a potential gubernatorial candidate in 1966, waging a spirited campaign against Pat Brown as a law-and-order populist. But in 1970, Yorty's reactionary style failed in part because Reagan's popularity had influenced many California conservatives to formally join the GOP, leaving the state's Democratic Party more uniformly liberal. Nevertheless, Reagan's pragmatic and centrist record during his first term, coupled with his conservative reputation, gave the Republican a clear win over Unruh, and another term in the governor's office in Sacramento. As expected, Reagan's strongest showings were in the suburban strongholds of San Diego and Orange Counties. Like Nixon in 1968, he also carried several other counties within the greater Los Angeles metro area.[42]

In Texas, George Bush's campaign for a seat in the U.S. Senate was not as successful. Instead, Texans sent moderate Democrat Lloyd Bentsen to the Senate, replacing the liberal Ralph Yarborough,

[41] Lassiter, *The Silent Majority*, 269–271.
[42] Cannon, *Governor Reagan*, 322–347.

whom Bentsen had defeated in the Democratic primary. It was Bush's second failed attempt to win a Senate seat. Six years earlier, he had lost to Yarborough, thanks largely to Johnson's landslide over Goldwater, which Yarborough capitalized on by labeling Bush a "darling of the John Birch Society." Bush had no such affiliation, but in the political climate of post-JFK assassination Texas, the trick worked and Yarborough won. Six years later, Bush planned vengeance against Yarborough, buoyed by the context of a rejuvenated, post-1960s anti-liberalism. But Bentsen beat Bush to the punch, ousting Yarborough in the Democratic primary by hammering the incumbent's support for Great Society programs and opposition to the war in Vietnam. Bentsen claimed the Democratic Senate nomination on the strength of suburban moderates and conservatives, then defeated Bush by suggesting that the Republican was a Texan in name only – an unacceptable product of the Northeast and the Ivy League. Bentsen even attacked Bush's support for the Equal Rights Amendment and abortion. Ironically, these were all strategies that Bush would use against Bentsen eighteen years later on his way to the White House. Meanwhile, Bill Archer, a Republican whose conservatism was unimpeachable, replaced Bush as Houston's congressional representative of the Seventh District.[43]

Ultimately, the election of 1970 went poorly for Republicans, especially in the Sunbelt, where Ronald Reagan was the party's only major success story. Nixon's decision to employ a blatantly racist Southern Strategy had backfired. The suburban strategy Nixon had used so well in 1968 now seemed open to bipartisan application, especially in the South, where the impact of the Voting Rights Act of 1965, coupled with advancements in political gamesmanship and advertising, had dealt a severe blow to the politics of white supremacy, segregation, and overt race-baiting. Not only had Nixon failed to bring more Republicans into Congress, he had also temporarily stunted the party's growth in the South. As 1972 approached, Nixon's approval ratings were dangerously low and his prospects for reelection, slim.

---

[43] Cunningham, *Cowboy Conservatism*, 65–66, 122–124.

THE ELECTION OF 1972 AND ITS AFTERMATH

Luckily for Richard Nixon, the Democratic Party chose George McGovern as its 1972 nominee for president of the United States. McGovern won the Democratic Party's nomination thanks to a truly grassroots campaign that openly appealed to the antiwar Left and took advantage of liberalized rules governing the party's convention. It also did not hurt McGovern's quest for the nomination that several of his opponents – including George Wallace, who barely survived an assassination attempt in May that left him paralyzed, and Ted Kennedy, whose campaign ended before it even began as a result of personal scandals involving the controversial drowning death of one of his female aides – were forced out of the race before the summer. The son of a Methodist minister and senator from South Dakota, McGovern was easily the most radically progressive presidential nominee in the history of the Democratic Party to that time. Not simply did McGovern appeal to the antiwar Left by advocating an immediate and unilateral withdrawal from Vietnam, as well as amnesty for draft-evaders, he also proposed severe cuts to the defense budget; a wealth-redistribution plan that guaranteed every American a minimum income designed to eradicate poverty; and supported gay rights, feminism, abortion, and busing. At one point, he even suggested support for the legalization of marijuana, though he backed off such statements later in the campaign.[44]

Although inspiring for many on the Left, McGovern was simply un-electable by 1972 standards. Democrats across the Sunbelt rejected him, giving Nixon significant latitude in terms of campaign strategy. Ultimately, Nixon chose to wage an anti-liberal war against McGovern. Conservatives in both parties labeled the Democratic nominee the candidate of "acid, amnesty, and abortion." Aside from its failure to effectively defend itself against such attacks, McGovern's campaign fell into disarray for other reasons, as well. He was plagued with funding shortfalls; disorganized and

---

[44] See again Perlstein, *Nixonland*; for a comprehensive, journalistic account of the presidential election of 1972, see Theodore H. White, *The Making of the President, 1972* (New York: Atheneum, 1973).

unenthusiastic campaign managers in several states; and an almost comical crisis in which Thomas Eagleton of Missouri, his original running mate, was forced off the ticket because he had received electroshock therapy as a treatment for psychological disorders. Meanwhile, Nixon re-embraced the suburban strategy that had worked so well for him in 1968, ran not as a "Republican" but as "the President," and essentially pinned to McGovern the same "extremist" label that Johnson had used so well against Goldwater eight years earlier.[45]

The results were definitive. Nixon won reelection, defeating McGovern with 61 percent of the popular vote, carrying forty-nine of fifty states, losing only in Massachusetts. The 1972 presidential election reflected an overwhelming repudiation of entitlement-liberalism. That repudiation momentarily unified the entire Sunbelt into a single Republican bloc. And for at least a year, it also unified a majority of voters across the entire nation against what was perceived to be the dangers of the radical Left. Ironically, however, Nixon's was a very lonely victory. Despite the land-slide, Republicans were actually two Senate seats poorer after the election than before, despite picking up seats in New Mexico, Oklahoma, Virginia, and North Carolina, where Jesse Helms began a career in the Senate that would last until 2003. North Carolina also elected James Holshouser as its first Republican gov-ernor since 1896; in Texas, John Tower – in the process of winning a third term in the U.S. Senate – became the first Republican in state history to carry a plurality of Mexican American voters in a statewide race. These successes notwithstanding, Republicans fared surprisingly poorly in down-ballot races in 1972. Many in the GOP blamed Nixon for these failures, charging that the presi-dent had not campaigned as aggressively as he ought for fellow Republican candidates.[46]

---

[45] Ibid.
[46] Ibid.; for more on McGovern and Tower in Texas, see Cunningham, *Cowboy Conservatism*, 134–148; for more on Helms and North Carolina, see Link, *Righteous Warrior*, 125–130.

These political animosities came back to haunt Nixon when his
administration was embroiled by Watergate – a scandal related to
the June 1972 burglary of the Democratic Party's national headquarters in Washington. Though acknowledged by both camps
during the campaign, the Watergate scandal did not erupt in earnest
until December, more than a month after Nixon had already won
reelection. Watergate quickly proved quite damaging. By the spring
of 1973, Nixon's White House was in disarray, wracked by charges
of corruption related to illegal wiretapping, surveillance, and persecution of perceived political enemies; blackmail; and rampant
cover-up. By the summer of 1974, Nixon's presidency had completely collapsed. Facing the undeniable reality of impeachment
and conviction in a hostile Congress, Nixon resigned on August
9, 1974 – the first president in U.S. history ever to do so. It was an
ignominious end to one of the most influential political careers in
American history, and certainly one of the most important in the
political history of the postwar Sunbelt.[47]

The Nixon years were both divisive and profoundly influential to
the political cultures of the Sunbelt and the United States, more
broadly. On the one hand, Nixon's ability to capture suburban,
middle-class whites in 1968 through a campaign focused on law
and order undercut both moderate Democrats and reactionary
racists, while intensifying the public's hostility toward entitlement-
liberalism. With the exception of 1970, Nixon effectively used a
suburban strategy to nurture a growing conservative ascendancy
across the Sunbelt – one that in 1972 resonated with the entire
country. The politics of the still-thriving metropolitan Sunbelt –
libertarian, suburban, middle class, and racially moderate –
increasingly reflected the political impulse in places well beyond

[47] The literature on Watergate is abundant, though journalists, not scholars, have
produced most of it. For a brief but scholarly overview of Watergate, see
Melvin Small, *The Presidency of Richard Nixon* (Lawrence: University Press of
Kansas, 1999), 269–296. For more on the Nixon presidency, see Melvin Small,
ed., *A Companion to Richard M. Nixon* (West Sussex, UK: Wiley-Blackwell
Publishing, 2011); see also Robert Dallek, *Nixon and Kissinger: Partners in
Power* (New York: HarperCollins, 2007).

the South or the West. In essence, Nixon's suburban strategy could be considered a Sunbelt Strategy – one that represented a tremendous shift in the political, social, and cultural milieu of the United States in the approaching post-Vietnam era. On the other hand, Republican growth in the Sunbelt hit another bump in the road thanks to Nixon's paranoia and the related Watergate scandal. Republicans fared badly in the midterm elections of 1974, but as time would tell, Watergate only deepened Americans' growing frustration with the federal government. Trusted and admired when Lyndon Johnson took office, the federal government no longer commanded Americans' faith. Instead, government seemed to have failed at almost everything since 1964 and had lied about it in the process. Such a culture was ripe for a renewal in anti-establishment populism. Over the next several years, Sunbelt candidates in both parties would attempt to tackle the nation's problems from the position of a self-proclaimed "outsider."[48]

Meanwhile, as the Watergate scandal was destroying the Nixon presidency, another development surfaced to further reshape the nature of American politics – and once again did so most powerfully and visibly in the Sunbelt. An undercurrent within conservative circles throughout most of the twentieth century, it was not until the mid-1970s that the full force of evangelical Christian political mobilization emerged as yet another destabilizing variable in the ongoing evolution of American politics in the postwar Sunbelt.

[48] Lipset and Schneider, "The Decline of Confidence in American Institutions," pp. 379–402.

5

Mobilizing the Religious Right in the Politicized "Bible Belt"

On the afternoon of January 22, 1973, Lyndon Johnson suffered a massive heart attack and died. Coming just two days after Richard Nixon's second inauguration, Johnson's death was a painful irony for those whose political philosophy had been embodied by the man whose presidency was practically synonymous with both liberalism's postwar apex and its demise. For parts of four decades during the middle of the twentieth century, Johnson's long political career almost perfectly spanned the era of liberal consensus. As president from 1963 to 1969, Johnson promoted a vision for progress and reform that captured the highest ambitions of postwar liberalism. But discontentment on both the Left and the Right, much of it related to the size of government and the war in Vietnam, killed Johnson's Great Society before it could achieve most of its goals. Meanwhile, Johnson's actions on civil rights cost him and the Democratic Party the loyalty of many white conservatives in the South, while expediting partisan realignment across the entire Sunbelt. In the wake of Nixon's greatest political triumph, Johnson's death in early 1973 seemed to symbolize what many already knew: the long-dominant New Deal coalition was dead.

Not surprisingly, Johnson's death was front-page news all across the country. Ironically, however, it was not the only major political story to command front-page headlines that day. Also on January 22, 1973, just hours before Johnson died, the United States

Supreme Court issued its widely anticipated ruling in *Roe v. Wade*, an abortion case originating out of Dallas, Texas. In *Roe*, as well as its Georgia-based companion case *Doe v. Bolton*, the Supreme Court declared state laws restricting abortion to be unconstitutional in view of due process clauses and privacy rights as interpreted through the Fourteenth Amendment. The ruling, therefore, guaranteed a woman's right to abortion until the point of fetal "viability," a term ambiguously defined as the beginning of a pregnancy's third trimester. *Roe* was a political triumph for feminists and other pro-choice activists who, for decades, had been quietly fighting to legalize abortion as part of a larger fight to control their own bodies and lives. For others, however, *Roe* represented the high stakes of a very different type of political fight.[1]

Roe alone did not create the political mobilization of conservative Catholics and Protestant evangelicals that accelerated with surprising fervor during the 1970s and early 1980s, especially in the Sunbelt. But the legalization of abortion through *Roe* did accelerate and impassion that mobilization. During the 1970s, as the politics of civil rights and Vietnam entered less volatile and certainly less prominent phases, the politics of religion – often publicly synonymous with the politics of sexuality, family values, and the so-called culture wars – emerged with greater force to further reorient the nation's constantly evolving postwar political discourse. In doing so, the rise of the Religious Right added yet another element of power to the ever-expanding Sunbelt. Home to millions of newly affluent, home-owning, middle-class families, the Sunbelt was the perfect breeding ground for a political culture centered on the protection and preservation of the oft-idealized patriarchal American family. Not surprisingly, therefore, the fusion of a metropolitan, business-oriented, and modern Sunbelt with a politically charged, actively mobilized, and tradition-centric "Bible Belt" transformed political agendas at the local, state, and national levels. It also gave many Sunbelt conservatives – especially

[1] For more on *Roe v. Wade* and the politics of abortion, see Donald T. Critchlow, *Intended Consequences: Birth Control, Abortion, and the Federal Government in Modern America* (New York: Oxford University Press, 2001).

Republican ones – yet another new weapon in their fight to remake the essential character of postwar American politics.[2]

RISE OF THE RELIGIOUS RIGHT: PART I

The convergence of South and West during the late nineteenth and early twentieth centuries did not simply meld regional ideas about politics and economics; it also transformed the dynamic between politics and religion at both the regional and national levels. Historians have long grappled with the origins of the South's deep religiosity, citing, for instance, the connections between agricultural economics, Jeffersonian populism, and evangelical and congregational democracy. Whatever the ultimate explanation for the South's strong historical commitment to the related but sometimes competing traditions of Protestant fundamentalism and evangelicalism, suffice it to say that most of the white southerners who migrated west in the decades between the Civil War and World War II steadily carried with them these religious sensibilities. These beliefs profoundly shaped the future Sunbelt's spiritual and cultural nature, as well as its relationship to the volatile dynamic between religion and the rise of Sunbelt conservatism.[3]

---

[2] Among the many excellent studies on the politics of family, include J. Brooks Flippen, *Jimmy Carter, the Politics of Family, and the Rise of the Religious Right* (Athens: University of Georgia Press, 2011); May, *Homeward Bound*; Robert O. Self, *All in the Family: The Realignment of American Democracy Since the 1960s* (New York: Hill & Wang, 2012); and Natasha Zaretsky, *No Direction Home: The American Family and the Fear of National Decline, 1968–1980* (Chapel Hill: University of North Carolina Press, 2007). For a shorter, but still insightful analysis of the Religious Right, see Robert Freedman, "Uneasy Alliance: The Religious Right and the Republican Party," in Robert Mason and Iwan Morgan, eds., *Seeking a New Majority: The Republican Party and American Politics, 1960–1980* (Nashville: Vanderbilt University Press, 2013), 124–142.

[3] The best discussion of the South-to-West migration of politics and religion is found in Dochuk, *From Bible Belt to Sunbelt*, xv–xviii, 6–26. For more on distinctions between fundamentalists and evangelicals, see Williams, *God's Own Party*, 1–18. Generally speaking, fundamentalists emphasized a literal interpretation of the Bible, viewed the Bible as inerrant and inspired, and prioritized social conservatism through the preservation of traditional Christian morals. Evangelicals typically agreed with fundamentalists on these basic issues but paid

Fundamentalists were among the most powerful influencers shaping the political mobilization of the Religious Right in the early postwar Sunbelt. Among other things, fundamentalists demanded a literal interpretation of the Bible, emphasized the Scriptures as divinely inspired and inerrant, and called for individuals to live lives of strict discipline and morality. Within a postwar context, they also saw in communism not simply a threat to liberty and individuality, but one to the social and cultural authority of traditional Protestant Christianity in American life more broadly. Typically, fundamentalists were more overtly political, resolutely conservative, and culturally engaged than most mid-century evangelicals and included men such John R. Rice. Rice began his politically charged ministry in Dallas during the 1930s, where he balanced pastoral responsibilities with the publication of his widely circulated newsletter, *Sword of the Lord*. Unlike many Texans and southerners during the 1930s, Rice was quick and eager to denounce the New Deal as dangerously complicit with socialism. Later, after a stint at Wheaton College in Illinois, Rice took his ministry to Murfreesboro, Tennessee, where he continued to preach both the Gospel of Jesus Christ and the vital importance of Republican-led anticommunism.[4]

Another of the Religious Right's fundamentalist Sunbelt pioneers was Bob Jones Jr. of South Carolina. During the 1950s, Jones managed the intractably fundamentalist university founded by his father of the same name and increasingly associated that university with anticommunism and conservative Republicans. He routinely organized conferences on "Americanism" that featured Strom Thurmond and other southern conservatives, many of whom were not yet Republicans, but most of whom already supported the GOP in national elections. Meanwhile, fundamentalist preachers including Carl McIntire and Billy James Hargis took their messages of anticommunism and patriotic nationalism

more attention to individual spiritual conversions and personal growth than they did to culture wars. These loose definitions aside, creating a definitive standard for the terms "fundamentalist" and "evangelical" is a slippery and almost impossible task.

[4] Williams, *God's Own Party*, 34–43.

to the radio airwaves, pioneering – along with men such as Clarence Manion and Dan Smoot – the powerful practice of generating conservative grassroots energy through right-wing broadcasting. Both McIntire and Hargis enjoyed widespread popularity across the Sunbelt South, although McIntire based most of his work in New Jersey, whereas Hargis – a transplanted Texan – worked out of Oklahoma. Both circulated popular newsletters and also freely cooperated with other anticommunist agitators including Joseph McCarthy, Edwin Walker, and Robert Welch.[5]

These and other influential men like them, including radio preacher J. Vernon McGee of Pasadena, California, carried an uncompromisingly fundamentalist message about the imperativeness of cultural Christianity and the dangers of secular relativism, which they argued was being surreptitiously entrenched through the same liberal consensus that guided the mainstream of both major parties during the early postwar years. McGee, in particular, reflected the transplantation of southern fundamentalism to the modern Sunbelt West, establishing a popular radio following in 1967 after relocating to Southern California from Texas. McGee's radio ministry continued to reach tens of thousands of listeners well into the twenty-first century, despite McGee's death in 1988.[6]

These fundamentalist anticommunists were a powerful influence on the evolving nature of Sunbelt conservatism during the early postwar period. However, no individual had a greater impact on the postwar growth of conservative Protestantism in the region (or the nation) than the evangelist Billy Graham. Born in Charlotte, North Carolina, in 1918, Graham was, by the 1950s, a far more transcendent figure in the world of American Christianity than any of his more politically charged, fundamentalist contemporaries. Though perhaps most popular across the emerging Sunbelt, Graham established himself during the early Cold War as the nation's (and the world's) leading Gospel evangelist. His revivalist "Crusades" attracted hundreds of thousands of worshipers in the

---

[5] Ibid.
[6] Dochuk, *From Bible Belt to Sunbelt*, 154–166.

nation's largest cities and resulted in tens of thousands of spiritual conversions. Like most evangelicals, and more than most fundamentalist anticommunists, Graham emphasized the importance of individual faith in and personal dedication to Jesus Christ. Though unquestionably engaged with postwar politics, he was less overtly political than most fundamentalists of the time. For example, he willingly cooperated with many mainline Protestants and Catholics, including some that conservative fundamentalists rejected as heretics. During the 1950s, Graham also developed a strong relationship with Dwight Eisenhower, significant because, at the time, many on the conservative Right had grown sharply critical of moderate Republicans. He also openly prayed with Martin Luther King Jr., while offering cautious support for the civil rights movement. For the rest of the twentieth century, Graham was among the nation's most highly respected men – patriotic, anticommunist, sincerely committed to Gospel evangelism, and more moderate in his political style than many of the Sunbelt's more fiery and politicized personalities – Jones, McIntire, Hargis, and McGee among them. For these reasons, every president from Harry Truman to Barack Obama, regardless of party, took the time to befriend or at least publicly counsel with Graham.[7]

Predominantly because of style, evangelicals like Graham were more influential in the long-term rise of postwar conservatism across the Sunbelt than were most fundamentalists. Typically less apocalyptic, conspiratorial, or fiery than most prominent fundamentalists, evangelicals like Graham more easily commanded bipartisan respect, while usually avoiding the divisive and retrogressive politics of race that still tinged fundamentalism, especially in the South. One reason for the popularity of Sunbelt evangelicals was their increasing willingness to tailor sermons to the affluent ambitions of the region's growing middle class. While fundamentalists were busy fighting communism and cultural relativism, and

---

[7] Historical literature on the political influence of Billy Graham is vast. For example, see Steven P. Miller, *Billy Graham and the Rise of the Republican South* (Philadelphia: University of Pennsylvania Press, 2009). Among other things, this literature is increasingly aware of Graham's connections to the conservative Southern business community.

Graham was busy becoming a global icon, several Sunbelt preachers turned their attention to the suburbs and the culture of consumption that seemed to drive much of the middle class's behavior
during these decades.[8]

Rejecting the Social Gospel that had guided liberal mainline
Protestantism and church-sponsored public welfare since the turn
of the century, a new breed of evangelical Protestants began to
preach the much more appealing, timely, and family-oriented message of "health, wealth, and prosperity." Popular with upwardly
mobile suburbanites, evangelical preachers such as Robert Schuller
of Garden Grove, California – who, in 1955, established the
nation's first "drive-in" church – spoke passionately not simply
about the virtues of American patriotism, but also of God's desire
to bless his followers with material abundance. Neatly compatible with corporate America's postwar vision for the free market,
Schuller and other Sunbelt evangelicals like him – including Tulsa,
Oklahoma's charismatic televangelist Oral Roberts – attracted
loyal audiences not simply because they were conservative in the
age of Cold War anticommunism, but because they told their
followers that it was okay to be rich. Some even went so far as to
suggest that God's desire for American families was entirely synonymous with the comforts of modern suburbia. Therefore, it was
not a stretch for residents to see their flourishing postwar Sunbelt
as both evidence of this blessing and as a "promised land" set
aside by God for a people whose ultimate responsibility was to
preserve and expand that blessing to the rest of the nation. In
other words, as more individuals enjoyed the fruits of Sunbelt
modernity, the more convinced those individuals became that
their experiences were representative of the American Dream at
its very best.

In a related development, religious conservatives across the
Sunbelt increasingly suggested that although communism was a
serious problem, liberalism – because of its mainstream credibility
and its power to secularize the American mind – was actually the

[8] For more, see Lizabeth Cohen, *A Consumer's Republic: The Politics of Mass
Consumption in Postwar America* (New York: Alfred A. Knopf, 2003).

more dangerous and urgent threat to the American Dream's preservation and expansion. Liberalism, they argued, was anathema to the Sunbelt because it undermined independence and initiative, while threatening individual liberty and parental authority. In each of these ways, the growth of what became the Religious Right powerfully enhanced, enabled, and benefited from the simultaneous growth of Sunbelt libertarianism.[9]

The mobilizing Religious Right gained steam during the early 1970s. This acceleration was due in part to the ongoing success of fundamentalist radio personalities, evangelists, and "Prosperity Gospel" preachers across the Sunbelt, but it was also the result of breakthrough contributions such as Hal Lindsey's 1970 book, *The Late Great Planet Earth*. A Christian Zionist and passionate eschatological dispensationalist, Lindsey used his book to offer an apocalyptic vision of impending American doom. Lindsey's vision was driven by contemporary geopolitics, particularly unrest in the Middle East, which he connected to end-times prophecies found in the Bible, especially in the books of Daniel, Ezekiel, and Revelation. Unlike similarly themed books published in earlier years, *The Late Great Planet Earth* was a runaway bestseller, outselling every other work of nonfiction published during the entire decade of the 1970s. Lindsey's ability to connect modern politics with prophecies related to the rise of the Antichrist, Christ's second coming, and the "Tribulation" resonated with Sunbelt conservatives who were already primed to see in liberalism a slippery slope of moral decay, escalating government tyranny, and religious persecution.[10] *The Late Great Planet Earth* propelled Lindsey toward a long career as one of the nation's most influential and controversial Christian personalities. It also

---

[9] For more on Schuller, Roberts, and evangelical influence in the Sunbelt more broadly, see again Dochuk, *From Bible Belt to Sunbelt*, 167–195; and Williams, *God's Own Party*; see also McGirr, *Suburban Warriors*, 101, 105–107.

[10] "Tribulation" as mentioned here refers to an eschatological belief among some Christians that prior to the Second Coming of Jesus Christ, the world will bear witness to a variety of ever-worsening circumstances, trials, and sufferings, in accordance with Biblical prophecy, and specifically in accordance with prophecies in the book of Revelation. There are multiple variations of this interpretation, all depending on different theological perspectives.

inspired a new generation of Christian authors, including Tim LaHaye and Jerry B. Jenkins, whose *Left Behind* series of fictional novels re-created many of Lindsey's apocalyptic themes for millions of new readers in the 1990s and 2000s.[11]

Like LaHaye and so many others, Lindsey based his work out of Southern California. Also like so many others during the postwar decades, Lindsey had relocated to Southern California from Texas. A graduate of Dallas Theological Seminary, Lindsey moved to Southern California during the late 1960s to work with Bill Bright's revolutionary parachurch ministry, Campus Crusade for Christ. Founded at UCLA in 1951, by the early 1970s Campus Crusade for Christ had established itself as the nation's premier campus ministry, and one of the most influential evangelical organizations in the world. Under Bright's visionary leadership and market-driven strategy, Campus Crusade for Christ established a model for evangelism on the modern college campus that other organizations would attempt to replicate or build from, while transforming the way that similar ministries organized and administered staffs and raised funds. Throughout his adult life and with some important moments of exception, Bright lived with a single-minded commitment to Gospel evangelism. Though not always successful – especially during the late 1970s – he usually tried to avoid overtly political engagements that would compromise that mission. At the same time, however, the postwar growth and success of Campus Crusade for Christ often paralleled and unintentionally fueled the rise of politically mobilized evangelical Sunbelt conservatives, many of whom increasingly connected the hedonism and widening secular relativity of university life with the ominous march of political liberalism.[12]

[11] Hal Lindsey, *The Late Great Planet Earth* (Grand Rapids, MI: Zondervan, 1970); Dochuk, *From Bible Belt to Sunbelt*, 315; Tim LaHaye and Jerry B. Jenkins, *Left Behind: A Novel of the Earth's Last Days* (Colorado Springs, CO: Tyndale House Publishers, 1995); Williams, *God's Own Party*, 161.

[12] Several recent studies into the religious influence on modern conservatism have highlighted Bill Bright and Campus Crusade for Christ, but the best and most comprehensive treatment is John G. Turner, *Bill Bright and Campus Crusade for Christ: The Renewal of Evangelicalism in Postwar America* (Chapel Hill: University of North Carolina Press, 2008).

More to the point, by the early 1970s, Bright and others in the Campus Crusade circle argued that Americans had been lulled into spiritual poverty by both the quest for material abundance and the pursuit of existential meaning through non-Christian avenues. Proactively battling this trend, Campus Crusade took its message of Christ-centered purpose and meaning to the streets of San Francisco during the summer of 1967, hoping to intervene with the hippie counterculture's so-called Summer of Love. These and similar efforts during the late 1960s yielded some evangelical success, but far more impactful was Campus Crusade's staging of an event known as Explo '72. Also known as the Great Jesus Rally – or "Godstock" to some – this event attracted more than 85,000 young worshipers to the Cotton Bowl in Dallas, Texas, during the summer of 1972. There, the mostly college-aged crowd listened to preachers, singers, politicians, and athletes – including Billy Graham, Johnny Cash, Florida Governor Reuben Askew, and Dallas Cowboys quarterback Roger Staubach. These and other men shared testimonies about the power and fulfillment of a life dedicated to Christ. It was a remarkable moment in the history of postwar American Christianity – one that blended conservative sensibilities and evangelical fervor with countercultural images, music, and style. The event was widely covered in the press and even made the cover of *LIFE* magazine.[13]

Explo '72 was not an overtly political event. But as a stylistically youthful alternative to the many secular rallies that had become common during the 1960s and early 1970s, it helped mobilize thousands of individuals who shared with Sunbelt conservatives the broadly defined values of family, patriotism, and Christian morality. Polls conducted at Explo '72 showed that the vast majority of attendees supported Nixon over McGovern in the upcoming presidential election of that year and did so by a wide margin. Yet, unlike conservatives who may simply have been expected to passively lament the relentless progression of modernity, as the *Dallas Morning News* observed, these youthful and "modern conservatives" had in mind a more proactive vision for

[13] Ibid.

changing the nation. Similar to the vision espoused by youth in the emerging New Left, the young people who attended Explo '72 wanted to engage the world, not retreat from it. In doing so, they hoped to promote a spiritual antidote for existential waywardness. Unlike most of those on the Left, however, this message was compatible with both a traditionally Biblical and largely Protestant interpretation of the ideal American lifestyle and the Right's prescription for social and economic survival. Again, the message of Campus Crusade for Christ – like that of other fundamentalists and evangelicals who gained popularity during the 1960s and 1970s – resonated across much of the Sunbelt, especially in places where the growth of the white, suburban middle class had fertilized a conservative commitment to the preservation of individual liberty and family values.[14]

As Campus Crusade for Christ was rallying tens of thousands of young conservatives at Explo '72 in Dallas, Phyllis Schlafly was rallying even more Christians into active political engagement by establishing a grassroots organization called STOP ERA. Long focused on geopolitics, anticommunism, and factional tensions within the GOP, Schlafly's new interest in 1972 was the threat of radical leftist feminism and, specifically, the fight over ratification of the Equal Rights Amendment (ERA). A constitutional amendment designed to eliminate sex discrimination, ERA had enjoyed bipartisan support since first being proposed during the early 1920s. In 1972, ERA finally passed both houses of Congress. Over the next twelve months, thirty states ratified the amendment, leaving ERA just eight states short of formal ratification to the Constitution. Through STOP ERA, however, Schlafly successfully rallied millions of conservatives, the vast majority of whom were actively affiliated with a Christian church, and all of whom were dedicated to the preservation of family values while broadly opposing the advance of liberalism and "cultural socialism."

---

[14] Ibid., 119–146; see also Paul S. Boyer, "The Evangelical Resurgence in 1970s American Protestantism," in Bruce J. Schulman and Julian E. Zelizer, eds., *Rightward Bound: Making American Conservative in the 1970s* (Cambridge, MA: Harvard University Press, 2008), 41.

STOP ERA represented the emerging power of grassroots activism on the socially conservative Right. It also represented an emerging trend that would see the political salience of social and religious issues elevated to a new position of prominence among conservative Sunbelt Republicans. Thanks largely to Schlafly's efforts and the support of social conservatives who were concerned about its potential ramifications – ranging from women in the military to unisex bathrooms and the destruction of traditional gender roles – the ERA failed to win enough remaining states to achieve formal ratification. ERA officially died in 1982.[15]

STOP ERA was a major moment in the emerging mobilization of the Religious Right, but few things stirred evangelicals and other social conservatives into the mainstream of political action quite like the Right's growing hostility toward the United States Supreme Court. Social conservatives had been increasingly wary of Supreme Court action since at least the early 1960s, though in the South – where social conservatism was more intimately connected to the politics of race – modern hostility against the Supreme Court could be traced back to at least the *Brown* decision of 1954, if not earlier. But so far as the Court's specific attention to religion was concerned, it was the coupled impact of two cases – *Engel v. Vitale* (1962) and *Abington v. Schempp* (1963) – that enlisted a rising number of religious conservatives into active combat against what was widely seen as federally mandated secularism. In *Engel*, the Court determined that formally recited prayer by state officials in public schools was unconstitutional – essentially a violation of the separation of church and state. Although many Catholics were immediately upset, a fair number of evangelicals, including surprisingly the Southern Baptist Convention, cautiously accepted the ruling, hoping that the Court's decision would have no impact on individual, unorganized, or spontaneous prayers. But a year later, when the Court ruled in *Schempp* that public schools could not lead students in Bible readings, evangelicals and Catholics alike protested much more forcefully, sensing the

---

[15] Critchlow, *Phyllis Schafly and Grassroots Conservatism*, 214–227.

emergence of an unwelcomed trend.[16] In 1966, when the Court ruled in *Miranda v. Arizona* that statements made by suspected criminals were inadmissible as evidence without law enforcement officers having first informed the suspect in question of his or her legal right to an attorney, these same religious conservatives saw yet additional evidence of eroding traditions promoted through Court-mandated secularization. In this way, *Miranda* helped further unite religious and law and order conservatives under broader worldviews that opposed liberalism, moral relativism, and cultural secularization.[17]

With these and related Supreme Court decisions serving as a fertile backdrop, the growing national debate over abortion provided yet another incendiary catalyst for the formation of the Religious Right. Feminist activism related to the legalization of abortion had been gaining steam throughout much of the 1960s. Then, in 1965, conservative Catholics received with significant disgruntlement the Supreme Court's decision in *Griswold v. Connecticut*, which overturned state laws regulating the distribution of birth control. Seeing *Griswold* as another unwanted federal intrusion, as well as a potential precedent for overturning state abortion laws, Catholics began to more forcefully agitate against the legalization of abortion. Conservative Protestants, meanwhile, were generally less concerned about the issue. Some, including Pastor W. A. Criswell of the First Baptist Church of Dallas, even quietly and surprisingly supported abortion rights during these years. However, such attitudes began to change in 1967 when, ironically, a pair of Sunbelt Republican governors – Ronald Reagan of California and John A. Love of Colorado – signed two of the nation's first liberalizing abortion rights laws. As many Catholics had for years, a growing number of conservative Protestants began to worry more about the Court's consistent intervention with religion, family, and sexuality. Still, most

---

[16] Williams, *God's Own Party*, 62–67.
[17] For more on the *Miranda* case, see Gary L. Stuart, *Miranda: The Story of America's Right to Remain Silent* (Tucson: University of Arizona Press, 2004).

Protestants remained hesitant to join their Catholic brethren in the nascent but emerging "pro-life" movement.[18]

Then, in 1970, two young Texas attorneys and feminist activists – Sarah Weddington and Linda Coffee – identified a young woman from Dallas named Norma McCorvey. Single, poor, and pregnant, McCorvey wanted a safe and legal abortion but was denied that wish by Texas laws that, at the time, held that abortion was illegal unless extreme circumstances, such as the endangered life of the mother, warranted medical intervention. McCorvey, who in legal documents assumed the name of *Jane Roe*, eventually gave birth and placed her newborn child up for adoption before her legal challenge made its way through the courts. But in 1973, the U.S. Supreme Court issued its ruling in McCorvey's case, which had been filed as *Roe v. Wade*.[19] Essentially legalizing abortion by overturning the Texas statute and others like it, the *Roe* decision was an unmistakable sparkplug for the joint political mobilization of Catholics and conservative Protestants who increasingly found common cause on issues related to religion, sexuality, family values, and the perceived consequences of cultural and secular liberalism. This was true all over the country, but became more important in the conservative Sunbelt, which had a long history of being more religiously fervent than the national mainstream, and which had already hosted the growth of fundamentalist and evangelical awareness during the early postwar decades. In the years immediately after *Roe*, pastors and preachers across the Sunbelt more frequently espoused political anti-liberalism from the pulpit, much of which was driven by the fear that the nation's oft-exaggerated historical commitment to Christian heritage was more vulnerable than ever.[20]

From radio personalities and televangelists to Supreme Court cases and specific policy debates, the early postwar Sunbelt both

---

[18] For more on *Roe v. Wade* and the politics of abortion, see again Critchlow, *Intended Consequences*.

[19] Ibid.

[20] For more on the Sunbelt's religiosity compared to that of the nation-at-large, see Lyman A. Kellstedt and James L. Guth, "Religion and Political Behavior in the Sunbelt," in Nickerson and Dochuk, *Sunbelt Rising*, 110–138.

witnessed and hosted many of the most important battles that defined and inspired the rise of the Religious Right. It was no surprise, therefore, that the Sunbelt also produced the first openly "born-again" evangelical president of the United States. What did surprise many in 1976, however, was that this individual was the former governor of Georgia, Jimmy Carter.[21]

YEAR OF THE EVANGELICAL

Being born-again was nothing if not trendy during the mid-1970s. Evangelical churches and affiliated personalities had been growing more popular since at least the 1950s. But the nation's collective disillusionment – stemming from Watergate and the end of the Vietnam War – noticeably deepened Americans' spiritual wandering. Not all of those wandering souls made their way to evangelical Protestantism, but many did. Public declarations of personal faith in Jesus Christ became much more common during the mid-to-late 1970s and included a number of relatively big names. For example, convicted Watergate conspirator Chuck Colson made headlines in 1975 when he published a best-selling book from prison called *Born Again*, in which he detailed his spiritual conversion. Later, former Black Panther militant Eldridge Cleaver professed a similar conversion, as did Bob Dylan. These celebrities were hardly alone. According to polls conducted in 1976, roughly 34 percent of all Americans claimed to have been born again. For these and related reasons, both *Time* and *Newsweek* magazines proclaimed 1976 to be the "Year of the Evangelical."[22]

If 1976 was the Year of the Evangelical, then Jimmy Carter – easily the most famous self-professing born-again Christian in the United States – was a major reason why. Carter's ascension to political stardom as a confessing southern evangelical was probably the most striking reason for *Time*'s and *Newsweek*'s declaration about the religious flavor of the nation's bicentennial.

[21] Ibid.
[22] Flippen, *Jimmy Carter, the Politics of Family, and the Rise of the Religious Right*, 61–106.

A native of rural Georgia and a lifelong Baptist, Carter experienced a spiritual awakening in 1966 shortly after losing his first
bid to win the governorship of his home state. Carter then spent
the next several years evangelizing door-to-door in several northern cities, a dedication mitigated only by his equally passionate
commitment to winning the governorship of Georgia in 1970.
Carter succeeded in that goal and was among the wave of New
South governors to win office in 1970. Upon entering the governor's mansion, Carter routinely peppered his political speeches
with the theology of Reinhold Niebuhr and Martin Luther King
Jr. After four years of service at the state-level, he turned his
attention to capturing the White House.

Americans' confidence in their political system – and their trust
in politicians – reached new lows in the 1970s. In this mixed,
post-Watergate climate of collective social discouragement and
renewed interest in personal spirituality, Carter understood that
his blend of southern populism, evangelical dedication, personal
integrity, and Democratic-affiliation was a rare but timely prescription for political success at the national level. Beginning his
campaign as a virtual unknown, Carter gained early momentum
by winning the Iowa caucuses and the New Hampshire primary;
as a result, he quickly emerged as the front-runner for his party's
nomination. Running an authentically grassroots campaign,
Carter won Democratic supporters by highlighting his experience
as a moderate governor in a southern state, his work as a local
Sunday School teacher at the Plains Baptist Church, his commitment to faith and family, and his equally valuable status as a
Washington outsider.[23]

Carter's strategy in 1976 was not terribly dissimilar from that
of another former Sunbelt governor and insurgent presidential
candidate, Ronald Reagan. While Carter ran for the Democratic
Party's nomination, Reagan mounted an almost unprecedented
challenge for the Republican nod, seeking to unseat the incumbent
president and his fellow-Republican, Gerald Ford. So far as religion goes, far more was made of Carter's faith in 1976 than

---

[23] Ibid.; Kalman, *Right Star Rising*, 180–201.

was made of Reagan's. Both candidates drew strength from the
Sunbelt South, though Reagan's appeal was much more libertarian,
corporate, and anticommunist than was Carter's. In Republican
primaries across the Sunbelt, the conservative Right flocked
to Reagan, including most notably in North Carolina, Georgia,
Texas, California, and Nevada. Carter, meanwhile, claimed
Florida as his most valuable early prize, winning the Sunshine
State's Democratic primary that March, at the same time ending
George Wallace's last bid for the White House. Eventually,
Reagan's challenge to unseat Ford fell narrowly short, but not
before the former governor of California had widened the
already dangerous ideological crack that still divided the GOP
into conservative and moderate (or establishment) factions.
Meanwhile, Carter's efforts to win the Democratic Party's nomination ended triumphantly. Shortly after accepting that nomination in July, polls showed Carter holding a more than 30-point
lead over Ford in the general election. With the GOP fissured and
still reeling from Watergate-related unpopularity, Carter seemed
well on his way to becoming the first Deep South candidate to
successfully capture the White House.[24]

Carter's relaxed waltz into the Oval Office was nearly derailed
in late September, however, when news leaked that he had given
an interview to *Playboy* magazine. Worse, it was reported that
certain subjects were discussed in the interview that many of
his evangelical supporters would not condone. Most famous
was Carter's admission that he had "committed adultery in [his]
heart many times." Carter was actually referring to standards
made clear by Christ during his Sermon on the Mount, but conservative fundamentalists and many evangelicals nevertheless
objected. Conservatives criticized Carter's choice of language –
he had used the word "screw" in the interview – and also criticized
his decision to even grant *Playboy* an interview in the first place.
Widely considered by conservatives to be a pornographic magazine, some considered Carter's willingness to grant the interview
as a tacit endorsement of obscenity. Almost immediately, Carter's

[24] Ibid.

support among evangelicals began to dip. W. A. Criswell was only one of many prominent Sunbelt preachers to take the *Playboy* incident as an opportunity to make political statements from the pulpit. On October 10, with Ford in attendance, Criswell publicly endorsed the incumbent Republican during that Sunday morning's sermon, making specific reference to the *Playboy* issue. The Ford campaign quickly incorporated clips from that sermon into a 60-second television advertisement. Less than three weeks later, Criswell spoke in Dallas at the National Prayer Congress, an event organized and sponsored by Campus Crusade for Christ. Criswell's tone was explicitly political, though he – like most of the other speakers – largely avoided mentioning specific candidates. Instead, the tone of the National Prayer Congress was one of deep concern for the spiritual health of the country. Prominent evangelicals seemed to be suggesting that although it was good to have political candidates who openly proclaimed a personal relationship with Jesus Christ, such declarations – if not accompanied by a rededication to fundamentalist principles and direct action – would leave the United States in a position of continued moral vulnerability and inevitable declension. Criswell and others urged those in attendance to pray for the country, and to pray specifically that it would evade the dangers of modern secularism so intimately connected to modern liberalism. Much more so than Campus Crusade's Explo '72, the National Prayer Congress in Dallas just before the 1976 election was a call to political action.[25]

The *Playboy* incident nearly killed Jimmy Carter's entire career. At the very least, it compromised his image of being authentically born-again, at least among many conservative evangelicals and fundamentalists. In Carter's favor was that a good number of religious conservatives were just as unhappy with Ford as they now were with Carter. Most religiously oriented Republicans had preferred Reagan to Ford during the primaries. Many of these "values voters" shared the libertarian Right's view of the GOP's moderate wing as conservatism's most immediate and strategically

---

[25] Flippen, *Jimmy Carter, the Politics of Family, and the Rise of the Religious Right*, 99–101; Nickerson and Dochuk, *Sunbelt Rising*, 1–3.

important enemy. Ford understood this, wanted to reunify the GOP, and believed that rallying evangelicals in both parties was a key step in that process. Choosing not to rely solely on the *Playboy* backlash or Criswell's public endorsement, Ford personally tried to woo evangelicals. He invited several prominent preachers to the White House, publicly cited his own born-again experience and dedication to the Episcopal Church, and even agreed to the addition of a stronger pro-life plank to the GOP's 1976 platform, despite being a relative moderate on the issue. Each of these efforts helped Ford with the emerging Religious Right, but not enough. Most of these religious conservatives simply did not trust Ford. This lack of trust stemmed, in part, from disagreements over issues related to the size of government, economic regulations, and foreign policy. But it also stemmed from a vehement dislike of the First Lady. Well before 1976, Ford's wife, Betty, had developed a national reputation as a liberal on social issues. A longtime supporter of the ERA, Betty Ford's liberal reputation was enhanced during a nationally televised interview in 1975 in which she passively endorsed premarital sex, abortion, and marijuana, among other things. For each of these reasons, Ford struggled with religious voters far more than most Republicans typically did in national elections.[26]

At the end of the day, Ford managed to win a slim majority of self-described evangelical voters – 51 percent to be precise. But among white Southern Baptists – a demographic most prominent in the South – Ford did poorly, capturing only 43 percent, compared to Carter's 56 percent. Overall, Carter won the presidency in 1976, taking barely 50 percent of the nation's popular vote, and 297 electoral votes, compared with Ford's 240. Carter did well in the South, carrying every state of the old Confederacy, with the exception of Virginia. In Texas, Carter won by just more than 3 percent. (Texas has not voted for a Democratic presidential candidate since.) Carter did far less well in the Sunbelt West, losing California to Ford by less than 2 percent, in addition to

[26] Williams, *God's Own Party*, 123.

losing Nevada, Arizona, and New Mexico. Elsewhere, U.S. House and Senate races resulted in very little change, with the notable exception of conservative Republican Sam Hayawaka's victory in the race for a U.S. Senate seat representing California. President of San Francisco State University, Hayawaka defeated California's incumbent and liberal Democratic Senator John Tunney by running as a political outsider. For the conservative Right, Hayawaka's surprising victory was a welcomed sign of things to come.

Nevertheless, for the fourth straight election, Americans sent a Sunbelt politician to the highest office in the land and, for the second time in four elections, that politician was a Democrat. In many ways, Jimmy Carter's campaign for the presidency in 1976 was a reflection of the times. It reflected the rise of politicized evangelicalism. It was also a harbinger for just how intimately connected the dynamics of religion and politics would become over the next several decades.

RISE OF THE RELIGIOUS RIGHT: PART II

Religious conservatism continued to gain momentum during the late 1970s. In many ways, that momentum was simply a carryover from earlier ERA and abortion-inspired activism at the grass roots, as well as the influence of several key fundamentalist and evangelical personalities. The presidential election of 1976 – particularly the role of religion in it – was also a major contributing factor. In other ways, however, the nascent Religious Right's surge was also a reflection of the nation's deepening sense of demoralization and fear. In 1979, President Carter referred to this climate of unrest as a "crisis of confidence." For many in the Sunbelt, the nation's sagging economy, coupled with its apparent impotence overseas in places ranging from Vietnam to the Middle East, did not simply suggest that the nation was facing eminent decline; it also suggested that to avoid that decline, people would need to rediscover their individual moral compasses. For many conservatives, this meant nothing short of a national rededication to Christian values and the preservation of the traditional family. Once again, the evolving nature of postwar American politics seemed increasingly rooted in the microcosmic debates and struggles taking place on Sunbelt soil.[27]

One of the most influential of these struggles took place in South Florida and concerned the issue of gay rights. In early 1977, Anita Bryant – a former beauty queen from Oklahoma and a nationally recognized pop singer and citrus spokesperson – began leading a movement to repeal an ordinance in Dade County, Florida, that guaranteed certain civil liberties to homosexuals. Through what became known as the Save Our Children campaign, Bryant rallied religious conservatives in South Florida against homosexuality on the premise that openly gay men and women had proclivities toward pedophilia, and that legal measures validating such lifestyles should be rejected and repealed. Bryant's crusade in South Florida was interesting for several reasons, not the least of which was the fact that the greater Miami metropolitan area had a sizable and relatively open gay population, which is what had made passage of the original county ordinance so easy in the first place. Despite Miami's diversity in terms of race, ethnicity, and sexual orientation, Bryant's campaign struck a nerve among local conservatives who answered Save Our Children's call by overwhelmingly voting to repeal the gay rights laws, 69 percent to 31 percent.[28]

Bryant's campaign against gay rights made her one of the nation's most recognizable and, among many religious conservatives, admired women in America. It also catalyzed gay rights militancy in places all across the country, especially in cities and states where Bryant's success in South Florida was seen as a model for similar restrictions in other communities. The clearest manifestation of this contestation came in California. In 1978, a self-described born-again conservative Republican named John Briggs introduced a law to essentially ban homosexuals from jobs in public schools in California. Eventually known on the ballot as

[27] Nickerson and Dochuk, *Sunbelt Rising*, 4. For more on the concepts of family protectionism, suburban "containment," and national decline, see among others May, *Homeward Bound*; Self, *All in the Family*; and Zaretsky, *No Direction Home*.
[28] Dominc Sandbrook, *Mad as Hell: The Crisis of the 1970s and the Rise of the Populist Right* (New York: Anchor Books, 2011), 350–352.

Proposition 6, the Briggs Amendment was the direct outgrowth of Bryant's struggle against gay rights in South Florida and, more importantly, the political partnerships that had been fostered between Bryant, Briggs, and a host of other Sunbelt Republicans and religious conservatives. The fight for Proposition 6 rallied thousands of newly mobilized religious conservatives in Southern California, Tim and Beverly LaHaye being among the most vocal. Having served as a pastor in San Diego since the late 1950s, Tim LaHaye was heavily involved in the rise of the Religious Right throughout the 1970s, founding a private Christian college in San Diego in 1971 before he and his wife emerged more noticeably into the public eye as a result of the fight over Proposition 6. Religious conservatives throughout California supported the measure, though many libertarian conservatives – including Ronald Reagan – openly rejected the proposal as unfair, discriminatory, and silly. Eventually, most voters agreed with Reagan and the measure was overwhelmingly rejected. Nevertheless, whether it was in Florida, California, or elsewhere, the fight over gay rights – typically couched as an effort to protect children and families from "gay liberation," which Briggs said was "more dangerous than communism" – had invigorated a significant corps of pastors and grassroots religious conservatives.[29]

Despite (or perhaps because of) Proposition 6's defeat, the LaHayes continued to successfully mobilize Christian voters in the fight against secular liberalism. In 1978, Beverly LaHaye formed Concerned Women for America (CWA), an organization designed to mobilize conservative women in the fight against radical feminism. A year later, Tim LaHaye joined others, including Paul Weyrich and Robert Grant, in forming Christian Voice, a political action committee (PAC) dedicated to supporting Republican candidates friendly to the Religious Right's vision for American security. Among the first of many similar PACs, CWA and Christian Voice became meeting places for conservative pastors, grassroots activists, and GOP political aspirants in

[29] Dochuk, *From Bible Belt to Sunbelt*, 381–387.

Southern California and elsewhere across the broader Sunbelt and nation.[30]

Southern California remained a hotbed of evangelical growth and conservative activism throughout the late 1970s and early 1980s. James Dobson, for instance, founded his enormously impactful ministry, Focus on the Family, in Arcadia, California, in 1977. Like so many others, Dobson had grown up in small towns across Oklahoma and Texas before making his way to Los Angeles in the late 1950s. From there, he attended Pasadena College before completing his Ph.D. in psychology from the University of Southern California. He spent the next several years as a professor of pediatrics at Los Angeles Children's Hospital. Thanks to Dobson, Focus on the Family quickly became one of the nation's most popular resources for Christian parents. It also became a broadcasting mouthpiece for socially conservative political values. Unable to use Focus on the Family for direct political action in Washington, however, Dobson capitalized on his newfound popularity by organizing the Family Research Council (FRC), a lobbying group founded in 1981. FRC quickly became one of the nation's leading lobbyist groups for family values issues. Focus on the Family and FRC enjoyed tremendous cultural and political success throughout the 1980s. In 1991, Dobson moved Focus on the Family to Colorado Springs, Colorado, where it continued to influence both Christian parents and Republican politicians well into the twenty-first century.[31]

The same year Dobson founded Focus on the Family, John Wimber founded a new church in suburban Los Angeles that would eventually be known as the Anaheim Vineyard Fellowship. Launched in 1977, Wimber's Vineyard Fellowship was crucial to the growth of charismatic Christianity during the last decades of the twentieth century, and it quickly became one of the Los Angeles metro area's largest churches. Wimber's church was actually an offshoot of Chuck Smith's equally huge Calvary Chapel, also based in Orange County. Smith founded Calvary Chapel in 1965, and by

[30] Ibid.
[31] Ibid., 303–305; Self, *All in the Family*, 354.

the late 1970s – along with Wimber's Vineyard Fellowship – was a national leader in the emerging Jesus Movement, which incorporated countercultural styles and hippie-like communalism with existential pursuits of spiritual meaning through deeper relationships with Christ. Even Rick Warren, eventually the best-selling author of *The Purpose Driven Life*, began his path toward megachurch stardom in Southern California during the late 1970s. A California native, Warren moved to Orange County in 1979 after completing a master of divinity degree at Southwestern Baptist Theological Seminary in Fort Worth, Texas. Heavily influenced by W. A. Criswell, but equally sensitive to the power of modern and "authentic worship" as expressed by his far more charismatic colleagues, Warren founded Saddleback Church in 1980. Within twenty years, Warren's church would boast more than 20,000 weekly attendees. A clear reflection of his national influence, in 2008, Warren even moderated the first (though unofficial) "debate" between presidential candidates John McCain and Barack Obama, both of whom he referred to as "friends."[32]

The rise of the Religious Right was not simply a matter of Sunbelt pastors and preachers becoming more involved in and outspoken about politics. It was also about partnerships. Increasingly, leading Christian influencers openly cooperated with Republican strategists and candidates. It was a symbiotic relationship. Christian influencers believed they were making friends in high places who could influence policy, and Sunbelt Republicans believed they were making friends who could influence thousands, if not millions, of socially conservative voters at the grass roots. According to conflicting reports, one such partnership emerged in 1974 when a Republican congressman from Arizona named John Conlan allied with Bill Bright to create Third Century Publishers, a publishing house designed to promote and distribute socially and fiscally conservative political literature. Bright later denied having partnered with Conlan in the founding of Third Century Publishers

---

[32] Dochuk, *From Bible Belt to Sunbelt*, 313–314; Boyer, "The Evangelical Resurgence in 1970s American Protestantism," in Schulman and Zelizer, *Rightward Bound*, 42; Williams, *God's Own Party*, 265–276.

and adamantly maintained that neither he nor Campus Crusade for Christ was seeking anything close to a direct engagement with politics. However, the mission of Third Century Publishers was, for a time at least, certainly in keeping with Conlan's vision for changing America by winning politicians for Christ. Bright's convictions did not prevent him and Campus Crusade for Christ from sponsoring the National Prayer Congress in Dallas just weeks before the 1976 presidential election.[33]

One year after that election, as Betty Ford and Rosalynn Carter joined hands with other feminist activists on a stage during the National Women's Conference in Houston, Phyllis Schlafly made headlines by organizing a rogue and competing Pro-Family Convention in Houston at the very same time. Schlafly's Pro-Family Convention seized much of the national attention away from the feminist happenings of the National Women's Conference and, once again, deepened the partnerships between grassroots religious conservatives and the Republican Party. Whereas the feminist activists meeting in Houston chose to highlight the importance of explicitly "women's issues" – abortion, day care, equal pay, workplace equality, and so on – Schlafly's Pro-Family Convention published a manifesto that read more like a first draft of the Republican Party's platform for 1980. Schlafly skillfully conflated radical feminism with threats to the traditional family and then connected those threats with the encroachment of federal authority into private lives. Thanks to Schlafly's vision and leadership, thousands of conservative women grew politicized not simply in reaction to feminist agitation, but to the broader values of secular liberalism, perceived collectivism, and even national security.[34]

Back in Southern California, Pepperdine University's annual Founding Four Hundred banquet became yet another breeding ground for these developing partnerships. Beginning in 1977, Pepperdine's president, Bill Banowsky, began inviting conservative

[33] Dochuk, *From Bible Belt to Sunbelt*, 362–365; Turner, *Bill Bright & Campus Crusade for Christ*, 161–165.
[34] Self, *All in the Family*, 311–317.

speakers, including Milton Friedman and William F. Buckley Jr., to headline the school's most important annual fund-raising event. Long considered a bastion of Christian conservatism, Pepperdine University was among the best examples of Christian intellectualism's merger with fundamentalist doctrine and Republican politics during the late 1970s. Benefiting from a steady stream of leadership and financial assistance from supporters in Texas, Pepperdine – as Darren Dochuk has explained – was also a meeting place for the ongoing convergence of South and West, as well as the growing partnerships between religious conservatives and Republicans. Both of these factors were central to the development of the Sunbelt's political culture and its expanding power.[35]

Private Christian education was also at the heart of one of the most divisive and influential controversies to shape the Sunbelt's surge toward Republican conservatism during the late 1970s. In 1978, the Internal Revenue Service (IRS) announced that in accordance with civil rights laws, it would begin investigating private Christian schools that could not demonstrate evidence of having attempted to recruit and enroll sufficient numbers of minority students. Private Christian schools were not isolated to the Sunbelt, but they were most abundant there, especially in the South. Many of these schools had been established during the late 1950s and early-to-mid-1960s, seemingly in response to federally mandated public school desegregation. Tax exempt as religious institutions, the IRS declared that such schools would no longer receive tax benefits unless proactive and aggressive efforts were made to desegregate what liberals viewed as discriminatory all-white academies. As busing had done in the early 1970s, this issue mobilized Sunbelt parents against both the federal government

---

[35] Dochuk, *From Bible Belt to Sunbelt*, 376–377; for more on the partnerships between Republicans and the Religious Right, see Thomas Frank, *What's the Matter with Kansas: How Conservatives Won the Heart of America* (New York: Owl Books, 2005). See also Clyde Wilcox, *God's Warriors: The Christian Right in Twentieth-Century America* (Baltimore: Johns Hopkins University Press, 1992).

186 *Cunningham*

and Jimmy Carter specifically and did so most powerfully through
the offices of strategically minded Sunbelt Republicans, including
Senator Jesse Helms of North Carolina and Representative Robert
Dornan of California, a former television personality turned
conservative politician from Los Angeles. Not surprisingly, Helms,
Dornan, and other Sunbelt Republicans capitalized on the Religious
Right's anger over the IRS's decision by redirecting hostilities to
Carter, liberalism, and the evils of "big government." Along these
lines, Paul Laxalt, a Republican senator from Nevada, introduced
to the Senate a bill known as the Family Protection Act of 1979,
designed to prohibit federal funds for sex education, public school
desegregation, and legal subsidies for divorce and abortion cases
and an outright ban on all funding for gay rights initiatives. During
the late 1970s, Sunbelt conservatives like Laxalt increasingly
linked the protection of families not with economics, as liberals
had done since the Great Depression, but with morality and
opposing federal intervention of any kind on the ground that
such intervention threatened the private sanctity of families.[36]

Each of these partnerships was important, but the single most
important one that formed between Christian activists and conservative political strategists during the late 1970s was the one
that developed between Jerry Falwell and a small cadre of men
leading what became known as the New Right. For more than a
decade, issues including school prayer, gay rights, abortion, and
feminism had catalyzed Christian conservatives into increasingly
direct political engagement. During the same years, concerns over
the global spread of communism, the growth of government, and
the struggles of a postindustrial economic recession had not gone
away, neither had the anticommunist, libertarian, and law and
order conservatives to whom these issues mattered most. Seeking
to create a new political coalition capable of winning national
elections, the New Right – essentially led by Paul Weyrich, Robert
Grant, direct-mail guru Richard Viguerie, Howard Phillips, and
Terry Dolan – recruited Falwell to become the bullhorn of this

[36] Kalman, *Right Star Rising*, 272–273; Self, *All in the Family*, 336.

aspirant coalition. The result was an organization known as the Moral Majority.[37]

Falwell had not always been an obvious choice to lead such a group. Pastor of the Thomas Road Baptist Church of Lynchburg, Virginia, since 1956, Falwell had long preached that it was not his job to change the outside world but to convert the individual souls who attended his church. A segregationist during the 1950s and 1960s, and certainly a fundamentalist conservative through-out his career, Falwell slowly grew more interested in and vocal about politics during the mid-1970s. Like W. A. Criswell, he was disappointed in Jimmy Carter's interview with *Playboy* and, as a result, publicly endorsed Gerald Ford in 1976. In 1977, he pro-vided Anita Bryant a national platform via his *Old-Time Gospel Hour* television show, which by the late 1970s was generating roughly $35 million in annual revenue while being broadcast on more television stations nationally than Johnny Carson's *The Tonight Show*. In 1978, the war between private Christian schools and the IRS gave Falwell yet another reason to take a stand on policy issues, and by 1979, he was a major player in several Christian PACs operating all across the country. So, when Paul Weyrich and other New Right organizers approached him about becoming the leader of a new, nondenominational organization – the Moral Majority – Falwell was already primed to accept.[38]

Under Falwell's leadership, the Moral Majority actively dis-tributed voter education guides; registered millions of new voters into the Republican Party; staged well-attended rallies; and mag-nified the dangers of secularism, economic and cultural liberalism, and the Democratic Party for untold numbers of American Christians. Its influence was most powerfully felt across the Sunbelt, where megachurch pastors – including Charles Stanley, pastor of the First Baptist Church of Atlanta, Georgia, and James Kennedy, pastor of the Coral Ridge Presbyterian Church of Fort

[37] Ibid., 21–37; Flippen, *Jimmy Carter, the Politics of Family, and the Rise of the Religious Right*, 228; Sandbrook, *Mad as Hell*, 353–360; Williams, *God's Own Party*, 167–179.

[38] Ibid.

Lauderdale, Florida – enthusiastically abandoned the idea that politics and the pulpit should not mix. Both Stanley and Kennedy, in fact, were original members of the Moral Majority's board of directors, as was San Diego's Tim LaHaye. In 1979 and 1980, Falwell and the Moral Majority were firmly positioned within the national discourse on faith, politics, and conservative family values.[39]

As Weyrich and Falwell were building the Moral Majority out of Virginia, Ed McAteer was building another (but theoretically more ecumenical) political action group in California called the Religious Roundtable. In 1980, with the help of several executive board members who, including Falwell, had input in multiple like-minded organizations, McAteer identified James Robison, a fiery and controversial preacher from Pasadena, Texas, to become the new national figurehead of the Religious Roundtable. Throughout most of the 1970s, Robison's impassioned sermons were broadcast on television stations across the state of Texas and routinely included dire warnings about the evils of homosexuality and nontraditional families. In 1979, WFAA of Dallas pulled Robison's sermons off the air after he said that homosexuals liked to murder small boys and that the assassinations of San Francisco Mayor George Moscone and Board of Supervisors' member Harvey Milk were actually the divine judgment of God against gay America. (Milk was the first openly gay man ever elected to public office in the state of California and had become famous in 1978 through his debates with John Briggs over Proposition 6.) Robison vehemently protested the station's decision and pleaded with Christian conservatives across the country, including Falwell, to come to his rescue.[40]

They did. Over the course of the following year, Robison's stature in the Religious Right grew. In August 1980, his Religious Roundtable commanded national attention when it staged an event at Reunion Arena in Dallas known as the National Affairs Briefing. In front of more than 15,000 attendees, Robison called on

[39] Ibid.
[40] Flippen, *Jimmy Carter, the Politics of Family, and the Rise of the Religious Right*, 230, 284; Williams, *God's Own Party*, 182–184, 187–188.

"God's people to come out of the closet" to reverse the slide of moral degradation that he and others like Falwell were convinced was at the heart of the nation's problems. Robison had invited all three presidential candidates – including John Anderson, who was running as a third-party Independent – to attend the event at Reunion Arena. Only one candidate accepted the invitation. During his speech, Robison stopped short of endorsing any single presidential candidate, but it was clear who he and those on stage supported, for sitting mere feet behind Robison at the time was the former governor of California, Ronald Reagan.[41]

The rise of the Religious Right was one of the most critical developments in the history of postwar American politics. The enlistment of conservative evangelicals, fundamentalists, and a good many Catholics into active combat in the war against secularism and cultural liberalism was the result of both the concerted efforts of numerous pastors, preachers, and public personalities and the response of millions of concerned citizens at the grass roots all across the nation. Make no mistake, the Religious Right had a national following, but it was primarily in the Sunbelt, and especially in the Sunbelt's major metropolitan areas, that this following was strongest and most influential. Such hotbeds of activity included, but were not limited to, San Diego, Los Angeles, Dallas, Miami, Atlanta, and Virginia Beach, where Pat Robertson's Christian Broadcasting Network began reaching millions of politically minded viewers in 1977. It was in these cities that the Bible Belt and the Sunbelt became most forcefully synonymous.

The Sunbelt's importance to the rise of the Religious Right is no small point. The mobilization of politically engaged Christians within the context of an economically thriving, suburban-oriented, libertarian, and patriotic Sunbelt profoundly shaped the flavor of (especially) Protestant Christianity during the last decades of the twentieth century. Many of the issues that became important to fundamentalist and evangelical activists in the Sunbelt – the relationship between federal taxes and private

[41] Ibid.

entities, for instance – were also important to less-religious libertarians. This fact helps explain the strengthened partnership that
emerged during these years between two such historically unrelated constituencies. By 1980, the Republican Party was eager to
become the "church" in which these constituencies married, and it
was Sunbelt conservatives who most often performed the wed-
ding. Simply put, the late-1970s fusion between the Religious
Right and the libertarian and anticommunist Right enabled the
Reagan Revolution of the 1980s. It also encouraged the power
shift that Kirkpatrick Sale forecasted in 1975; by the end of the
1970s, the future of American politics, it seemed, lay in the hands
of Sunbelt power brokers.[42]

This is not to say, however, that the Religious Right represented
the sum total of American Christianity during the last decades of
the twentieth century. Neither would it be accurate to say that the
Religious Right represented the sum total of fundamentalist or
evangelical thought on American politics. In fact, many conservative
pastors rejected the call of the Moral Majority and similar organizations into active combat with the Left. Additionally, a good
many libertarian conservatives, including Barry Goldwater, recoiled
at the idea that Christian clergy should have so strong a voice in
shaping the nation's political agenda. At the same time, it should
also be clear that racial minorities across the Sunbelt, many of
whom actively identified themselves as committed Christians, were
excluded from the political agenda of the Religious Right. In
this way, the Christian Left – part-Catholic, part-Protestant – was
a relatively small but still important voice for dissent among
Christians during the postwar decades. Such exceptions noted, however, it remains true that in the multifaceted and diverse story of
American politics and religion in the postwar Sunbelt, it was the rise
of the Religious Right that most profoundly altered that narrative.[43]

[42] Sale, *Power Shift*.
[43] For more on the evangelical Left, see David R. Swartz, *Moral Minority: The
Evangelical Left in an Age of Conservatism* (Philadelphia: University of
Pennsylvania Press, 2012). See also Rossinow, *The Politics of Authenticity*. For
more on Barry Goldwater's hostility toward the Religious Right, see Goldberg,
Barry Goldwater, 315.

6

Reagan's Sunbelt, Reagan's America

The Sunbelt's social, cultural, and economic development from the 1940s through the 1970s foreshadowed the region's emergence as a nationally dominant political force during the 1980s and beyond. From roughly 1945 until the close of the 1970s, the Sunbelt was transformed into an economically vibrant, culturally diverse, and bitterly contested battleground on which many of the most divisive and important political struggles of the postwar era were waged. The Sunbelt's development also correlated with an important trend in American politics – one in which the nation's political culture, over time, came to resemble and reflect the Sunbelt's. Put another way, by the 1980s, the Sunbelt seemed to encapsulate the very essence of American politics, if not American history more broadly – sentimentally patriotic, nostalgic, and dedicated to middle-class expansion on the one hand, divisive, polarized, and passionately contested on the other. These were not necessarily new characteristics in the history of American politics, but so far as the twentieth century was concerned, it was the contested but predominantly conservative nature of the Sunbelt's development that entrenched these characteristics at the forefront of the nation's political stage. If the first three decades following the end of World War II were a story about the Sunbelt's remarkable rise from obscurity (or nonexistence) to prominence and power, then the last two decades of the twentieth century were a story about how the rest of the United States came to see the Sunbelt not as an anomaly, but as a pacesetter and role model.

The protagonist in this drama – at least from the Right's perspective – was Ronald Reagan. Reagan personified the Sunbelt's role in the transformation of American politics at the end of the twentieth century. More to the point, Reagan's presidency, but especially his campaigns for the presidency, articulated a hopeful and appealing vision for America – one ostensibly rooted in a reverence for the nation's revolutionary past, but one that was actually more powerfully organized around the ideals of the postwar Sunbelt. During the 1980s, with Reagan as their popular figurehead, Sunbelt conservatives finally seized control of the national Republican Party. In doing so, the GOP also successfully co-opted the Democratic Party's traditionally populist image, retooled that image along both cultural and economic lines, and re-branded itself as a new and far more conservative home for the idealized and Jeffersonian-styled "common man." Having matured through decades of intense contestation and national tumult, the conservative Sunbelt of the 1980s was unquestionably "Reagan Country." More importantly, the United States – after consecutive Republican landslides in the presidential elections of 1980 and 1984 – clearly seemed to have become "Reagan's America."[1]

Meanwhile, Sunbelt Democrats struggled to withstand the surging tide of anti-liberalism that threatened to sink their national party through mass defections across the region. Responding to the GOP's success, these Democrats labored to repackage liberalism through a Sunbelt lens. Their efforts did not initially pay off. Thanks largely to Reagan's overwhelming popularity, the 1980s was, in national elections, a Republican decade. In state and local elections, the Sunbelt remained divided, though it increasingly leaned to the conservative Right, with Republicans winning more elections than in decades past, and with conservative Democrats often eager to abandon ship. Democratic remodeling eventually

[1] Garry Wills, *Reagan's America* (New York: Doubleday, 1987); Frank, *What's the Matter with Kansas?*; Kazin, *The Populist Persuasion*, 245–268.

paid off during the 1990s, but at the height of Reagan's America, such payoffs seemed far away.

On the whole, American politics during the 1980s reflected the Sunbelt's growing economic, demographic, and electoral clout. That clout accelerated partisan realignment and polarized the nation's political culture, making the Sunbelt of the 1980s both a reflective microcosm of American politics and a prescriptive one.

ECONOMIC SURGE

Sunbelt conservatism's political ascendancy during the 1980s was prefaced by another important economic surge across the region during the 1970s. What differentiated this latest surge from the one that followed the immediate aftermath of World War II, however, was that it contrasted the rest of the nation's economic free fall. For most of the United States, the 1970s was a decade of recession. Thousands of jobs were outsourced overseas; union membership crumbled; unemployment spiked; runaway infla- tion decimated savings accounts; soaring interest rates made home ownership less possible for more Americans; and cities such as Detroit, Philadelphia, Newark, and others across what was becoming known as both the "Frostbelt" and the "Rustbelt" struggled to withstand the onslaught of postindustrial economic change. Even New York City limped through the decade, almost declaring bankruptcy in 1975. When the film *Taxi Driver* was released in 1976, the dominant image of New York City – as depicted in that film – was one of decay, depression, and degra- dation. In the public relations fight for new investors, the entire Rustbelt struggled to overcome these and similar perceptions, whereas the Sunbelt seemed all the more vibrant in comparison.[2]

The apparent dichotomy between the Rustbelt's floundering economy and the Sunbelt's flourishing one was an essential aspect of the nation's political realignment toward conservatism during

---

[2] James T. Patterson, *Restless Giant: The United States from Watergate to* Bush v. Gore (New York: Oxford University Press, 2005), 58–59; Schulman, *The Seventies*, 106–114.

the 1970s and 1980s. As the once-dominant Rustbelt's infrastructure crumbled, so too did that region's status at the forefront of American politics. For employees whose jobs were not
outsourced overseas, relocating to the Sunbelt became a very real
and sometimes necessary option. Doing so often meant abandoning union cards because – California and Nevada being
notable exceptions – organized labor's strength in the Sunbelt
was typically subordinated to conservative right-to-work laws.
The lack of strong labor unions in the Sunbelt added to the
region's reputation among employers as being business friendly.
In 1975, the Fantus Service – a highly influential workplace
relocation consulting firm – buttressed that reputation when
it released a report on state business climates. In that report,
Fantus ranked Texas, Alabama, Virginia, South Carolina, North
Carolina, and Arkansas at or near the top of its list of best places
to do business. During the 1970s, thousands of corporations
relocated their offices to Sunbelt cities because of this positive
image, not to mention the abundant supply of cheap and available land. NASA's strong presence in the region – with major
operations centers in Texas and Florida – only added to the Sunbelt's
reputation as the wave of the future. With its smooth highways,
modern homes, educated middle class, controllable workforce,
low taxes, and space-age industries, the Sunbelt's economy soared
during the late 1970s at the same time that the Rustbelt's crashed.
The Sunbelt's growth also made trendy ideas about the free market,
self-help, and traditional family values in essence the ideological
cornerstones of Sunbelt conservatism.[3]

Nowhere were these trends any clearer than in Texas. Between
1973 and 1981, Texas added 2.2 million new jobs. Just from 1979
to 1982, Texas added 800,000 new jobs. This latter number is
especially stark when contrasted with the net 200,000 jobs lost
nationally during the same years. Postwar economic growth in
Texas manifested across diversified sectors, but during the
1970s, it was primarily saturated in oil. Long a national leader
in oil production, the Texas oil industry benefited from the

[3] Ibid.

destabilization of U.S. foreign relations in the Middle East. The
first major moment in this destabilization came in 1973 when
the Organization of Petroleum Exporting Countries (OPEC) –
responding to American intervention on Israel's behalf during
the Yom Kippur War – placed an embargo against oil shipments
to the United States. This embargo prompted a spike in oil prices,
the result of reduced supplies and speculative fear. Long gasoline
lines soon plagued American drivers. Such annoyances were as
common in Texas as they were anywhere else. But unlike most
other places across the country, in Texas those annoyances were
offset by the economic surge being fueled by rising oil prices,
widespread exploration, and increased production. By no means
were all Texans benefiting from this surge in corporate oil profits,
but at least indirectly, many did. The influx of oil revenue into the
state's economy created new jobs and trickled down to rising
home prices, housing construction, commercial real estate development, and growth in related sectors including finance, banking,
insurance, retail, and agribusiness. Political instability in the
Middle East continued throughout the decade, and in 1979, an
Islamic revolution in Iran – and a prolonged hostage crisis involving Americans in Teheran – prompted yet another round of
oil shocks to the U.S. economy. All the while, Texas boomed.
Between 1970 and 1980, the state's population grew by more than
27 percent.[4]

   The capital of the Texas oil industry – and the nation's, for that
matter – was Houston. Home to companies such as Shell, Texaco,
and Gulf, Houston during the late 1970s was, in the words of
U.S News & World Report, nothing short of a "phenomenon."[5]
Soaring oil prices created windfall profits for hundreds of corporations, 125 of which boasted more than 1,000 employees in the
greater Houston area alone. One estimate of Houston's infrastructure in 1980 suggested that roughly three-quarters of the

[4] For more on Texas economic growth during the 1970s, see Campbell, *Gone to Texas*, 438–447. For more on the Iran hostage crisis, see David Farber, *Taken Hostage: The Iran Hostage Crisis and America's First Encounter with Radical Islam* (Princeton, NJ: Princeton University Press, 2006).
[5] Campbell, *Gone to Texas*, 404–408.

entire city had been built since the end of World War II. In 1980, Houston became the nation's sixth largest industrial producer. In 1970, Houston ranked seventy-sixth in per capita income; by 1980, it ranked sixteenth. Houston also became a major port city, shipping oil and manufactured products all over the globe, its largest trading partner being Saudi Arabia. Not surprisingly, the city's population also boomed. Between 1975 and 1980, Houston led the nation in new housing starts. Rather than allow for new suburban municipalities, Houston annexed most of these new housing developments into the city. Annexation expanded the number of white, middle-class voters at the same time that it diluted the political clout of the city's abundant, impoverished, and still effectively disfranchised black and minority populations. The most dramatic example of oil-related corporate growth across the Sunbelt, Houston's expansion during the 1970s was indeed phenomenal.[6]

The Sunbelt's prosperity was especially obvious in relation to the Rustbelt's decline. Still, Houston's experience during the late 1970s was more atypical than typical so far as corporate and industrial growth in the Southwest was concerned. Take, for instance, the cities of Phoenix and Las Vegas. Like Houston, both those cities boomed in the decades after World War II and grew substantially again during the 1970s, at least in terms of population. This was particularly true in Las Vegas, which saw its population increase by nearly 70 percent during the 1970s. But unlike Houston, neither Phoenix nor Las Vegas benefited all that much from the rising price of oil. Instead, the new jobs coming to them were primarily lower-paying, unskilled, service-oriented jobs related to recreation and tourism, resorts, hotels, and conference centers. By the end of the century, Phoenix and Las Vegas – along with San Diego and Orlando – were among the nation's premier destinations for business conferences, recreational travel, and vacation leisure. None of those cities, however, fared well at attracting higher paying, white-collar jobs during the late 1970s or early 1980s.

[6] Bernard and Rice, *Sunbelt Cities*, 197–201.

The infusion of outside capital certainly boosted economies all across the metropolitan Sunbelt, but when that capital came from corporations unrelated to sectors such as oil, defense, technology, or finance – the sectors most responsible for the region's dramatic postwar growth in the first place – wealth did not tend to distribute itself evenly. In places where tourism and leisure were not as influential, service-oriented jobs in commercial retail resulted in misleading statistics about job creation and the depth and breadth of regional affluence. In late-1970s Los Angeles, for instance – once the Sunbelt's industrial capital – unemployment consistently straddled, within a point or two, the depressing 10 percent mark. Still, even in Sunbelt cities where added capital failed to promote employment or an expanding middle class, images of an escalating skyline, vibrant night life, convenient strip malls, and modern infrastructure furthered the Sunbelt's reputation as America's best hope for the future – a reputation conservative Republicans were quick to embrace. For the same reasons, the Sunbelt became home to an increasing number of corporate executives and wealthy investors, eager to preserve and expand their prosperity, and happy to invest in Republican candidates willing to support those efforts.[7]

Sunbelt cities also competed with one another for corporations' affections. The foot soldiers in that fight were typically civic boosters, local political officials, and befriended corporate executives – all parties interested in promoting economic development where potentially profitable. During the late 1970s and early 1980s, these boosters, officials, and executives advanced the Sunbelt's image as a business-friendly region. Essentially, this was a loosely coordinated public relations campaign grounded in economics, but laced with political overtones. The shared goals were simple: lower taxes and fewer regulations. To accomplish these goals, business interests cooperatively lobbied state

---

[7] For more on Phoenix, see Shermer, *Sunbelt Capitalism*; and VanderMeer, *Desert Visions and the Making of Phoenix, 1860–2009*. For more on Las Vegas and the economic impact of tourism in the West, see Rothman, *Devil's Bargains*; see also Self, *All in the Family*, 324–327.

and federal governments for more corporate tax breaks. They also promoted a vision of the free market that was in keeping with the broadly defined American values of liberty, hard work, and growth – values always contrasted to the Rustbelt's short-comings. Sunbelt boosters usually focused on local projects, but occasionally their messages were also remarkably ideological and national. Such messages were often tailored according to the central tenets of modern conservatism and aggressively promoted by Republican activists.[8]

The public relations of economic theory were an important component of Sunbelt conservatism's rise to power. During the 1970s, cooperating business interests across the country saw an opportunity to rehabilitate the public's perception of free-market capitalism. Among many Americans, the concept of a truly free market had lost almost as much luster since the 1930s as the unregulated stock market had lost at the end of October 1929. The perceived successes of the New Deal coalition and subsequent liberal consensus had made most Americans at least relatively comfortable with the idea of a semi-regulated and managed economy. But with the national economy mired in recession during the late 1970s, conservative economists including Milton Friedman and Arthur Laffer began garnering more attention, even among liberal Democrats, many of whom were beginning to be called "neoliberals" for their willingness to use spending cuts and deregulation in a prioritized fight against inflation, as opposed to more traditionally Keynesian ideas that would have targeted unemployment through job creation. As conservative economists more frequently bent Washington's ear, corporate activists eagerly capitalized on the rejuvenated interest. Rather than apologize for the more brutally Darwinist aspects of capitalism, corporations and other business interests argued for capitalism's virtues, depicting their economic philosophy as one of the nation's most important founding creeds.

[8] For more on the relationship between civil boosters, local political officials, and corporate executives, see Phillips-Fein, *Invisible Hands*. See also Lotchin, *Fortress California, 1910–1961*, 319–345.

Capitalism, in this view, was made to be virtually synonymous with individual liberty.[9]

Seeking to advance the cause of free-market libertarianism, cooperating business interests also founded, funded, and utilized several conservative think tanks, the most famous being the Heritage Foundation. Founded in 1973 by business leaders and GOP activists – including Colorado brewing magnate Joseph Coors and future Moral Majority organizer Paul Weyrich – the Heritage Foundation (and other think tanks like it) influenced municipal politics and promoted conservative economic theories all over the country. In the process, these think tanks referenced the postwar Sunbelt as the best evidence in support of free-market capitalism and libertarian government, overemphasizing the connections between the region's affluence and its conservative political climate, while underemphasizing the region's historical dependence on federal subsidies.[10]

Conflating the virtues of capitalism with broadly conceived notions of freedom was among corporate America's most impressive achievements of the postwar era. Championing the virtues of the free market also made the Sunbelt appear more "American" than other places across the country, especially the heavily regulated and unionized Rustbelt. The Sunbelt's "Americanness" was further enhanced by the more than 140 military bases dotting the region, more than the rest of the country combined.[11] Military bases helped infuse the region with patriotism, while local chambers of commerce, city councils, and area business leaders worked with corporations to champion the unfettered free market as the purest, fairest, and quickest way to achieve widespread affluence. Among millions of voters, these efforts seemed to work. The revival in unregulated capitalism's popularity coincided with the popular demonization of the regulatory welfare state, increasingly

---

[9] For more on economic growth in the South, see Bartley, *The New South, 1945–1980*; and Schulman, *From Cotton Belt to Sunbelt*.

[10] For more on the Heritage Foundation, corporate influence on municipal politics, and the rise of conservative economic thought, see again Phillips-Fein, *Invisible Hands*.

[11] Judis and Teixeira, *The Emerging Democratic Majority*, 71.

seen as burdensome and counterproductive to economic expansion. As Sunbelt cities competed with one another within this corporate-friendly paradigm, they advanced the free market's cause across the entire region, encouraged the implementation of ever-more conservative policies, pressured Rustbelt cities to conform or suffer, and further solidified the region's image as a place for thriving economic development. The tax breaks came, and so did corporations. Regardless of where in the country you were seated, it was hard not to notice the Sunbelt's booming economy.[12]

The growing popularity of libertarian and free-market economic thought reflected both the Sunbelt's surging prowess and its emerging influence over the nation's cultural identity. The Sunbelt boom of the late 1970s paralleled the popularization of country music and auto racing; the expansion and relocation of professional sports franchises into the region; and even the country's mythical love affair with the National Football League's Dallas Cowboys, dubbed "America's Team" in 1976. In sum, the Sunbelt became fashionable in the 1970s. That fashionableness underscored the region's reputation for opportunity and growth, thereby creating a crucial backdrop for conservatism's ascendancy to the forefront of national politics during the 1980s.[13]

TAX REVOLTS

The renaissance in free-market capitalism that was manufactured by corporate America during the 1970s also coincided with a grassroots uprising against taxation. Anti-tax hostilities had been brewing across the country for decades, but they were especially prevalent across the Sunbelt during the 1960s and 1970s. Such forces had helped inspire Barry Goldwater's presidential

---

[12] See again Bartley, *The New South, 1945–1980*; Phillips-Fein, *Invisible Hands*. For more on economic growth in the South, see again Schulman, *From Cotton Belt to Sunbelt*.

[13] Cowie, *Stayin' Alive*; Schulman, *The Seventies*; Campbell, *Gone to Texas*, 444–447. See also Thomas Borstelmann, *The 1970s: A New Global History from Civil Rights to Economic Inequality* (Princeton: Princeton University Press, 2011).

campaign of 1964, not to mention the rise of "color-blind" conservatism across the metropolitan South in places such as Atlanta
and Charlotte. Federal spending increased during the 1960s and
1970s, regardless of which party controlled the White House.
As it did, conservatives saw taxation as yet another example of
government's heavy and very visible hand in economic management. Americans' mainstream tolerance for that heavy hand disappeared when the economy slipped into recession during the
1970s. Always part of a broader conversation about the size
and scope of government, the question of taxation created yet
another wave of momentum for Sunbelt conservatives seeking to
change the way the country did business.[14]

The tax revolt of the 1970s manifested in different ways across
the Sunbelt. In 1972, it showed up in Dallas, Texas, when activists
recruited a young Republican congressional candidate named Alan
Steelman to be the face of their opposition to a federally sponsored
plan to transform the Trinity River into a shipping canal. Known
as COST (Citizens' Organization for a Sound Trinity), these activists worked with Steelman to undermine what had previously
been a widely endorsed plan to spend $1.6 billion to canalize the
Trinity River from Dallas to the Gulf of Mexico. Such a canal, it
was hoped, would enable Dallas to compete more effectively with
Houston and other port cities along the Gulf and southeastern
Atlantic coasts. Dallas business leaders enthusiastically adopted
the project as their own, working with leaders in Austin and
Washington to ensure public funding. Thanks to COST, however,
Dallas citizens began to object to the project's expense and ineffi-
cient management, not to mention its environmental ramifications.
More than anything, COST objected to the proposed tax hikes that
would be needed in order to pay for the project. In October 1972,
Steelman used the canal issue as the basis for his campaign
against Democratic incumbent Earle Cabell, who had served
Dallas as a U.S. representative since defeating Bruce Alger in

---

[14] For a short, but insightful overview of the tax revolt, see Iwan Morgan,
"Taxation as a Republican Issue in the Era of Stagflation," in Mason and
Morgan, *Seeking a New Majority*, 179–196.

1964. Connecting the Trinity River Canal Project to other allegations of wasteful spending and bureaucracy run amok, Steelman –
in quite an upset – defeated Cabell easily in the November election.
Less than a year later, Dallas voters officially killed the canal
project, rejecting a related bond proposal in March 1973. As a
case study in the power of anti-tax activism across the region,
the Trinity River Canal Project rallied grassroots conservatives in
Dallas to unseat an incumbent Democrat in favor of a young
Republican in the Sunbelt Right's strengthening mold.[15]

Three years after the Trinity River Canal Project went down
to defeat in Dallas, Gerald Ford unintentionally ignited a prairie
fire across the American West when he signed a bill known as
the Federal Land Policy and Management Act of 1976. That law
declared that publicly held land – of which the federal government
claimed a disproportionate amount in western states – was to be
"perpetually" held, thereby eliminating prospects for state control
or privatization. The issue of federally controlled land in the West
had long been a source of severe irritation to many of those
living in the West, but in the context of the growing conservative
backlash against regulation, taxes, and the general growth of
government, this new law was received with considerable angst.
As a result, a grassroots movement calling itself the Sagebrush
Rebellion sprang to life, rallying anti-tax, anti-regulation, and
anti-government animus across the entire West, including most
notably in Sunbelt states such as Nevada, New Mexico, Colorado,
and California.[16] Self-described Sagebrush Rebels did not simply
argue against the federal government's perpetual ownership of
public lands. They also decried the regulations that accompanied
that ownership, including the highly unpopular enforcement of
a 55-mile-per-hour speed limit on public highways, various
environmental restrictions, and other laws inhibiting trade and

[15] Cunningham, *Cowboy Conservatism*, 131–134.
[16] "The Sagebrush Rebellion," *U.S. News & World Report*, December 1, 1980;
for a more comprehensive examination of the Sagebrush Rebellion and its
political legacy, see R. McGregor Cawley, *Federal Land, Western Anger: The
Sagebrush Rebellion and Environmental Politics* (Lawrence: University Press of
Kansas, 1993).

related forms of business development. In each of these ways, the Sagebrush Rebellion reflected the growing conservative and libertarian sentiment against high taxes, federal oversight, and excessive regulation. It was not surprising, therefore, to hear Ronald Reagan tell a group of Sagebrush Rebels in August 1980, "count me in as a [Sagebrush] Rebel!"[17]

The importance of the anti-tax backlash in Texas and other parts of the Southwest notwithstanding, the epicenter of the late-1970s tax revolt was California, specifically the state's expanding cities and suburbs. For white, middle-class Californians, the primary source of discontent lay in escalating property taxes. Hostilities related to rising property taxes had been bubbling up in California since at least the 1950s. Originally concentrated in the Los Angeles suburbs, grassroots organizations dedicated to reducing property taxes spread all across the state in the late 1960s, gathered momentum during the early 1970s, and began to win victories at the ballot box in the late 1970s and early 1980s. The most important of these victories came in 1978 with the success of Proposition 13. A reaction to rapidly escalating property taxes, as well as excessively inflated home values, Proposition 13 proposed an immediate cut in property taxes, a cap on how much home value assessments could increase in a single year, and an amendment to the state constitution requiring a two-thirds approval in the state legislature before any new taxes could be enacted. When it went to voters in June 1978, Proposition 13 achieved an overwhelming two-to-one victory. One year later, California conservatives won yet another policy fight at the ballot box, successfully passing Proposition 4, which severely restricted state and local spending, in addition to requiring that state budget surpluses be refunded to taxpayers. The short-term success of tax revolts in California inspired similar movements across the Sunbelt, most notably in Tennessee, Louisiana, South Carolina, Nevada, and Texas, each of which passed spending caps similar to California's Proposition 4. Though it certainly had its roots in the libertarian Sunbelt, the tax revolt of the late 1970s and early

---

[17] Quoted in Cawley, *Federal Land, Western Anger*, 1–3.

1980s was not limited to these states. Rather, anti-tax activism in
the Sunbelt also inspired conservative economic policy making in
states as far-reaching as Hawaii, Michigan, and Massachusetts.[18]

The economic context of the 1970s – especially the late 1970s –
predicated the conservative Republican ascendancy of the 1980s.
As the Sunbelt withstood the economic recession that seemed
to cripple the rest of the country, its conservative ethos of limited
government, low taxes, and free-market economics gained a measure of credibility it had not enjoyed since, arguably, the 1920s.
Despite the fact that discrimination and economic inequality persisted across the region – and in some cases grew worse – the
popular image of the Sunbelt as a land where hard work mattered
and where opportunity was abundant inspired droves of Americans
to migrate to that region. Many of these Americans came from
declining Rustbelt states and were eager to invest in the Sunbelt's
conservative worldview. The most important element of that
worldview was that the federal government was no longer aiding
economic growth but was instead stifling it through high taxes and
burdensome regulations. Tax revolts such as those reflected in the
Sagebrush Rebellion and the fight for Proposition 13 effectively
connected wasteful spending with inefficient management. Those
connections opened the door for conservatives to criticize welfare
spending, public housing, immigration policies, public education,
and a host of other government-supported or subsidized programs.
Within this context, it made perfect sense that issues like affirmative
action also exploded during the late 1970s, and did so in places
such as California where race-based admission into public universities became a wildly hot source for political controversy and
conservative angst.[19]

[18] Schneider, The Conservative Century, 142–143; Schulman, The Seventies,
205–217.
[19] For more on affirmative action, and for specific information about the Supreme
Court case University of California Regents v. Bakke (1978), see Howard Ball,
The Bakke Case: Race, Education, and Affirmative Action (Lawrence: University
Press of Kansas, 2000). See also Brilliant, The Color of America Has Changed,
257–258; and Kalman, Right Star Rising, 184–201.

As their region's conservative worldview increasingly gained national popularity, Sunbelt Republicans conveniently found it much easier to graft into their growing movement the less progressive elements of right-wing political culture that, in some places, continued to rally supporters through issues related to race, religion, and sexuality. For the conservative Sunbelt Right, it was a perfect storm.[20]

THE ELECTION OF 1980

In November 1980, the conservative Sunbelt Right capitalized on this perfect storm and achieved one of its greatest political victories when Ronald Reagan was overwhelmingly elected the fortieth president of the United States. Reagan's importance to the history of American politics in the postwar Sunbelt cannot be overstated. As a politician, Reagan bridged almost every gap that existed in the multifaceted and often contradictory nature of conservative Sunbelt politics. He appealed to white, middle-class suburbanites in metropolitan areas ranging from Los Angeles to Atlanta, where many residents understood their primary political identity to be as parents, homeowners, and property taxpayers. He also appealed to conservative intellectuals and ideologues – anticommunists, traditionalists, and libertarians who, like him, had cut their teeth in the Goldwater campaign of 1964. In the Deep South, he won many (but certainly not all) ex-Wallace supporters for whom the nation's problems were still largely racial and cultural. At the same time, he also won most corporate executives and the extremely wealthy. He also appealed to the Religious Right, which saw Reagan as a moral figure whose faith in America mirrored its own convictions about God, country, and the importance of keeping God in the country. Reagan even appealed to blue-collar workers outside the Sunbelt, many of whom were

[20] For more on the anti-tax surge, as well as middle America's hostility toward government during the late 1970s, see, for example, Sandbrook, *Mad as Hell*. For more on the Carter presidency generally, see Burton I. Kaufman and Scott Kaufman, *The Presidency of James Earl Carter, Jr.* (Lawrence: University of Kansas Press, 2006).

206   Cunningham

facing the consequences of a severe economic downturn, and
some of whom were in the process of moving into the region or
who had already seen former neighbors do just that. For these
Americans, Reagan emphasized the Democratic Party's failure to
protect them, citing modern liberalism's obsession with the marginalized, impoverished, and oppressed. Above all else, Reagan
personified the Sunbelt's quintessential characteristics, those that
gave the region its soul – a reverence for the past, optimism about
the future, and a rhetorically patriotic embrace for individual
liberty and local control.[21]

In the wake of multiple political assassinations, urban violence,
Vietnam, Watergate, economic recessions, and a hostage crisis in
the Middle East, Reagan's optimism in 1980 mirrored for the rest
of the nation the conservative Sunbelt's attitudes about hard
work, faith, and family. But Reagan's strategy for capturing the
White House was not simply one of unwavering optimism. He
and his conservative strategists also went on the attack, blaming
liberals in the Democratic Party for most of the nation's ills.
Conservative attacks against liberals were hardly new in 1980,
but in the immediate context of national decline, those attacks
were especially effective. Reagan criticized liberal tax policies,
citing excessively progressive marginal income tax rates as funda-
mentally unfair. He also argued that high corporate tax rates
discouraged creativity and risk by punishing success. He also
criticized federal spending habits by pointing out areas where
social programs had either failed or duplicated existing programs,
and he used examples of inefficiency and waste to highlight the
need for local control and limited government. Whereas Jimmy
Carter had succeeded in 1976 by exploiting his image as an outsider from a southern state in order to capitalize on the nation's
animosity toward the Washington establishment, Reagan won

[21] Historians have given the election of 1980 extensive coverage over the years,
particularly in the growing historiography on modern conservatism. For effective
narrative overviews, see among others Elizabeth Drew, *Portrait of an Election: The
1980 Presidential Campaign* (New York: Simon & Schuster, 1981); and Theodore
H. White, *America in Search of Itself: The Making of the President, 1956–1980*
(New York: Harper & Row, 1982). See again, McBee, *Don't Shoot the Easy Rider*.

in 1980 by doing almost the exact same thing. Against Carter, Reagan positioned himself as a Washington outsider, a man of faith and family (though once divorced, not terribly close with his children, and an irregular church attendee) and a leader with executive experience in a Sunbelt state. With national morale at a dangerous low, Reagan captured the Sunbelt and the nation in 1980, defeating Carter by ten percentage points in the popular vote, and 489 to 49 in the Electoral College. Reagan carried every state in the Sunbelt with the exception of Carter's Georgia. It was a sweeping victory for Reagan, conservatism, and Sunbelt Republicans who hoped to finally and permanently wrestle control of their party out of establishment moderates' hands.[22]

In terms of his emotional connection with the majority of American voters, Reagan was an amalgam of old-fashioned, blind-eyed optimism mixed with passionately negative expressions of frustration, fear, and anger. Reagan was most effective as an optimist, but other conservatives found attitudes of frustration, fear, and anger to be more politically beneficial. Such attitudes manifested in places like Texas where, for instance, Eddie Chiles – a conservative businessman and co-owner of the Texas Rangers baseball franchise – used radio commentaries to rail against Jimmy Carter, the eastern establishment, and the evils of liberalism. Most famously, Chiles used his radio time to proclaim – as the fictional Howard Beale had similarly cried in the 1976 film *Network* – "I'm Eddie Chiles, and I'm mad as hell!" Many fans adopted Chiles's anger, displaying bumper stickers that read, "I'm Mad Too, Eddie." Another popular bumper sticker read, "I Love America Too, Eddie" – a not-so-veiled insinuation that liberals did not. In Chiles's Texas, as was true elsewhere across the Sunbelt, Reagan succeeded in 1980, in part, by stripping traditional populism of its economic egalitarianism and replacing it with cultural tradition and unwavering patriotism. At the same time, this brand of populist conservatism also redefined establishment elitism – historically understood as the domain of the very wealthy. But in Reagan's America, establishment elitism was more commonly understood

[22] Ibid.

as a collection of "pointy headed bureaucrats," "ivory tower" intellectuals, and other liberals who used government to control people's lives. In essence, populist conservatism went mainstream during the 1980s by redirecting middle America's frustrations away from Wall Street and toward Washington. Once years ahead of the rest of the nation, by 1980 the rest of the nation seemed to have caught up to the Sunbelt's more conservative political culture.[23]

Reagan's landslide victory in 1980 also resulted in major Republican gains in down-ballot elections. In the U.S. Senate, Republicans picked up twelve seats and seized control of that legislative body for the first time since 1955. Notable Republican victories included Paula Hawkins in Florida, John Porter East in North Carolina, Mack Mattingly in Georgia, and Jeremiah Denton in Alabama. Both Mattingly and Denton were the first Republicans to win a U.S. Senate seat from their respective states since Reconstruction. Tennessee Republican Howard Baker was named Senate Majority Leader. In the other chamber, Republicans fell short of regaining control of the U.S. House of Representatives but dramatically cut the Democratic Party's majority, picking up 34 seats. Notable Republican victories included four wins in California and three in Virginia.

The GOP also gained two seats in South Carolina, in addition to retaining one held by conservative Floyd Spence. Running for a sixth term, Spence easily defeated former George Wallace campaign manager and repentant liberal convert Tom Turnipseed. Spence would likely have defeated Turnipseed under any circumstances, but he left nothing to chance in 1980, embracing the controversial tactics of Lee Atwater, a new campaign advisor. A rising star in GOP circles since 1972, a former aide to Strom Thurmond, and an advisor to Ronald Reagan's 1980 presidential campaign in South Carolina, Atwater effectively destroyed the Turnipseed campaign by floating false stories about the Democratic candidate's mental competence. He also insinuated that Turnipseed was a member of the NAACP. The tricks

---

[23] Ibid.; Cunningham, *Cowboy Conservatism*, 238; see also again Kazin, *The Populist Persuasion*.

Ronald Reagan campaigns with his wife and Strom Thurmond in South Carolina during the 1980 presidential campaign. (Courtesy of the Ronald Reagan Presidential Library.)

worked and Spence easily won reelection. Atwater was subsequently hired as a political strategist for the Reagan administration, where his aggressive style contributed to ever-increasing levels of responsibility. Atwater's loyalty to Reagan throughout the 1980s, as well as a close relationship with George W. Bush, earned him a managerial role in George H.W. Bush's campaign for the presidency in 1988. After orchestrating that victory – one of the most negative campaigns in modern history – Atwater was named chairman of the Republican National Committee in 1989. A controversial and (to many on the Left) a reviled figure, Atwater set a new standard for aggressive conservative campaign tactics at the end of the twentieth century. Atwater's time on the national stage was cut short, however, when he succumbed to brain cancer in 1991. He was only 40 years old.[24]

---

[24] For a highly critical account of Lee Atwater's career, see John Brady, *Bad Boy: The Life and Politics of Lee Atwater* (Boston: Addison-Wesley, 1996). See also Alexander Lamis, ed., *Southern Politics in the 1990s* (Baton Rouge: Louisiana State University Press, 1999).

Lee Atwater's most important protégé was Karl Rove. Having studied under Atwater's tutelage since the two were leaders together in the national College Republicans organization, Rove broke out as a rising star in the world of campaign strategy during the mid-1970s, working as a legislative aide to Fred Agnich, a Republican state representative from Dallas. Then in 1977, Rove began working for a political action committee based out of Houston under the direction of James Baker, at the time a local attorney and aspiring candidate for Texas attorney general. Baker's friendship with George H. W. Bush positioned Rove for a long career of influence inside Texas GOP circles. That career got off to a dramatic start in 1978 when Rove was a central figure in Bill Clements's stunning victory over John Hill in the race for Texas governor. Running a campaign premised almost exclusively as a battle against Jimmy Carter and national liberalism, Clements used Rove's guidance to become the first Republican since Reconstruction to win a gubernatorial election in Texas. That same year, Rove advised Baker during his bid to become the state's attorney general. He also helped manage George W. Bush's first political campaign, a bid for the state's 19th congressional district representing Lubbock, Midland, and much of the surrounding South Plains. Neither of those campaigns ended successfully. Baker lost to future governor of Texas Mark White, and Bush lost to Kent Hance, a conservative West Texas Democrat who famously depicted his opponent as a product of Ivy League privilege, unfamiliar with the true nature of West Texas values, and undeserving of the region's trust. Rove learned valuable lessons in both the Baker and Bush campaigns, despite losing both. In 1979 and 1980, he worked for Governor Clements while also managing George H. W. Bush's bid for the Republican presidential nomination, a campaign that ended with Bush being tapped as Reagan's running mate. In 1981, Rove began a direct-mail operation out of Austin designed to assist Republican candidates across the state. Rove received generous financial support from, among other donors, Bob Perry, an ultra-wealthy and very conservative homebuilder whose fortunes had helped Clements make history in 1978, and whose money would continue to finance Rove's business

interests and the fortunes of conservative Republican politics in
Texas for the rest of the century.[25]

Reagan's coattails, Perry's money, and Rove's ideas also contributed to Jack Fields's surprising victory over multi-term congressman and Houston liberal Bob Eckhardt. As Lee Atwater had
done to Tom Turnipseed in South Carolina, the Fields campaign
used dirty tricks to undercut Eckhardt's support in Houston.
Emphasizing broadly national issues, Fields went after Eckhardt
as a reflection of liberalism's affinity for homosexuality, gun control, forced busing, and secular humanism. The Fields campaign
even staged a phony financial contribution to Eckhardt in which
an envelope addressed to Eckhardt was "mistakenly" delivered
to the Fields campaign, supposedly revealing an East Coast resi-
dent's affection for Eckhardt as a liberal in the style of Ted
Kennedy. The campaign contribution was a meager five dollars
and the letter, which cited Eckhardt's support for gun control and
opposition to defense spending, had actually come from a conservative activist in Virginia named Mark Florio. Florio was
working with Fields to create the false image that Eckhardt was
a tool of the liberal eastern establishment. The Fields campaign
quickly leaked news of the contribution and the accompanying
"letter of support" to the local press, which in turn used the letter
to attack Eckhardt as a national liberal whose values no longer
represented the average Texas voter. Fields won the election and
subsequently became quite wealthy thanks to an investment in
Bob Perry's latest business venture, Perry Contractors, Inc.,
founded in Houston just three weeks after the election.[26]

During the late 1970s and early 1980s, strategists like Lee
Atwater and Karl Rove helped unify the conservative message
across the Sunbelt and the nation. Meanwhile, donors like Bob

[25] Cunningham, *Cowboy Conservatism*, 194–208, 237–239; see also Kenneth
Bridges, *Twilight of the Texas Democrats: The 1978 Governor's Race*
(College Station: Texas A&M University Press, 2008); for more on Bob Perry,
Karl Rove, and campaign financing, read, "Bob Perry: GOP ATM," unpub-
lished paper produced by Texans for Public Justice, October 2012 [http://info.
tpj.org/reports/pdf/BobPerryGOPATM.pdf].
[26] Ibid.

Perry funded GOP campaigns, while state and local candidates
like Floyd Spence and Jack Fields dutifully delivered the message
to voters. This reality does not, however, undercut the simultaneous reality that conservative Republicans appealed to a wide
swath of the American electorate and received millions of dollars
in small campaign contributions from ordinary citizens, many of
them in the Sunbelt, who sincerely believed in the Right's mantra
of low taxes, local control, and family values. It was Reagan's
popularity, however, that made each of these developments possible, or at least successful. Without Reagan's presence at the top
of the Republican ticket in 1980, the rise of modern conservatism –
and the Sunbelt's quickly developing status as the center of
national political power – would have looked very different. The
circumstances that contributed to Jimmy Carter's failure, coupled
with more than three decades of evolution and contestation within
the Republican Party, created a moment in 1980 that was ripe
for the ascendancy of modern, Sunbelt conservatism. As much or
more than anything else, though, it was Reagan's personification
of the Sunbelt that made the election of 1980 the climactic moment
that it was in the history of postwar American politics.

THE REAGAN REVOLUTION

Ronald Reagan's tenure as president has been popularly described –
and occasionally romanticized – as a "revolution." According to
most conservatives, Reagan used the presidency between 1981 and
1989 to undo many of the excesses and mistakes of the postwar
liberal consensus. Under Reagan's watch, federal taxes were
lowered, inflation was halted, rising unemployment levels were
reversed, and stock values increased. Even more dramatically,
the Cold War virtually ended. Reagan's aggressive first-term
posturing and arms buildup, followed by his more diplomatic
and carefully developed relationship with Soviet Premier
Mikhail Gorbachev, played an important role in bringing more
than four decades of nuclear tension to a close. More than anything, however, Reagan restored America's confidence in itself as
a world leader, as a beacon for freedom and hope, and as a land

of opportunity and success. Reagan entered office in an electoral landslide, won an even greater landslide in 1984, set the stage for George H. W. Bush to become president through another landslide triumph in 1988, and left Washington in January 1989 with approval ratings well above 60 percent.[27]

For all its successes, the Reagan Revolution also produced its fair share of shortcomings and failures. Budget deficits soared during Reagan's time in office, as did the corresponding national debt, which reached nearly $3 trillion by 1989 – three times greater than the debt had been when Reagan took office. Economic growth during the decade was strong, but by most measurements, it disproportionately benefited the wealthy. Before Reagan took office, the richest 1 percent of Americans controlled approximately 22 percent of the nation's aggregate wealth. By the time Reagan left office, that same 1 percent of Americans controlled just less than 40 percent of the nation's aggregate wealth. In a related problem, middle-class Americans were saving half as much money at the end of the decade as they were when Reagan took office and in fact began slipping into ever-dangerous levels of debt in order to maintain a lifestyle of material affluence and comfort. Meanwhile, by the time Reagan left office, 15 percent of Americans lived below the poverty line, the highest percentage since the early 1960s. Homelessness became a national plague. Speaking of plagues, Reagan and his conservative advisors were tragically slow to respond to the HIV/AIDS epidemic that burst onto the national scene during the early 1980s.[28]

Reagan's top priority upon entering office was economic recovery. Initially, his chief strategy for accomplishing that recovery was a massive tax cut. It did not take Reagan long to channel the anti-tax hostilities of the late 1970s into a major tax bill during his first months in office. In 1981, Reagan worked with

[27] For a scholarly overview of the Reagan years, see Critchlow, *The Conservative Ascendancy*, 184–219; and Sean Wilentz, *The Age of Reagan: A History, 1974–2008* (New York: HarperCollins Publishers, 2008). For a general, journalistic narrative of the Reagan White House, see among others Lou Cannon, *The Role of a Lifetime* (New York: Simon & Schuster, 1991).

[28] Ibid.

congressional Democrats like Texas's Kent Hance – among a group of more than 60 conservative southern Democrats known as "boll weevils" – to slash investment and personal income tax rates. All taxpayers had their rates reduced by the Economic Recovery Tax Act of 1981, but the most dramatic cuts were reserved for the wealthy. In addition to cutting capital gains rates by 40 percent, Reagan also slashed the highest income bracket from 70 percent to 50 percent for 1982. Top marginal rates were further cut to 38.5 percent for 1987 and reduced all the way to 28 percent for 1988. Reagan focused on cutting taxes for the wealthy on the theory that tax cuts would stimulate investment, which would then trickle down to the middle and working classes through new jobs. Whereas Reagan cut 20 percentage points off the top marginal rate in his first year alone, he conversely reduced the lowest income tax bracket from 14 percent to 12 percent for 1982, down to 11 percent for 1983. However, in 1988 the lowest marginal rate was actually raised to 15 percent, meaning that over the course of Reagan's entire administration, taxes on the highest marginal bracket had been reduced 42 percentage points, whereas the lowest income tax bracket was actually 1 percentage point higher. Reagan did not always treat organized labor kindly either. For example, Reagan fired more than 11,000 striking federal air traffic controllers during the summer of 1981, a clear signal that his administration – like the Sunbelt from which he came – would not coddle labor unions. On the whole, there is no question that the Reagan Revolution was a political success, just as there is little question that it achieved many more positive results during its two terms in power than its harshest critics at the time would have thought possible. However, it is just as clear that Reagan also failed in a number of areas, thereby leaving – as all presidents do – a mixed record.[29]

Referred to by some as the "Great Communicator," Reagan remained popular with middle- and working-class families, despite enacting economic policies that did not always benefit those constituents. Much of that popularity was the result of

[29] Ibid.

Reagan's charm and rhetorical skill, which he typically used to champion libertarian and free-market ideals couched in patriotic and nostalgic overtones. Having been emotionally drained by the events of the previous two decades, most Americans were happy to receive Reagan's optimistic message.[30] Though his critics often ridiculed such optimism as baseless and naive, and despite some evidence of economic mismanagement, Reagan's unwavering commitment to stay the course was validated to at least some degree by economic developments that began to take hold just one year before his reelection. The national economy struggled during the first two years of Reagan's first term but rebounded in late 1983, before embarking on the largest peacetime economic expansion in American history, lasting through most of 1987. In large part because of that expansion, many middle-class Americans did very well in the 1980s. During Reagan's time in office, home and auto sales increased, inflation dropped, 18 million new jobs were created, real income and consumption levels rose, more Americans moved into the middle and upper classes, and the aggregate value of the stock market tripled. These successes helped entrench a culture of material affluence and individual ambition as one of the stereotypical hallmarks of the 1980s.[31]

Despite its mixed and oft-debated record, the Reagan Revolution's popularity with voters was undeniable. That popularity was never clearer than in November 1984 when Reagan crushed former Minnesota senator, vice president, and avowed liberal, Walter Mondale, achieving the greatest Electoral College landslide in American history. Reagan won an astounding 525 electoral votes against Mondale's laughable 13. Reagan also won nearly 60 percent of the popular vote on his way to a second term, carried every state with the exception of Mondale's Minnesota (which Reagan lost by less than 1 percent of the vote), and

---

[30] For a unique spin on Reagan "mythology," see Slotkin, *Gunfighter Nation*, 643–654; see also Farber, *The Rise and Fall of Modern Conservatism*, 159–208; and Gil Troy, *Morning in America: How Ronald Reagan Invented the 1980s* (Princeton, NJ: Princeton University Press, 2007).

[31] See again Critchlow, *The Conservative Ascendancy*, 184–219; Wilentz, *The Age of Reagan*; and Cannon, *The Role of a Lifetime*.

made "tax-and-spend" liberalism the butt of many jokes. One of Reagan's most effective campaign themes in 1984 proclaimed that it was "Morning in America." Advertisements depicted the nation finally on the upswing after more than a decade of decline. Flag-waving children, church-centered marriages, and even white picket fences peppered Reagan's campaign imagery, reflecting the aspirations of Reagan's core constituency – the coalition of suburban, middle-class whites and hopeful blue-collar families that had also rallied to the Republican message four years earlier. Even more so than the election of 1980, Reagan's reelection in 1984 loudly declared that the social, cultural, economic, and political values previously understood as the domain of the conservative Sunbelt were now just as illustrative of the entire country – or at least the vast majority of the country's voters. If Ronald Reagan's election in 1980 was not the conservative Sunbelt's greatest triumph, his landslide reelection in 1984 likely was.[32]

Looking back on the Reagan years, conservatives have been quick to point out two things about the decade's economy. First, they note that the economic boom from 1983 to 1987 followed the enormous tax cuts of 1981. Second, they cite Reagan's impulse for widespread deregulation, such as on his first day in office when he ordered a freeze on all federal hiring, then followed that order by restricting federal regulatory agencies from issuing new regulations. Over the next several years, Reagan eliminated or softened many other regulations, including those that inhibited mining, drilling, and timber cutting. He also eliminated or weakened other regulations designed to protect the environment. All told, Reagan's deregulation initiatives reshaped the Securities and Exchange Commission, the Federal Communications Commission, the Commerce Department, and the Department of the Interior, just to name a few. Conservative business interests – and many in the middle class who believed their own fortunes were directly tied to corporate America's unfettered ability to conduct business as it saw fit – cheered loudly. Meanwhile, many of those on the Left lamented the rapid loss of environmental

---

[32] Ibid.; for more on the presidential campaign of 1984, see also Jamieson, *Packaging the Presidency*, 446–458.

protections and economic regulatory gains made during the 1960s and 1970s, not to mention the apparent disparity in tax cuts that they argued disproportionately favored the rich. Many of those same liberals also cried foul in 1987 and 1988, blaming Reagan-backed deregulations for a disastrous meltdown of the nation's savings and loan industry, a financial debacle that was especially destructive in Texas. Liberals, however, largely ignored the fact that most of these banking deregulations had originally been initiated during Carter's presidency, just as they ignored other examples of deregulatory policies initiated under Carter and popularly supported during the late 1970s by congressional liberals including, in several cases, Ted Kennedy.[33]

Whereas conservatives have been quick to bracket Reagan's success with conservatism's viability, they have not been as quick to point out that although Reagan reduced corporate, capital gains, and marginal income tax rates for individual payers, he also frequently raised taxes in less obvious ways to stem the tide of an increasingly unbalanced budget. For instance, in 1982, he signed the Tax Equity and Fiscal Responsibility Act, which for all intents and purposes undid many of the secondary tax cuts passed in 1981. Reagan also raised taxes on gasoline and, to avoid default, raised the nation's debt limit eighteen times in eight years. On that note, conservatives have largely refused to accept blame for escalating budget deficits during the 1980s, pointing out that the Democratic-controlled Congress refused to reduce spending on entitlements and social programs to the degree that the White House asked. In 1981, for instance, Reagan – with the support of boll weevils in the House like Phil Gramm of Texas – proposed a $47 billion cut to Carter's final budget but in the end achieved only a $35 billion cut. However, liberals argued that soaring budget deficits had far more to do with increased spending on defense. In fact, Reagan increased military spending by 34 percent during his first term alone, whereas over the course of two terms,

---

[33] Wilentz, *The Age of Reagan*, 139–140, 194–200; Critchlow, *The Conservative Ascendancy*, 189.

cutting spending on social and economic programs for the impoverished by an estimated $70 billion.[34]

Increased defense spending helped re-ignite a boom in subsidized prosperity across the Sunbelt, where weapons research, development, and manufacturing created jobs and boosted an already healthy economy. Increased defense spending also undoubtedly escalated tensions with the Soviet Union. At the same time, however, there is an argument to be made that increased defense spending also put pressure on the Soviet Union, and that this pressure contributed – even if only slightly – to the Soviet Union's disastrous economic problems during the latter half of the decade. Although he certainly heightened international tensions during his first term in office, Reagan also pursued disarmament during his second term, a shift in policy that also played a role in bringing the Cold War to a surprisingly early end. Either way, Reagan's condemnation of communism as "evil" during a 1983 speech to the National Association of Evangelicals in Orlando, Florida, as well as his public demand that Mikhail Gorbachev "tear down" the Berlin Wall in 1987, resonated with conservatives all across the Sunbelt and the nation who believed in peace but also believed that liberals' pursuit of détente during the 1970s had confused peace with surrender.[35]

Ultimately, the Reagan Revolution was not just about economics, nor was it just about the relationship between economics, federal spending, and the Cold War. Social conservatives also ascended to national power under Reagan's watch. But as was true during the 1960s and 1970s, social conservatism was far more than just Jerry Falwell, Pat Robertson, and the most visible elements of the Religious Right. Rather, during the 1980s, a widespread coalition of cooperative but independent and largely grassroots forces – defined by their attention to issues including

[34] Cannon, *The Role of a Lifetime*, 253–256; Wilentz, *The Age of Reagan*, 148–149, 152–155, 274.
[35] Ibid.; for more on Reagan, the Cold War, and the politics of disarmament, see the provocative and controversial Beth A. Fischer, *The Reagan Reversal: Foreign Policy and the End of the Cold War* (Columbia: University of Missouri Press, 1997).

abortion, school prayer, homosexuality, feminism, crime, gun control, immigration, and race, just to name a few – rallied behind Reagan, confident that their president understood and sympathized with their concerns for America's moral health. Reagan did sympathize with the socially conservative Right's agenda, but he was more libertarian and anticommunist at heart than he was a moral traditionalist. He backed antiabortion measures, such as a bill proposed by Jesse Helms of North Carolina to legally classify life as beginning at conception. But despite Reagan's support, the Helms bill never made it out of the Senate. By the end of the decade, many religious conservatives had grown vocally disappointed in the lack of progress under Reagan. As early as 1984, that disappointment manifested in a wave of extreme violence, as more than thirty abortion clinics were either bombed, set on fire, or peppered with bullets, including several clinics in Texas, Florida, Georgia, and Virginia. Most Sunbelt conservatives condemned such violence, as did Reagan. Nevertheless, social issues like abortion remained an emotional topic of political conversation throughout the 1980s.[36]

Far more than policy making, the Religious Right's influence on American politics was most powerfully electoral and strategic in nature. In other words, what the politics of the Religious Right did for Reagan and the Republican Party was offer an alternative gateway for socially and culturally frustrated Americans to enter the GOP's ever-increasing political fold. Strategists such as Lee Atwater, Pat Buchanan, Richard Viguerie, and Paul Weyrich – building on the work of former Nixon advisors Harry Dent and Kevin Phillips – used the emotive power of cultural issues to embolden conservative supporters and then fused those supporters' concerns with the party's more broadly ideological values – those that emphasized local control, limited government, and the free market. This had been Phyllis Schlafly's strategy during

[36] Link, *Righteous Warrior*, 230–231; Self, *All in the Family*, 311, 368–369, 396; for more on the Sunbelt's religiosity compared to the rest of the nation, see Lyman A. Kellstedt and James L. Guth, "Religion and Political Behavior in the Sunbelt," in Nickerson and Dochuk, *Sunbelt Rising*, 110–138.

the late 1970s and continued to work well during the 1980s, as
conservatives linked the decline of the family – often understood
synonymously with rising divorce rates – with the failures of
liberalism. More religious on the whole than other parts of the
country, the Sunbelt provided Republicans with a healthy supply
of enthusiastic new voters, eager to wage war against what
they perceived to be liberalism's godless and socialistic pursuit of
welfare redistribution, moral relativism, and unilateral weakness.[37]

Despite its relatively mixed record, the Reagan Revolution of
the 1980s remains a major moment in the history of American
politics, especially in the postwar Sunbelt. In representing the
multi-factional conservative Right, Reagan inspired a new political coalition, not quite as strong as Franklin Roosevelt's had been
during the 1930s and 1940s, but one that was certainly strong
enough to encourage several boll weevil Democrats, including
Texans Kent Hance and Phil Gramm, to finally switch parties.
Other boll weevils, including Alabama's Richard Shelby, consistently backed Reagan without formally switching parties, though
Shelby did eventually join the GOP in 1994. Conservative Democrats
across the South had been switching to the GOP since at least the
1960s, but it was not until Reagan made Republicanism fashionable during the 1980s that the floodgates of partisan realignment
grew wide enough to significantly reshape the regional and
national political landscapes.[38]

The Reagan Revolution also illustrated the electoral power of
patriotic and nostalgic optimism. Capturing the entrepreneurial
spirit of the conservative Sunbelt, then projecting that spirit onto
the rest of the nation, Reagan communicated a message of hope
and change, using success stories from the mythically free-market

[37] Ibid.; see also, Frank, *What's the Matter with Kansas?* On the whole, Frank
tends to argue that conservatives used cultural issues to distract voters away
from economic issues, whereas Self argues that conservatives used cultural
issues in tandem with free-market economic ideas to forge what he refers to as
"breadwinner conservatism."

[38] For more on political realignment in the South, see Black and Black, *The Rise of
Southern Republicans*; Shafer and Johnston, *The End of Southern Exceptionalism*;
and Feldman, *Painting Dixie Red*; see also again Troy, *Morning in America*.

Sunbelt in order to reinforce that spirit. Reagan's brand of populist conservatism converged and, in some ways, perfected the
disparate streams of conservative populism that had been flowing
somewhat unpredictably through the nation's political culture since
the end of World War II. In 1986, several Sunbelt Republicans
used that spirit as a springboard into state office, winning gubernatorial elections, for instance, in Alabama, Florida, Oklahoma,
Texas, and South Carolina. In the years that followed, conservatives recalled the 1980s as a sort of golden age, not simply
because Reagan enacted (or at least publicly supported) much
of the Right's social, cultural, and economic agenda, but also
because he left office with approval ratings in the 60s and gave
popular credibility to a movement that had long been marginalized and ridiculed.[39]

THE PEAK OF ANTI-LIBERALISM

In 1964, liberals effectively convinced the vast majority of
American voters that Barry Goldwater and the conservatism
he represented was radical and extreme. In 1972, conservatives
accomplished the same thing in reverse, depicting George
McGovern as the candidate of "acid, amnesty, and abortion."
Reagan's win over Mondale in 1984 furthered liberalism's eroding reputation not as a philosophy of uplift and equality, but one
of moral permissiveness and entitlement.[40] But the peak of anti-
liberalism in postwar American politics came in 1988, when
George H. W. Bush easily defeated Michael Dukakis, the governor of Massachusetts, to win what many viewed as a third term
for Ronald Reagan. The presidential election of 1988 was a
referendum on the national popularity of Sunbelt conservatism
and, especially, the voting public's preference for Sunbelt conservatism over establishment liberalism. As such, it was also a statement about just how much the nation's political culture had

---

[39] Ibid.
[40] For more on popular associations between liberalism and permissiveness, see
again Petigny, *The Permissive Society*.

changed since World War II, and how much the Sunbelt's emergence had contributed to that change.

A Texan, but also a longtime moderate on several issues,
George H. W. Bush did not easily or quickly earn the conservative
Right's unwavering endorsement in 1988. In fact, in Republican
primaries across the Sunbelt, Bush struggled to overcome his
reputation as ideologically soft. One of Bush's most visible opponents during those primaries was Pat Robertson, a popular televangelist from Virginia Beach, Virginia, whose *700 Club* news and
talk show was seen by an estimated 27 million viewers monthly at
its height during the mid-1980s. A former Democrat who endorsed
Jimmy Carter in 1976, Robertson formally switched to the GOP in
1984 before unofficially launching his campaign for the White
House in 1986. Believing he could unite Christian conservatives
and blue-collar populists, Robertson campaigned on everything
from family values to debt cancellation to Social Security privatization. Robertson did, in fact, garner a significant chunk of support
among conservatives, particularly from those in the Sunbelt who
primarily emphasized social issues. But despite some early organ-
izational success in South Carolina and his home state of Virginia,
Robertson's campaign quickly floundered, in part because of unrelated sex scandals involving other televangelists, including North
Carolina's Jim Bakker and Baton Rouge, Louisiana's Jimmy
Swaggart. Meanwhile, Bush continued to survive and advance,
eventually outlasting other Republican challengers including
Kansas's Bob Dole and New York's Jack Kemp.[41]

Meanwhile, the Democratic Party nominated Michael Dukakis,
the liberal governor of Massachusetts. Dukakis won his party's
nomination after early frontrunners, including civil rights leader
Jesse Jackson and former Colorado senator Gary Hart, stumbled.
In Hart's case, it was an extramarital sexual dalliance that undid
his once very credible bid for the White House. The Hart affair
did not help liberalism's growing image as morally permissive.
Nevertheless, as Bush struggled to reunite conservatives who had
been hesitant to jump on his bandwagon during the primaries,

[41] Williams, *God's Own Party*, 132, 213–220.

Dukakis surged to a seventeen-point lead after the Democratic National Convention in Atlanta that summer. However, thanks to Bush's campaign advisors – Lee Atwater chief among them – the GOP quickly erased Dukakis's head start in the polls, undermining the Massachusetts governor's reputation as a competent, business-oriented technocrat. Instead, the Bush team targeted their Democratic opponent by emphasizing issues like Dukakis's veto of a bill that would have required Massachusetts schoolteachers to lead their students in the Pledge of Allegiance. Republicans also portrayed Dukakis as "soft on crime" and used a Massachusetts program that allowed weekend furloughs to convicted criminals as evidence of a "revolving door policy" that coddled violent offenders at the expense of law-abiding citizens. Reviving the Nixon-era spirit of law and order, Bush ran racially charged television advertisements – paid for by independent political action groups but tacitly endorsed by Atwater and the official campaign –to connect Dukakis with weakness, and weakness with liberalism. The most memorable of these ads featured Willie Horton, an African American and a convicted murder serving a life sentence, but furloughed under Dukakis's watch. Horton used his furlough to flee to Maryland, where he kidnapped and tortured a young man for seven hours before repeatedly raping the man's fiancée. Despite the fact that Dukakis's Republican predecessor had started the Massachusetts furlough program, and despite the fact that several other states utilized similar programs, conservatives effectively capitalized on the story's horrific details to further connote liberalism with a propensity for immorality and lawlessness. Bush also called Dukakis a "card-carrying member" of the ACLU, a phrase strikingly similar to McCarthy-era warnings about communism during the early postwar Red Scare.[42]

In the end, Bush successfully tied himself to Reagan; reunited the conservative coalition of suburban middle-class whites, blue-collar families, and the Religious Right; and demonized liberalism as essentially synonymous with un-Americanism. In November,

[42] For more on the 1988 presidential election, see among others Critchlow, *The Conservative Ascendancy*, 221–227; Jamieson, *Packaging the Presidency*, 459–484; and Patterson, *Restless Giant*, 218–225.

Bush won the election easily, carrying the Electoral College 426
votes to 111, and the popular vote by a margin of 54 percent to
45 percent. Not surprisingly, Bush was strong in the Sunbelt,
easily sweeping the entire region. He won more than 60 percent
of the vote in Florida and South Carolina, and between 55 percent
and 59 percent of the vote in Nevada, Arizona, Texas, Oklahoma,
Arkansas, Mississippi, Alabama, Georgia, Tennessee, and North
Carolina. Most of these voters more than likely cast their ballots
in the hope that Bush's first term would be, essentially, Reagan's
third.[43]

Beginning in the late 1970s and continuing through the 1980s,
American politics moved sharply to the right. It did so in conjunction with the passage of yet another stage in the Sunbelt's
vibrant postwar economic ascendancy. That economic ascendancy paralleled the national political culture's adoption of several
issues and ideas deeply rooted in the region's political culture,
namely a renaissance in free-market capitalism; an at-least rhetorical adherence to the principles of limited government and low
taxes; and a dedication to protecting families from the dangers
of moral relativism, increasingly connoted as the very essence of
liberalism itself. On each of these points, Sunbelt Republicans
and conservatives all over the nation benefited from the widespread appeal and popular image of Ronald Reagan. The history
of Sunbelt conservatism since the end of World War II resembled
a rollercoaster ride, full of sudden ups, bumpy downs, surprising
turns, and quick accelerations. During the 1950s and early 1960s,
conservatism struggled to overcome negative perceptions that it
was irresponsibly extremist. Then, during the late 1960s and early
1970s, its fortunes mirrored Richard Nixon's rise, fall, and humiliation. But during Reagan's 1980s, conservatism finally enjoyed
an extended moment in the sun, gaining unprecedented popularity in the process. In short, conservatives across the Sunbelt found
Reagan's popularity and the GOP's corresponding growth during
the 1980s to be especially sweet.

Among Reagan's most important political legacies was the
partisan realignment he inspired across the Sunbelt, especially in

[43] Ibid.

the South. According to polls in 1980, 52 percent of white southerners identified themselves as Democrats, compared to only
24 percent who identified themselves as Republicans. Such numbers had long been meaningless in presidential elections. But in
state and local contests, loyalty to the Democratic Party was still
important. By the time Reagan left office, however, those numbers
were statistically dead even. Over the course of the next decade,
partisan identification among white southerners continued to
trend against the Democratic Party. So far as electoral behavior
was concerned, the once solidly Democratic South had become,
at best, a battleground region. But in presidential elections, it was
clear that the South was overwhelmingly Republican. Perhaps
even more striking – and certainly evidence in support of the
idea that, at least in the South, liberalism had become the new
extremism – 59 percent of southern moderates voting in presidential elections from 1980 to 1988 sided with the GOP.[44]

If the narrative of American politics in the postwar Sunbelt had
ended with George H. W. Bush's landslide victory over Michael
Dukakis in 1988, one could easily summarize Sunbelt political
history as a multifaceted drama of bipartisan competition eventually succumbing to a triumphant conservative ascendancy. But
the story of American politics in the postwar Sunbelt did not
end in 1988, nor did liberals and other Sunbelt Democrats easily
abandon their region to Republican conservatives. Rather, during
the 1990s, and then continuing well into the twenty-first century,
Sunbelt Democrats successfully remade themselves in order to effectively challenge conservatism's grip across the region. Eventually,
those Democrats created a Sunbelt that, once again, reflected the
rest of the country writ large – polarized but competitive, sometimes unwilling to compromise, but still typically desirous of
moderation. As Ronald Reagan had done during the 1980s,
yet another former Sunbelt governor commanded the nation's
political stage during the 1990s. His name was Bill Clinton.

---

[44] Black and Black, *The Rise of Southern Republicans*, 205–240.

7

Shades of Red, Shades of Blue

Few events more clearly illustrated the Sunbelt's powerful influence in national pop culture than the free concert staged by Garth Brooks on August 7, 1997, before approximately 50,000 fans in New York City's Central Park.[1] A Tulsa, Oklahoma, native, Brooks launched his career as a country music star in 1989. By the time of his Central Park concert, however, Brooks was already well on his way to becoming the third-highest-selling musical artist in United States history, behind only the Beatles and Elvis Presley. Like so many other country artists during the 1990s, Brooks owed a debt of gratitude to musical pioneers including Merle Haggard, Johnny Cash, and Waylon Jennings who had popularized the genre during the 1970s. Beyond Brooks's obvious status as a premier musical talent, however, his Central Park concert also made clear that country music at the end of the twentieth century had easily transcended regional borders.

---

[1] Attendance figures for this concert have varied dramatically. Initial estimates ranged from 750,000 to just under 1 million. Those estimates were later revised down to 250,000, then dramatically cut by officials in the New York City Parks Service, which estimated the attendance at closer to 50,000. This most dramatic revision was the result of analysis comparing different events in Central Park with events elsewhere, including Barack Obama's first presidential inauguration in January 2009.

Also like other country artists, Brooks made a living singing about populist and blue-collar – sometimes called "redneck" – values and experiences. Offering a window into mythical but idyllic worlds of tradition, nostalgia, and simple living, Brooks and other country singers attracted fans who identified with the music's oft-contradictory expressions of both frustration and hope, as well as its esteem for small town life. Two of Brooks's earliest hit singles, in particular, reflected such expressions, while articulating the dichotomous worldviews that made both the Sunbelt and the United States the competitively contested political battlegrounds that they were throughout the 1990s.

The first of these two songs, called "We Shall Be Free," was released in 1992 and immediately attracted attention for its surprisingly progressive lyrics. Among other things, Brooks sang about the connections between freedom and society's responsibility to fight hunger, homelessness, racism, pollution, homophobia, and the evils of moneyed power. The song also championed the beauty of religious tolerance while casting an almost John Lennon–esque vision of humankind as a single, unified race. With an African American gospel choir singing backup, "We Shall Be Free" suggested that if Brooks was still a reflection of the Oklahoma Sunbelt from which he came, then perhaps that Sunbelt was a more diversified and tolerant place than its critics might have thought. According to interviews, Brooks had been inspired to write the song in the aftermath of the famed Rodney King police brutality trial and subsequent rioting in Los Angeles during the spring of 1992.[2]

One year later, Brooks released another song, this one called "American Honky-Tonk Bar Association." This song's lyrics were far more in keeping with the Sunbelt's stereotypically conservative culture. Reflecting the frustrations of, as the song put it, the "hard hat, gun rack, achin' back, over-taxed, flag-wavin',

---

[2] "We Shall be Free." Song performed by Garth Brooks, Written by Garth Brooks and Stephanie Davis, *The Chase*, CD, Produced by Allen Reynolds, Liberty Records, 1992.

fun-lovin' crowd," Brooks attacked welfare recipients and bureaucratic "red tape," citing both as reasons to be "concerned about the
destination of this great nation." Above all, the song's message –
tongue-in-cheek, of course – was that frustrated Americans
should not look to the government for help but could easily
find solace among friends at their nearest locally controlled
drinking establishment.[3]

Far too much could be made of the contrasting messages
communicated in these two songs. But as a simple illustration,
comparing these songs suggests that the Sunbelt was not as uniformly conservative as the Reagan Revolution of the previous
decade might have suggested. Much more convincing as evidence
for this conclusion were the political developments that shaped
the Sunbelt and the nation during the 1990s. From Bill Clinton to
Newt Gingrich and George W. Bush to Al Gore, Sunbelt politicians
of varying stripes commanded the center stage of national politics
as the country moved into a new millennium. By December 2000,
American politics was already knee deep in the world of polarized
"red states" and "blue states." But a closer examination of the
political landscape reveals that within that world of red states
and blue states, there existed an ongoing desire for balance, cooperation, and moderation. Liberals had not abandoned the
Sunbelt, despite the region's long-standing conservative proclivities. Neither had all Sunbelt Democrats resigned themselves to a
life of subordination to liberal ideas. As conservative Republicans
continued to strengthen their positions across the Sunbelt, moderate Democrats across the region aggressively rebranded themselves and their party, reaching out to middle-class whites, small
business leaders, corporations, and even family values voters. At
the dawn of the twenty-first century, the United States was once
again a battleground nation, painted in competing shades of
red and blue. So was the Sunbelt.

---

[3] "American Honky-Tonk Bar Association." Song performed by Garth Brooks,
Written by Bryan Kennedy and Jim Rushing, *In Pieces*, CD, Produced by Allen
Reynolds, Liberty Records, 1993.

MAKING A THIRD WAY

The Reagan-fueled Republican ascendancy of the 1980s had not simply made conservatism more popular across the country; it had also made liberalism less popular. For many Americans, especially those in the Sunbelt, the liberal image of the late 1980s and early 1990s was one of a weak, immoral, tax-happy loser. This was certainly the image *Saturday Night Live* projected when it spoofed Michael Dukakis during the 1988 presidential campaign. Political sketches on the popular comedy program that fall depicted Dukakis as short, boring, and icy. In one particularly memorable skit, called "Dukakis After Dark," a who's who of the liberal Democratic establishment gathered in a luxurious penthouse apartment for a taxpayer-funded, end-of-campaign bash. Drinking excessively, lamenting the wild unpopularity of their ideas, and surrounded by *Playboy* bunnies, Dukakis – portrayed by actor Jon Lovitz – made the rounds at his party, speaking to an inebriated Ted Kennedy; a depressed Jimmy Carter; an ever-Utopian Joan Baez; and even Willie Horton, whom Dukakis had again "furloughed" for the convicted murder and rapist to attend. It was no small point that Horton was shown "dirty dancing" with Donna Rice, the white woman who had been caught having an affair with Gary Hart, the one-time front-runner for the Democratic Party's presidential nomination that year. "Dukakis After Dark" was only one of several satirical punches landed by *SNL* against liberals during the fall of 1988.[4]

SNL, however, was hardly the only production to mock liberalism and the Democratic Party during these years. For instance, during one scene in the popular 1991 comedic slapstick film *The Naked Gun 2 1/2*, the film's protagonist, Lieutenant Frank Drebin – portrayed by Leslie Nielson – is shown drowning his sorrows at a bar called The Blue Note. In order to convey the bar's depressing atmosphere, the camera slowly pans across the dimly lit establishment to reveal a series of decorative photographs recalling three of America's most tragic moments – the sinking

---

[4] Cunningham, *Cowboy Conservatism*, xi–xiii; see also Troy, *Morning in America*.

of the Titanic, the explosion of the Hindenburg, and Michael
Dukakis. During a different scene earlier in the film, Drebin assured
his ex-lover that their relationship was "ancient history . . . like the
Democratic Party."[5]

Despite what these satirical messages suggested, the Democratic
Party was not ancient history, even in the Sunbelt. In fact, liberal
and moderate Democrats had not disappeared at all, and in several
cases they continued to win elections across the Sunbelt throughout
the 1980s. Take California, for instance. When Ronald Reagan
left the California governor's office in early 1975, he was
replaced by Jerry Brown, the liberal Democratic son of Edmund
"Pat" Brown, whom Reagan had defeated in 1966. Brown
served as governor of California from 1975 to 1983 before
running for president of the United States in 1992. Even Tom
Hayden – a former Freedom Rider and SDS radical during the
1960s – served in the California State Assembly from 1982 to
1992, then in the California State Senate from 1992 to 2000. In
both stints, Hayden represented a district within the Los Angeles
metro area. Throughout the 1980s, California continued to elect
and listen to other liberal Democrats, including Nancy Pelosi –
first elected in 1987 – before sending both Barbara Boxer and
Diane Feinstein to the U.S. Senate in the early 1990s.

Democrats also continued to influence politics in Texas, where
liberal activists such as Jim Hightower and Molly Ivins earned
national reputations for their critical assessments of the Reagan
and Bush years. In some cases, Texans even elected progressive
minorities to state and local offices. In 1981, San Antonio voters
selected Henry Cisneros to be their mayor. A highly regarded
liberal Democrat and Mexican American activist who successfully
revitalized the city's economy, Cisneros served as mayor of San
Antonio until 1989, attracting several new high-tech industries to
the area while also improving the city's convention and tourism
industry. Meanwhile, Jim Wright, a Democrat from Fort Worth,
served as House Majority Leader from 1977 to 1987 before

[5] *The Naked Gun 2 1/2: The Smell of Fear*. DVD. Directed by David Zucker.
Paramount, 1991.

becoming Speaker of the U.S. House of Representatives. Wright served as Speaker until 1989, when he was forced to resign as a result of an ethics investigation led in part by Georgia Republican Newt Gingrich. From 1983 to 1987, the governor of Texas was Mark White, a moderate Democrat who had defeated James Baker in the race for Texas attorney general in 1978 before defeating Bill Clements in 1982. Clements exacted revenge on White in 1986, but Texas liberals won the governorship again in 1990, when Ann Richards completed a remarkable come-from-behind victory over Midland businessman and Republican nominee Clayton Williams – a Texas A&M graduate whose political incompetence reached new levels when, during a television interview, he compared bad weather to rape, suggesting that if something is inevitable, the best thing to do is simply "relax and enjoy it." Richards, however, was not simply an accidental beneficiary of Williams's bad judgment. She had earned national fame two years earlier when, during her delivery of the keynote address at the Democratic National Convention in Atlanta, she gave the famous line in reference to the GOP's nominee that year, "Poor George, he can't help it. He was born with a silver foot in his mouth." Even Michael Dukakis's running mate, Lloyd Bentsen, was from Texas. Bentsen had served the Lone Star State as a U.S. senator since 1971 and won reelection in 1988, despite simultaneously losing his bid for the vice presidency thanks to Dukakis's unpopularity.

Elsewhere in the Sunbelt, liberal Democrat and former United Nations ambassador Andrew Young served as the mayor of Atlanta from 1982 to 1990. In addition to his stint at the UN during the late 1970s, Young had previously served the city of Atlanta as a pastor, a civil rights activist, and a colleague of Martin Luther King Jr. From 1973 to 1977, Young was a congressman representing Georgia's 5th District. To Georgia's north, Fritz Hollings served as a U.S. senator representing the state of South Carolina from 1966 to 2005. A relatively moderate Democrat, Hollings conducted a widely publicized "poverty tour" in 1969 before publishing a best-selling book in 1970 called *The Case Against Hunger*. South Carolina voters seemed to appreciate the balance Hollings gave the state in the Senate, where for the duration of his career he served alongside Strom Thurmond. Meanwhile, voters in the state of Florida sent Lawton Chiles, a relatively moderate Democrat, to the U.S. Senate for three terms between 1971 and 1989 before electing him to two terms as governor, from 1991 to 1998. During those same years, the state legislature in Tallahassee remained relatively divided between liberals, moderates, and conservatives.

Examples such as these are important to the idea that the Sunbelt remained a politically contested battleground, even during the 1980s. That contestation intensified in 1985 when – at the arguable height of the Reagan Revolution – several regional Democrats founded the Democratic Leadership Council (DLC). Precipitated by the embarrassing campaign failures of both Jimmy Carter and Walter Mondale, the DLC was dedicated to rebuilding the Democratic Party's national image. As part of that rehabilitation, the DLC recruited and promoted candidates whose chief appeal was to middle-class moderates and corporate interests across the metropolitan Sunbelt. Very quickly, the DLC became a highly influential clearinghouse for strategic party politics. Early DLC leaders included Senators Joe Biden (Delaware), Sam Nunn (Georgia), and Al Gore Jr. (Tennessee), as well as Connecticut Attorney General (and future Senator) Joe Lieberman. Several Sunbelt governors, including Arizona's Bruce Babbitt, Florida's Lawton Chiles, and Virginia's Chuck Robb were also among the DLC's earliest pioneers. Robb was particularly influential. The governor of Virginia from 1982 to 1986, Robb had been born in Phoenix, Arizona and was a Vietnam veteran and husband to Lyndon Johnson's daughter Lynda. Like his DLC cohorts, Robb understood that the modern Democratic Party, in the majority of American voters' minds, had been taken over by the far Left, prioritizing the marginalized and impoverished at the expense of the white middle class. DLC leaders like Robb worked to reform their party's image in the populist mold that Republicans had been creating for themselves since at least the 1960s. The DLC emphasized economic growth, smaller government, strong national defense, and traditional values and at the same time approaching controversial issues including abortion with libertarian and moderately pro-choice positions. These Democrats did not shy away from charges that government was too big and inefficient. Instead, they blamed Republicans for bloated federal budget deficits and promised that, if elected, they would solve such problems.[6]

The DLC was immediately successful in its promotion of what it called "third way" candidates. In 1986, Florida Democrat Bob Graham defeated Republican Paula Hawkins for a seat in the U.S. Senate. Graham had previously served the Sunshine State as governor from 1979 to 1987. Elsewhere, Georgia Democrat Wyche Fowler defeated Republican Mack Mattingly for a Senate seat, and Democrat Terry Sanford did the same to Republican Jim Broyhill in North Carolina. Once in office, Graham, Fowler, and Sanford - governed as relative moderates. For instance, each took liberal positions on state funding for public education, while adhering to the DLC's emphasis on winning suburban whites by promoting middle-class tax breaks, strong national defense, and streamlined government.[7]

Though no longer the dominant force they had once been, Democrats continued to contest elections in the Sunbelt throughout the late 1980s. The DLC was responsible for much of that success. But the Democratic Party did not nominate a DLC candidate for president in 1988; instead, it chose a northeastern liberal. That decision had proved disastrous. Democrats would not make the same mistake twice. Less than two years after Dukakis's humiliating defeat in the presidential election of 1988, the DLC named a

---

[6] Kenneth S. Baer, *Reinventing Democrats: The Politics of Liberalism from Reagan to Clinton* (Lawrence: University Press of Kansas, 2000); Critchlow, *The Conservative Ascendancy*, 203–204; Judis and Teixeira, *The Emerging Democratic Majority*, 126–130; Michael Schaller, *Right Turn: American Life in the Reagan-Bush Era, 1980–1992* (New York: Oxford University Press, 2007), 69–70; see also Edsall with Edsall, *Chain Reaction*. The arguments presented in this book were particularly influential to Clinton's presidential campaign of 1992. Along these lines, see also Stanley B. Greenberg, *Middle Class Dreams: The Politics and Power of the New American Majority* (New Haven, CT: Yale University Press, 1996).

[7] Ibid.

new chair, one whose political career as a multi-term governor
from Arkansas suggested remarkable promise at the national level.

FROM A PLACE CALLED HOPE

Bill Clinton was part of America's great baby boom, born in 1946
in a small town in southwest Arkansas called Hope. This coinci-
dence would become one of the many marketable features of
Clinton's dramatic campaign for the White House in 1992.
Obsessed with politics from an early age, Clinton left Arkansas
to attend Georgetown University in the fall of 1964, the same
semester that Lyndon Johnson crushed Barry Goldwater in the
presidential election of that year. While at Georgetown, Clinton
earned a Rhodes scholarship, which he used upon graduation to
study at Oxford. He left Oxford early in order to attend Yale Law
School, where he met his future wife, Hillary Rodham. In 1972,
the not-yet-wed couple moved to Texas where they volunteered
with several area Democrats to work on George McGovern's
hopeless presidential campaign against Richard Nixon. In 1976,
barely 30 years of age, Clinton won the race for Arkansas attorney
general. Two years later, he won his first term as governor of
Arkansas, running as a populist moderate. Clinton lost his reelection bid in 1980, largely the result of Reagan's landslide over
Jimmy Carter. But he avenged the loss in 1982, defeating the
Republican incumbent, Frank White. Clinton remained governor
of Arkansas for the next ten years, during which time he operated
as a business- and middle-class-friendly moderate. In 1985, he
was among several Sunbelt Democrats to express interest in the
new DLC. By 1990, he was chairing the organization. That same
year, Clinton won his last reelection bid for governor of Arkansas,
easily defeating his Republican challenger, Sheffield Nelson.
Nelson ran an uninspired campaign, despite receiving free council
from Lee Atwater. Atwater feared Clinton's appeal in the upcoming presidential election and hoped to preempt such a contest by
defeating Clinton in Arkansas. Accordingly, Atwater instructed his
aides to help Arkansas Republicans tempt Clinton into a political
scandal, exhorting them to use "drugs, women, whatever works."

Nothing worked, and Clinton was easily reelected, setting the stage for his run at the White House in 1992.[8]

Clinton's experience with the DLC was essential to his staging as a national candidate. Understanding the nature of American political culture in the age of Reagan, Clinton carefully positioned himself as a "New Democrat," supportive of tax cuts for the middle class, in favor of the death penalty, insistent on welfare reform, and desirous of balanced budgets and fiscal responsibility. On social issues, Clinton toed a thin line. He declared himself a born-again Christian and claimed membership in a Southern Baptist church but also cautiously committed himself as pro-choice and supportive of gay rights. He supported organized labor but avoided over-identification with unions, which were still very unpopular in his home state, as well as the rest of the still-growing Sunbelt. Clinton also benefited from an easy, naturally gifted political style. He spoke conversationally, easily connected with voters, and gave inspirational speeches, all at the same

Jimmy Carter greets the newly elected governor of Arkansas, Bill Clinton, December 1978. (Courtesy of the Jimmy Carter Presidential Library.)

[8] Schaller, *Right Turn*, 69–70.

time. In this way, he seemed far more like Ronald Reagan than did his soon-to-be Republican opponent, the incumbent president, George H. W. Bush. Never missing an opportunity, Clinton also capitalized on the convenient fact that he had been born in a "place called Hope."⁹

As late as 1991, however, it did not appear likely that Clinton, or any Democrat for that matter, would be able to defeat Bush in the upcoming election. After the quick and successful conclusion to Operation Desert Storm – a military campaign in which U.S.-led coalition forces defended Kuwait against an attempted Iraqi takeover – Bush appeared almost untouchable, enjoying record-high approval ratings approaching 90 percent. Desert Storm – also commonly referred to as the Gulf War – was a particularly powerful opportunity for Americans to express their renewed patriotism and self-confidence, something the nation had been eager to do since the end of the war in Vietnam. Bush's victory in the Gulf, coupled with the official end of the Soviet Union on Christmas Day 1991, seemingly solidified the president's reputation as a strong commander in chief. Unfortunately for Bush, the economy – which had been growing steadily, more or less, since 1983 – slipped into a recession and struggled to recover. What made this recession particularly problematic for Bush was that its rising unemployment rate seemed to reflect the loss of white-collar jobs in the middle class more than losses in other sectors. Further irritating conservatives was the fact that Bush had chosen to deal with escalating federal budget deficits by reneging on a previous pledge not to raise taxes. Conservatives had been slow to support Bush in 1988 and began abandoning him when the economy slipped into recession not long after the tax increase.¹⁰

⁹ Patterson, *Restless Giant*, 248.
¹⁰ Ibid., 247; for a more comprehensive examination of Bush's presidency, see John Robert Greene, *The Presidency of George Bush* (Lawrence: University Press of Kansas, 2000). See also Ryan J. Barilleaux and Mark J. Rozell, *Power and Prudence: The Presidency of George H. W. Bush* (College Station: Texas A&M University Press, 2004); and Herbert S. Parmet, *George Bush: The Life of a Lone Star Yankee* (New York: Scribner, 1997).

Bush, therefore, began his reelection campaign in the midst of a deeply unhappy and very divided Republican Party. When Pat Buchanan polled a surprisingly strong 36 percent in the GOP's New Hampshire primary, it was clear that Bush had some bridges to rebuild within his own party. A native of Washington, D.C., Buchanan was a former speechwriter for Richard Nixon and communications director for Ronald Reagan.[11] Appealing primarily but not exclusively to the Religious Right, Buchanan rallied former Pat Robertson voters as well as libertarian isolationists and aggressive tax-cutting conservatives to undermine Bush's popularity with the Republican base. Social conservatives were especially enamored with the Buchanan campaign's renegade nature. In fact, shortly after the New Hampshire primary, Robertson conducted a poll of 700 *Club* viewers, revealing a 71–29 preference for Buchanan over Bush in the race for the GOP's presidential nomination. Eventually Bush still won the nomination rather easily, but he was pressured to give Buchanan a high-profile speaking role at the Republican National Convention in Houston that August. Buchanan's speech was an overly aggressive warning to convention goers about the dangers of secular liberalism and the vital importance of fighting with passion and unrelenting intensity what was beginning to be called the "culture wars." Well-received by many conservative delegates and viewers across the Sunbelt, Buchanan's speech alienated moderates all over the nation.[12]

Buchanan's speech proved troublesome for the Bush campaign. But Texas multi-billionaire H. Ross Perot was an even more painful thorn in Bush's side as the general election approached. Perot's personal fortune was the result of a data-processing company called Electronic Data Services (EDS), which he founded in Dallas during the early 1960s. Like so much else in the postwar

[11] For more, see Timothy Stanley, "Republican Populism in the Quest for a New Majority: Pat Buchanan in the White House," in Mason and Morgan, *Seeking a New Majority*, 90–106.

[12] Critchlow, *The Conservative Ascendancy*, 237; Williams, *God's Own Party*, 231; Patterson, *Restless Giant*, 250–251; Self, *All in the Family*, 402–404; Wilentz, *The Age of Reagan*, 315.

Sunbelt, EDS had grown lucrative because of government contracts, specifically contracts to process Medicare payments. During
the late 1970s, Perot used his fortune and elevated profile to lobby
the U.S. government to more actively pursue the repatriation of
P.O.W.s still presumably held in Vietnam. Over time, Perot grew
conspiratorial and paranoid on the issue. During the 1980s, he so
annoyed President Reagan that Reagan granted Perot access to
classified records on P.O.W.s in the hope of quelling the Texas
billionaire's agitated obsession. In 1987, Reagan even agreed to
send Perot on a trip to Hanoi in order to investigate the situation
for himself. But Perot returned home even more unsatisfied.
Exasperated, Reagan ordered then–Vice President Bush to inform
Perot that his security clearance had been revoked. The incident
inflamed an already tense relationship between Perot and Bush,
which manifested more clearly in 1992 when Perot announced his
candidacy for the presidency. Fueled by grassroots petitions, Perot
first ran in a handful of GOP primaries. He consistently outper-
formed expectations and then declared as an Independent after
Bush had sewn up the GOP nomination. Far more than anything
else, Perot's campaign emphasized the unsustainability of spiraling
budget deficits and the dangers of the escalating national debt.[13]

As Bush struggled to fend off attacks from his right on everything from social issues to the economy, Bill Clinton, who had
already astonishingly survived the first of what would be many
scandals in his personal life, added another Sunbelt moderate to
his ticket when he chose Tennessee Senator Al Gore Jr. to be his
running mate. Eschewing conventional wisdom suggesting that
a running mate ought to hail from a different part of the country
than the presidential nominee, Clinton instead looked into the
DLC to find a candidate who, like him, would appeal to middle-
class voters across the Sunbelt. Following a successful convention,
Clinton surged into the lead in polls, a position he only strengthened as a result of subsequent debate performances. Bush,
meanwhile, appeared increasingly tired and disconnected as the
campaign progressed. He was unable to unify his party or make

[13] Wilentz, *The Age of Reagan*, 315–317.

the emotional connection that his predecessor, Ronald Reagan, had achieved or even match the connection that his soon-to-be-successor, Bill Clinton, was already accomplishing.[14]

In the end, Clinton won a rather easy victory, taking 370 electoral votes to Bush's 168. In the Sunbelt, Clinton carried Nevada, Colorado, New Mexico, Arkansas, Louisiana, Tennessee, and Georgia. He also became the first Democratic nominee to carry California in a presidential election since Lyndon Johnson in 1964. (California has remained a solidly Democratic state well into the twenty-first century.) Bush, on the other hand, carried the rest of the Sunbelt – Texas, Florida, South Carolina, North Carolina, and Virginia most notably. Still, Clinton claimed only 43 percent of the popular vote in a three-way race. Bush won 38 percent of the vote, with Perot claiming an impressive 19 percent – the most for any Independent or third-party candidate during the twentieth century. Noting Perot's relative conservatism, analysts quickly speculated that Perot had likely cost Bush the election. Subsequent analysis has been less clear, though the best evidence suggests that Perot did in fact take a slightly higher percentage of votes away from Bush than he did from Clinton. Whether or not Perot's absence from the race would have resulted in a different outcome remains open to debate. Regardless, for the eighth consecutive time, Americans had voted a Sunbelt politician into the Oval Office.[15]

CONTRACT WITH AMERICA, TRIANGULATION, AND REELECTION

Having won the presidency by stressing the importance of economic reforms targeting mostly middle-class families, Clinton mistakenly used his first two years in office to push an agenda

---

[14] For more on Clinton's public appeal and GOP struggles during the 1990s, see Geoffrey Kabaservice, *Rule and Ruin: The Downfall of Moderation and the Destruction of the Republican Party, From Eisenhower to the Tea Party* (New York: Oxford University Press, 2012), 374–381; see also David Maraniss, *First in His Class: The Biography of Bill Clinton* (New York: Simon & Schuster, 1996).

[15] For more on the 1992 campaign, see Jamieson, *Packaging the Presidency*, 485–516. See also David H. Bennett, *Bill Clinton: Building a Bridge to the New Millennium* (New York: Routledge, 2014), 35–71.

that was more liberal than most Americans preferred. Rather than keep a campaign pledge to cut taxes for the middle class, he instead raised marginal tax rates by creating two new upper-tier brackets, one at 36 percent for Americans making more than $140,000 per year, and another at 39.6 percent for those making more than $250,000 annually. These rates were still much lower than top-tier rates had been as recently as 1980, but they were tax hikes nevertheless. He also raised corporate tax rates by 1 percent. These tax increases were designed to reduce budget deficits. Over time and in combination with a speedily recovering economy, they did. By the time Clinton left office in 2001, the federal government was running an annual budget surplus. However, such good news was yet unknown in 1993 when the unpopular tax increases were announced.[16]

Clinton also decided to spend an enormous amount of political capital on what amounted to a universal health care plan. Under the First Lady's leadership, that plan went nowhere. Instead, vitriolic attacks against the idea of a government-run "Hillarycare" system undermined Clinton's image as a moderate New Democrat who was opposed to the expansion of big government. Clinton also supported what became the "Don't Ask, Don't Tell" policy, implemented in an effort to deal with the issue of homosexuals in the military. This plan – which essentially asked all parties involved to pretend that homosexuality did not exist – pleased few. Gun control was also on Clinton's initial agenda, and in 1993 he signed into law what was known as the Brady Bill. Among other restrictions, the Brady Bill created background checks and a mandatory five-day waiting period on new handgun purchases. Meanwhile, Clinton bungled an international crisis in Somalia and allowed personal scandals to once again creep into his political life when he and Hillary were accused of participating in an improper real estate venture in Arkansas known as Whitewater. Shortly after the Whitewater story broke, Clinton was also confronted with allegations of sexual harassment, filed by a woman named Paula Jones. Jones charged that Clinton had propositioned her during his last

---

[16] See also Bennett, *Bill Clinton*, 72–103; Patterson, *Restless Giant*, 318–345.

term as governor of Arkansas. The Paula Jones case would haunt Clinton for the rest of his time in office.[17]

Clinton had won the presidency in 1992 by recapturing many of the suburban, middle-class voters who had flocked to Reagan during the 1980s. A healthy percentage of these voters resided in the Sunbelt, which Clinton and the DLC had targeted as a region crucial to the Democratic Party's future growth. But Clinton's performance in 1993 and 1994 undermined his image in the Sunbelt as anything but an old-fashioned liberal. His tax increases – not to mention his broken promise to cut taxes for the middle class – angered fiscal conservatives and middle-class voters alike; his stance on gun control angered the National Rifle Association and its millions of registered members, a sizable chunk of whom lived in Sunbelt states; his position on gays in the military upset social conservatives, especially in the Bible Belt; his support for universal health care reignited Red Scare visions of the slippery slope from liberalism to socialism; his failures in Somalia made him appear weak and indecisive; and his personal failings made him the butt of jokes on all late-night talk shows, while entrenching in the Religious Right's mind the image of Clinton as an immoral, lying philanderer.[18]

It was no surprise, therefore, when the Republican Party scored major victories against Clinton-backed Democrats in the midterm elections of 1994. What was surprising, however, was the scope of those victories. Coordinated into a single, national, and thoroughly partisan campaign led by House Republican Newt Gingrich of Georgia, the GOP made history in November 1994 by sweeping the Democratic Party out of majority control in both houses of Congress for the first time in four decades. In the House, Republicans picked up a whopping 54 seats to take a commanding 230–204 majority. Of particular note, Dick Armey was reelected in Dallas and Tom DeLay was reelected in Houston. Armey would quickly be named House Majority Leader, and DeLay was named House Majority Whip, expanding

---

[17] Ibid.
[18] Ibid.

conservative Texas Republicans' power in both regional and
national politics. Adding to this sense that Texas conservatism
was on the rise was Republican Steve Stockman's victory in southwest Houston over Democrat Jack Brooks, an NRA member
who had been in office since 1967. Despite his NRA membership,
Brooks lost in a stunning upset largely because of his support for a
bill that proposed a ban on semiautomatic assault weapons.[19]

The Gingrich-led revolution was national in scope, but most
dominant in the South, where Gingrich's alliance with Republican
National Committee Chairman Haley Barbour of Mississippi
helped accelerate Dixie's realignment into the GOP. Across the
old Confederacy, conservative Republicans won 119 congressional seats while seizing control over several state-level legislative
bodies, including those in Florida, South Carolina, and North
Carolina.[20]

Having spearheaded the Republican sweep with his famed
Contract with America plan – a conservative agenda that prioritized lower taxes and smaller government – Gingrich became
Speaker of the House. Elsewhere, Republican Senate candidates
fared very well in Tennessee, where Bill Frist defeated Jim Sasser,
a three-term incumbent Democrat. Tennessee voters also sent
Hollywood actor and conservative Fred Thompson to the Senate,
where he joined Frist by winning the seat vacated less than two
years earlier by Al Gore. In Arizona, Republican Jon Kyl won his
race for a Senate seat. He joined fellow-Republican John McCain,
who had replaced Barry Goldwater when Goldwater finally retired
from the Senate in 1987. Even Pennsylvania elected a conservative
in the Sunbelt's mold, sending Rick Santorum to the Senate, where

[19] Ibid.; Black and Black, *The Rise of Southern Republicans*, 268–293; Critchlow,
The Conservative Ascendancy, 244–248; Schneider, The *Conservative Century*,
191–196. For more on the recent history of the U.S. Congress, as well as a
good discussion on the midterm elections of 1994 and the aftermath of the
Republican takeover, see Julian E. Zelizer, *On Capitol Hill: The Struggle to
Reform Congress and Its Consequences, 1948–2000* (New York: Cambridge
University Press, 2006); see also Elizabeth Drew, *Showdown: The Struggle
between the Gingrich Congress and the Clinton White House* (New York:
Touchstone, 1997).
[20] Ibid.

he soon became one of the Religious Right's most outspoken supporters. Recognizing the writing on the wall, Richard Shelby – the conservative Democratic senator from Alabama – switched to the GOP the day after the midterm elections. All told, the GOP picked up eight seats in the Senate to take a 52–48 majority.[21]

Conservative Republicans also made waves in gubernatorial races. In Texas, George W. Bush easily defeated incumbent Democratic Governor Ann Richards, winning nearly 54 percent of the vote – an impressive margin due in large part to Karl Rove's nationally oriented campaign advice in which "Washington liberalism" became a chief issue, as did unfounded rumors of Richards's coddling of rampant homosexuality in the state capitol building. In California, Pete Wilson – the former mayor of San Diego – easily won reelection to a second term as governor in Ronald Reagan's home state. Conservative Republicans also won the governorship in South Carolina, Alabama, Tennessee, and Oklahoma, whereas moderate Republicans won in Pennsylvania, New York, Connecticut, and Rhode Island. The lone bright spot for Democrats in the Sunbelt was Florida, where Lawton Chiles squeaked past Jeb Bush in that state's gubernatorial contest, winning by less than 2 percent of the vote. Regardless, Chiles was sent to Tallahassee to work with a state legislature that had been overtaken by socially conservative Republicans. Seen by analysts at the time as another "revolution," the 1994 midterms affirmed Sunbelt conservatism as the Republican Party's ideological soul. In the South, post-election polls showed that 65 percent of whites now freely identified with the GOP. Among evangelical Protestants, that number reached 76 percent.[22]

Staring a one-term presidency in the face, Clinton turned to Dick Morris, an old friend and political strategist from his early days as governor of Arkansas. Morris, who had also previously worked as a Republican strategist, urged Clinton to more aggressively command the political center in an effort to strengthen

---

[21] Ibid.

[22] Ibid.; see also Marjorie Connelly, "Portrait of the Electorate: Who Voted for Whom in the House," *New York Times*, November 13, 1994, sec. 1, p. 24.

his position among southern whites and suburban moderates – a tactic Morris called "triangulation." Beginning in 1995, Clinton did just that. On social issues like school prayer, Clinton positioned himself as a centrist, recalling that prayer in public schools had been good for him when he was a youth, while also suggesting that school prayer should be considered acceptable as long as administrators did not require all students to participate. Emphasizing his own vision of family values, Clinton also spoke often of his and Hillary's role as parents of a teenage daughter, his support for school uniforms, and his support for parental rights related to blocking excessive sexual content and violence on television and in films. Strengthening his position among middle-class moderates who also self-identified as evangelical Christians, Clinton also signed the Defense of Marriage Act, a 1996 federal law that limited the definition of marriage – and its tax and insurance benefits – to relationships between one man and one woman. That law had been originally sponsored in the House by Georgia Republican Bob Barr and was widely supported by religious conservatives across the Sunbelt.[23]

Most famously, Clinton declared in his 1996 State of the Union address that "the era of big government [was] over," a statement met with great enthusiasm among conservatives. Later that year, Clinton signed the Personal Responsibility and Work Opportunity Act of 1996, a welfare reform law that, based on proposals introduced in Gingrich's Contract with America, appeased the vast majority of congressional Republicans by rolling back entitlements for the poor at the same time that work requirements were dramatically toughened. Welfare reform was a particularly symbolic political maneuver considering that antipoverty measures had been a cornerstone of liberal Democratic politics since the 1960s. Clinton's commitment to welfare reform – essentially a Republican

[23] Critchlow, *The Conservative Ascendancy*, 248–250; Judis and Teixeira, *The Emerging Democratic Majority*, 133–135; Patterson, *Restless Giant*, 375–376; Wilentz, *The Age of Reagan*, 358. For a general assessment of Clintonian politics, see again Kabaservice, *Rule and Ruin*, 374–381.

plan – brilliantly inoculated the White House against charges of "bleeding heart liberalism" as the 1996 election approached. Clinton also frequently reminded audiences that he had pushed for and signed into law a comprehensive new crime bill in 1994, one modeled on a California law that mandated stiff prison sentences for repeat offenders.[24]

After moving to the political center in the wake of the 1994 midterms, Clinton also benefited from the rise of several right-wing extremist organizations, as well as several tragic manifestations of violence, much of which seemed inspired by those same right-wing groups. For instance, membership in hate groups like the Ku Klux Klan and the Aryan Brotherhood rose dramatically during the mid-1990s. That growth was fueled in part by perceptions that the federal government was mandating multicultural secularism through heavy-handed regulations on public school curriculum and at the same time subsidizing "obscenity" through the National Endowment for the Arts, among other crimes against God and social tradition. Clinton also seized the political high ground in denouncing antiabortion militants who killed seven doctors and patients in various attacks on multiple clinics in 1994 and 1995. But the most obvious moment of right-wing zealotry going too far was the 1995 terrorist attack in Oklahoma City. On April 19, 1995, domestic terrorists and radical right-wing militia enthusiasts Timothy McVeigh and Terry Nichols unleashed a well-coordinated but isolated plot to detonate a massive bomb at the Alfred P. Murrah Federal Building in downtown Oklahoma City. The bomb killed at least 168 people, including 19 children younger than age 6. More than 680 others were injured. Before the attacks of September 11, 2001, the Oklahoma City bombing was the largest terrorist attack ever successfully carried out on U.S. soil. As a political event, the connections between McVeigh, Nichols, and right-wing anti-government militias gave moderates like Clinton an opportunity to once again command the vital center of the nation's political culture, while reigniting anti-Goldwater-esque fears of the radical and potentially violent far Right,

---

[24] Ibid.

still commonly associated with the worst of Sunbelt politics. Such associations were strengthened by images later shown of McVeigh wearing a neo-Confederate t-shirt emblazoned with the Latin phrase "Sic Semper Tyrannis" ("Ever Thus to Tyrants"), the words allegedly uttered by John Wilkes Booth just moments after he assassinated Abraham Lincoln. In the aftermath of Oklahoma City, Clinton worked with congressional Republicans to pass and sign the Antiterrorism and Effective Death Penalty Act of 1996, designed to deter and more harshly punish acts of terrorism conducted within the United States.[25]

Having struggled in 1993, suffered in 1994, and rebounded in 1995, Clinton – known widely by this time as the "Comeback Kid" – was well positioned for reelection as the 1996 campaign went into full swing. With the economy in much better shape than when he took office, Clinton's approval ratings steadily increased, while the Republican Party once again struggled to unite behind a single candidate. After indulging challenges from Pat Buchanan, Texas Senator Phil Gramm, former Tennessee Governor Lamar Alexander, and multimillionaire magazine editor and flat-tax evangelist Steve Forbes, the GOP settled on Kansas Senator Bob Dole. Widely seen by conservatives as a conciliatory moderate, Dole tried to solidify his standing with the GOP's base by winning Barry Goldwater's endorsement. Goldwater complied but openly lamented that he and Dole were now considered the party's new liberals. (Goldwater, by this time, had developed a hatred for the Religious Right, believing that social radicals had assumed total control of the GOP.)

Goldwater's fears aside, Republicans ran a much less vitriolic convention than they had four years earlier in Houston. Meeting in San Diego that summer, the Republican Party formally nominated Dole as its candidate for the presidency. Seventy-three years old at the time, Dole struggled to connect with younger voters, though his wife Elizabeth, who was thirteen years younger, delivered a very effective speech on her husband's behalf, setting the

[25] Link, *Righteous Warrior*, 357–358; Patterson, *Restless Giant*, 260–261; Wilentz, *The Age of Reagan*, 353.

stage for a future career as a Republican senator from North Carolina. For Bob Dole, however, age remained an issue. At one campaign stop, he inexplicably fell off the stage, suffering minor injuries. At another, he made reference to the Brooklyn Dodgers baseball team, failing to remember that the Dodgers had abandoned Brooklyn for Los Angeles in 1958.[26]

Dole's weak candidacy allowed the Clinton campaign to avoid substantive discussions on most issues. As a result, Clinton strolled to an easy reelection, expanding upon his 1992 victory in the Electoral College by winning a 379 to 159 landslide. Clinton took just more than 49 percent of the popular vote in a three-way race against Dole and Ross Perot, who ran again as a third-party candidate. Nevertheless, Clinton's popular vote percentage was six points higher than it had been four years earlier. Clinton also performed well in the Sunbelt, once again carrying California, Nevada, New Mexico, Arkansas, Louisiana, and Tennessee, while adding Arizona and Florida. Clinton's win in Arizona was the first for a Democrat in that state since Harry Truman had won there in 1948. On the other hand, he lost Colorado and Georgia, both states he had carried in 1992. Results in the House of Representatives showed just a two-seat net pickup for Democrats. Meanwhile, Republicans expanded their majority in the Senate, gaining two seats thanks to wins in Arkansas and Alabama. Gubernatorial contests that year produced little drama. Referencing his control of the nation's "vital center," Clinton spoke to Americans on election night as a man whose leadership was rooted in middle-class Sunbelt values. For the moment, Bill Clinton was firmly in command of an emerging Democratic majority.[27]

IMPEACHMENT, SURVIVAL, AND THE CLINTON LEGACY

Under normal circumstances, Clinton's second term would probably be remembered as a period of sustained economic growth

---

[26] Wilentz, *The Age of Reagan*, 368–370.
[27] Ibid.; see also Bennett, Bill Clinton, 103–105.

and federal budget surpluses. His record of economic achievement during these years was particularly strong. By the time Clinton left office in January 2001, unemployment levels were hovering around 4 percent, generally considered to be as close to full employment as the U.S. economy could achieve. During his eight years in office, U.S. gross domestic product (GDP) increased 80 percent and stock values spiked, as did home, 401k, and Individual Retirement Account (IRA) values. Much of the economy's vibrancy was a reflection of the proliferation of young, technology-based businesses, many of which – like amazon.com (founded in 1994) – were using the Internet to revolutionize the way Americans bought and sold consumer goods. The so-called dot-com boom accelerated economic growth but on the whole did not last long. Many dot-com startups went bankrupt shortly after they launched. Still, Internet-driven economics had clearly arrived. Such ventures were all part of the ongoing process of postindustrial economic change. By the end of Clinton's second term, consumer confidence in the economy was higher than at any point since 1952. Federal budget surpluses in 1998, 1999, and 2000 only validated such confidence. Clinton could – and did – take credit for these achievements, though Sunbelt conservatives also quickly pointed out that Clinton's post-1994 move to the political center, coupled with Republican leadership in both houses of Congress, had much to do with the economy's success.[28]

In most cases, an economic record such as this would dominate discussions about a president's second term. In Clinton's case, however, normal circumstances vanished under the dark clouds of a scandal involving the president's sex life and, more specifically, whether or not he had lied under oath about one particular sexual relationship involving a 21-year-old White House intern named Monica Lewinsky. The Lewinsky scandal became national

---

[28] Patterson, _Restless Giant_, 346–386, 400–402; Wilentz, _The Age of Reagan_, 405–407; for more on the Clinton presidency, see William Berman, _From the Center to the Edge: The Politics and Policies of the Clinton Presidency_ (Lanham, MD: Rowman & Littlefield, 2001); John F. Harris, _Bill Clinton in the White House_ (New York: Random House, 2006); and Maraniss, _First in His Class_.

news in January 1998 after Clinton was called to give a deposition in his ongoing sexual harassment lawsuit involving Paula Jones. Attempting to establish a pattern of infidelity and sexual promiscuity, Jones's attorney asked Clinton if he had ever had a sexual relationship with Lewinsky, to which Clinton replied that he had not, though his testimony was intentionally convoluted. In fact, Clinton had engaged in oral sex with Lewinsky on several occasions in the White House from late 1995 through early 1997.[29]

Having obtained evidence of the affair through a separate investigation, Independent Special Prosecutor (and future president of Baylor University) Kenneth Starr – originally assigned to the Whitewater case – turned his attention to the question of whether or not Clinton had perjured himself with his testimony about Lewinsky. For the rest of 1998, the Lewinsky scandal was easily the nation's top political story, even after Clinton finally confessed to the affair on national television that August. Unsatisfied, the Republican House of Representatives impeached Clinton on December 19, charging him with one count of obstruction of justice and one count of perjury. Two months later, Clinton was acquitted when the Republican-controlled Senate failed to achieve the 67 votes needed in order to convict the president and remove him from office. Fifty senators voted guilty on the obstruction of justice charge; of those, twenty-three came from senators representing Sunbelt states. Clinton had survived once again, but in the process he joined Abraham Lincoln's successor, Andrew Johnson, as the only presidents ever impeached.[30]

To a certain extent, Clinton's impeachment was a reflection of the degree to which the politics of morality had come to shape the nation's political culture in the years since Watergate. The scandal also reflected the heightened power that religious conservatives had come to wield since the 1980s, especially in the Sunbelt, where opinions running against the president were strongest. Presented

---

[29] Ibid.; for a thorough accounting of the Clinton impeachment and all related scandals, see Bob Woodward, *Shadow: Five Presidents and the Legacy of Watergate* (New York: Simon & Schuster, 1999), 227–513.
[30] Ibid.

with an opportunity to destroy a president for whom they held little but contempt, Sunbelt conservatives such as South Carolina's Lindsey Graham and Georgia's Bob Barr emphasized the scandal's lurid details in an effort to foment popular rage against Clinton, his infidelity, and his apparent lack of moral conviction. Ironically, however, the strategy backfired. Having once benefited from the politics of culture wars, conservative Republicans reached too far in their pursuit of justice with Clinton. Dismissed by many as a ridiculous investigation into the president's personal life, the tabloid nature of the Lewinsky scandal obscured the fact that Clinton had, indeed, perjured himself and also probably obstructed justice. But the perception that prudish conservatives were engaged in a witch-hunt against the president based on little more than his sexual indiscretions gained steam as the scandal wore on, and eventually contributed to the Senate's decision to acquit. Republicans lost popularity, as did the Religious Right.[31]

Newt Gingrich was especially hurt by his party's strategy to connect political worthiness with marital fidelity. Shortly after the 1998 midterms – an election in which Republicans lost ground in the House despite Clinton's moral failings – and in the wake of a separate ethics investigation, Gingrich resigned his congressional seat, doing so just days before it was revealed that he had also cheated on his wife. Republicans next chose Bob Livingston of Louisiana to replace Gingrich as Speaker of the House, but Livingston was promptly forced to resign before he could assume that position, also the victim of a scandal involving marital infidelity and sexual indiscretion.[32]

For all his accomplishments in office, Bill Clinton's immediate legacy was the reputation he had developed as an undisciplined,

---

[31] For an insightful examination of Washington politics in the 1990s, and the impact of the Lewinsky scandal on bipartisanship, see Steven M. Gillon, *The Pact: Bill Clinton, Newt Gingrich, and the Rivalry That Defined a Generation* (New York: Oxford University Press, 2008). For more on the notion that Republicans ceased to benefit from the culture wars during the late 1990s, see Matthew D. Lassiter, "Big Government and Family Values: Political Culture in the Metropolitan Sunbelt," in Nickerson and Dochuk, *Sunbelt Rising*, 99–109.
[32] Ibid.

scandal-ridden philanderer. Democratic candidates saw him as a liability, whereas Republicans continued to use him as a lightning rod for conservative mobilization. Curiously, however, Clinton also managed to leave office with a higher job approval rating than Ronald Reagan had enjoyed when he left office twelve years earlier. Such was the dichotomous nature of the Clinton years – moderate and successful on the one hand, polarized and scandalized on the other. Nevertheless, as the nation prepared to elect his successor, it was Clinton's personal failings and apparent lack of character that dominated the legacy of American politics during the 1990s.

Bush v. Gore

In 2000, both major political parties once again looked to the Sunbelt in search of a presidential nominee. Republicans eventually settled on the governor of Texas, George W. Bush. Bush won his party's nomination after defeating Arizona Senator John McCain in a bitterly contested primary fight. The bitterest of those fights came in South Carolina where, just days before that state's primary, Bush invited controversy by speaking at the fundamentalist and still racially regressive Bob Jones University. Having appealed to the state's most ardent fundamentalists, Bush's campaign – under the direction of former Lee Atwater protégé Karl Rove – indirectly led a smear campaign against McCain's family in which registered voters received a telephone call suggesting that McCain's wife, Cindy, was a drug addict and his (legally adopted) daughter was actually the product of an illicit biracial affair. Thanks in part to these dirty tricks, Bush won the South Carolina primary, destroyed McCain's campaign, and captured the Republican nomination. In the process, Bush raised more money than any other presidential candidate in American history to that point.[33]

---

[33] Critchlow, *The Conservative Ascendancy*, 257–263; Patterson, *Restless Giant*, 403–421; Wilentz, *The Age of Reagan*, 408–429.

Meanwhile, the Democratic Party united behind Vice President, former Tennessee senator, and DLC pioneer Al Gore. Hoping to capitalize on the Clinton administration's high job approval ratings while avoiding association with the far less seemly characteristics of life in the White House, Gore spoke passionately of family values during his acceptance speech at the Democratic National Convention in Los Angeles that August. For Gore, protecting family values meant preserving social programs such as Social Security and Medicare. Like Bush, Gore also emphasized the importance of education. Seeking to rally the same coalition that had elected Bill Clinton, Gore carefully positioned himself as a balanced Sunbelt moderate, an impassioned populist Democrat, and a relaxed but still born-again Christian. He also went out of his way to emphasize that he was in no way associated with the sex scandals that plagued Clinton. In an awkward effort to drive that particular point home, Gore essentially reaffirmed his martial vows by giving his wife, Tipper, a deep and sustained kiss just prior to delivering his speech. Like most of Gore's campaign, the moment seemed less than natural. Despite a widely recognized sense of humor, Gore struggled throughout the campaign to appear as anything but stiff and uncomfortable. Meanwhile, Bush – who also often appeared stiff and uncomfortable during speeches – seemed far more relaxed and approachable during less scripted moments.[34]

The campaign remained tight throughout the fall. Bush relied heavily on the support of religious conservatives and corporate funding, at the same time promoting himself as a man of "compassion" whose primary focus would be education. Gore, on the other hand, relied heavily on the support of special interest liberals, though his campaign – which also stressed education – was designed to appear sensibly centrist. The most expensive campaign in history to that point, both sides poured money into battleground states including Pennsylvania, Ohio, Missouri, and Florida. Ultimately, the race hinged on Florida. Late on election night, with the Electoral College showing Gore likely just three

[34] Ibid.

votes shy of the White House, all eyes turned to the Sunshine
State, where scrutiny over an unprecedentedly tight race quickly
revealed a number of voting irregularities and other problems.
Network news programs had awarded Florida to Gore earlier
that evening and then rescinded that declaration when it became
clear that the race was too close to call. They later awarded
Florida to Bush and then rescinded that declaration as well. The
confusion in projection rooms across broadcasting offices in New
York and Washington mirrored the confusion on the ground in
Florida, where Bush seemed to hold a margin of victory over Gore
in the range of just a few hundred votes out of nearly 6 million
cast. It took more than a month for a final tally to be certified,
and only then after the United States Supreme Court intervened,
ending the recount of votes in Florida in its *Bush v. Gore* (2000)
decision. At the end of the day, Bush carried Florida by less than
0.0005 percentage points – or just 537 votes. By winning Florida,
Bush won the presidency, having captured a 271 to 267 victory
in the Electoral College, though Gore actually won the national
popular vote, 48.4 percent to 47.9 percent. (Gore's final electoral
vote total was cut to 266 after one Democratic elector from
Washington, D.C., chose not to cast a vote for any candidate, a
protest motivated by reasons unrelated to the Florida situation.
Regardless, Gore was the first presidential candidate to win the
popular vote but lose the Electoral College since 1888.[35])

Democrats blamed their defeat on the situation in Florida, but
had Gore carried his home state of Tennessee, Florida's electoral
votes would have been meaningless. Instead, Gore lost Tennessee
and its eleven electoral votes by nearly four full percentage points.
Among Sunbelt states that Clinton had carried in 1996, Gore
also lost Nevada, Arizona, Arkansas, and Louisiana, in addition
to, of course, Florida. Conversely, Bush swept the rest of the
Sunbelt, losing only in New Mexico and California. In terms of
raw numbers, the race in New Mexico was even tighter than the

---

[35] Ibid.; see also, Jeffrey Toobin, *Too Close to Call: The Thirty-Six Day Battle to Decide the 2000 Election* (New York: Random House, 2001).

one in Florida, with Gore winning by a mere 366 votes amid allegations of voting irregularities.[36]

The election changed little in the House of Representatives, though Republicans temporarily lost control of the Senate, dropping six seats, including one in Florida to Democrat Bill Nelson, while picking up only two – one in Nevada and one in Virginia. In Virginia, Republican George Allen defeated the incumbent Democrat, former governor and DLC founder Chuck Robb. Despite supporting most of Gingrich's Contract with America, Robb had lost considerable favor among social conservatives in Virginia, having been the only southern senator to oppose the Defense of Marriage Act in 1996. He also supported allowing homosexuals to openly serve in the military. Though only narrowly so, Virginia remained a red state under the newly uniform system of electoral mapping adopted by news networks that year, and most famously promoted by NBC's Tim Russert. As he had promised so often during the campaign, Bush assumed the presidency by declaring himself a "uniter, not a divider." Unfortunately for Bush and for the country, keeping that promise proved difficult, even in the ever-contested Sunbelt.[37]

As the United States moved from the twentieth to the twenty-first century, it was clear that its political culture had changed dramatically in the more than five decades since the end of World War II. At one time under the control of a predominantly moderate liberal consensus, the nation seemingly unraveled during the 1960s and 1970s, precipitating new factions on both the Left and the Right. Those factions forced both major parties to respond, and in the process, the national electorate underwent a period of right-leaning realignment. Within this framework, Republicans successfully redefined the meaning of conservatism along more populist lines, poisoned many voters against "establishment" and "secular" liberalism (as they defined it), and achieved a level of electoral dominance not enjoyed by their party seen since the

[36] Ibid.
[37] Ibid.

1920s. Through it all, the Sunbelt – relatively unpopulated, economically backward, and politically impotent prior to World War II – grew in economic, social, cultural, and political power. At the dawn of the twenty-first century, the Sunbelt had become a reflective and trend-setting bellwether for American politics nationally. It was mostly conservative – seemingly filled with red states – but at no point was it uncontested. Electoral maps depicting red states and blue states could just as easily reveal that within each state there existed a healthy dose of purplish counties relatively balanced between competing shades of red and blue.

The contested nature of Sunbelt politics during the 1990s – typified by, among other things, the love-hate relationship the region seemed to have with Bill Clinton – was a harbinger of the political culture yet to come. During the first decade of the twenty-first century, the Sunbelt continued to look increasingly like the rest of the nation, filled with battleground counties, moderate voters, and polarizing politicians. At the same time, the Sunbelt's influence continued to expand, shaping not simply the nation's socioeconomic and cultural personality, but the world's as well.

Epilogue

Sunbelt Politics in the Twenty-First Century

The Sunbelt's political culture continued to evolve as Americans transitioned from the twentieth into the twenty-first century. Economic and political developments were still fueled by rapid population growth, which simultaneously sustained the region's history of metropolitan-based expansion. Meanwhile, the nation struggled to adjust to the paradigm-shifting implications of the War on Terror, brought on by deadly terrorist attacks in New York City, Pennsylvania, and Washington, D.C., on September 11, 2001, not to mention the transformative impact of the Bush administration's controversial response to those attacks. As the nation engaged a new set of global conflicts, the political attitudes of those in the Sunbelt also changed. Perhaps most importantly, the region's white, suburban middle class – so central to the Sunbelt's growth since the end of World War II – no longer seemed as powerful or as conservative as it had just a few decades before. Although still an influential epicenter for conservative political activism at the regional, state, and local levels, the Sunbelt of the early twenty-first century seemed increasingly ripe for greater political contestation and competitive balance.[1]

---

[1] Crichlow, *The Conservative Ascendancy*, 247; Judis and Teixeira, *The Emerging Democratic* Majority, 69–116. For a long history of American national security that includes U.S. interventions post-9/11, see, for example, Marvin Kalb and

One reason for this balance was the rise of what John Judis and Ruy Teixeira have called "postindustrial metropolises" – relatively younger cities driven by technology, university-based research and development, and a cultural willingness to re-embrace the trappings of a limited urbanity, while not entirely abandoning the comforts of modern suburbia. Such places included – but were not limited to – Boulder, Colorado; Austin, Texas; and the areas surrounding California's Silicon Valley, North Carolina's Research Triangle, and the Virginia Beltway suburbs adjacent to Washington, D.C. More racially and ethnically diverse than such communities had typically been in the past, these communities increasingly attracted a multicultural array of younger, white-collar, highly skilled professionals groomed in research institutions during the post–civil rights movement and postmodern eras. Many of these young professionals seemed to understand their own careers through a slightly right-of-center economic lens, embracing the concept of regulated capitalism, for instance, while typically rejecting the moral certitude of their parents' and grandparents' more socially conservative generations. These young professionals were statistically less likely to attend church on a regular basis and more likely to support liberal Democrats than many ambitious young professionals had been just two decades before.[2]

The rise of postindustrial metropolises across the Sunbelt also coincided with an influx of what Judis and Teixeira have called "progressive centrism," a quasi-political worldview that intersected with a rise in the proportional number of Hispanics and Asian Americans living in the region, especially in California, Arizona, Texas, and Florida. That mix has transformed the Sunbelt's

Deborah Kalb, *Haunting Legacy: Vietnam and the American Presidency from Ford to Obama* (Washington, DC: Brookings Institution Press, 2011); and Julian E. Zelizer, *Arsenal of Democracy: The Politics of National Security – From World War II to the War on Terrorism* (New York: Basic Books, 2009).

[2] Ibid.; for more on the spiritual wandering of younger, "postmodern" American voters, see Timothy Keller, *The Reason for God: Belief in an Age of Skepticism* (New York: Dutton, 2008), ix–xxii; for a broader and more academic look at this and other similar issues, see Daniel T. Rodgers, *The Age of Fracture* (Cambridge, MA: Harvard University Press, 2011).

demographic makeup in such a way as to give Democrats a great deal of confidence about their party's prospects for future success in the region. In essence, these social, cultural, demographic, and economic changes accelerated the Sunbelt's political nationalization, a process in which the region has increasingly looked less unique in contrast to the rest of the country.[3]

This process is reflected in, among other things, statistics on partisan affiliation. As seemingly strong as Republican conservatism was electorally during the last decades of the twentieth century, the partisan affiliation of individuals living in the region – though not always predictive of voter turnout – suggests a trend not toward conservative strength, but toward greater moderation and balance. According to one study, from 1960 to 1978 roughly 27 percent of all Sunbelt residents self-identified as Republicans, compared to 58 percent who self-identified as Democrats. Those numbers shifted radically during the 1980s. By 2004, the partisan affiliations of Sunbelt residents were statistically deadlocked at 43 percent Democrat and 43 percent Republican – a dramatic turnaround from four decades earlier, no doubt, but one that only leveled the historically uneven playing field. By 2008, however, those trends began to reverse. Democratic affiliation across the Sunbelt rose from 2005 to 2008, whereas Republican affiliation fell by 6 percentage points during the same period. Tellingly, those numbers mirrored trends at the national level.[4]

Put simply, changes in partisan affiliation across the Sunbelt during the first decade of the twenty-first century reflected the region's status as a political battleground. In some places, conservative Republicans continued to thrive. In other places, moderate and liberal Democrats much more vigorously competed for influence in states once considered reliably conservative. Such was the case, for example, in the region's three largest states – California, Texas, and Florida. In 2008, nearly 50 percent of all residents in

---

[3] Crichlow, *The Conservative Ascendancy*, 247; Judis and Teixeira, *The Emerging Democratic Majority*, 69–116.

[4] Kellstedt and Guth, "Religion and Political Behavior in the Sunbelt," in Nickerson and Dochuk, *Sunbelt Rising*, 120.

Richard Nixon's and Ronald Reagan's home state self-identified
with the Democratic Party, though Orange and San Diego Counties
continued to be hotbeds for nationally focused conservative
activism. Meanwhile in the strongly rightward-leaning state of
Texas, Democrats actually held a slight 42–41 percent advantage
in partisan affiliation among all residents, even as conservative
Republicans continued to dominate statewide elections. And in
Florida, Democrats were remarkably successful at winning new
converts, upping their percentage of state residents sharing their
partisan affiliation by nearly ten points in less than ten years. In
2008, some of the Democratic Party's most notable successes
came along Florida's "I-4 Corridor" connecting Tampa and
Orlando. Four years earlier, the three largest counties in this
corridor – Pinellas, Hillsborough, and Orange – had combined
to give George W. Bush a narrow bump of just more than 30,000
votes in his bid for reelection against John Kerry, a liberal
Democratic senator from Massachusetts. Just four years later,
however, those same three counties swung the other way, giving
Barack Obama, a liberal Democratic senator from Illinois, a
comfortable cushion of more than 161,000 votes in his presidential campaign against John McCain, a moderate Republican
senator from Arizona.[5]

Obama first came to the nation's attention in 2004 when
he delivered an impressive Keynote Address at the Democratic
National Convention in Boston. But Obama's speech was not
enough to help Kerry win the election that year. Instead, George
W. Bush won a second term in the White House, once again domi-
nating his liberal opponent across the Sunbelt. Despite Kerry's
selection of North Carolina Senator John Edwards as a running
mate, Bush did even better in the region in 2004 than he had in
2000, adding New Mexico to his column of Sunbelt prizes. Bush
also expanded his margin of victory in every other Sunbelt state,
with the lone exception of Edwards's North Carolina, which the
Republican still won with 52 percent of the vote. Overall, Bush
won reelection in 2004 in part by sweeping the entire Sunbelt,

[5] Ibid.

with the single exception of California. But even in California, Bush improved on his performance of 2000, winning more than 44 percent of the state's popular vote.

Impressive at the time, Bush's reelection in 2004 seemed more like Sunbelt conservatism's last hurrah when the nation went to the polls in 2008. Plagued by two prolonged and unpopular wars in Iraq and Afghanistan, a less-than-stellar response to the August 2005 crisis in New Orleans caused by Hurricane Katrina, and a crippling economic meltdown that called into question many of the libertarian Right's ideas about unregulated free markets, Bush's approval ratings reached near-record lows in the fall of 2008. Republicans, as a result, lost favor even in states and counties once reliably conservative in national elections. Tapping into this discontent, as well as progressive centrism's surging momentum in postindustrial metropolises across the region and nation, Barack Obama easily defeated John McCain for the presidency, notably carrying a majority of Sunbelt electoral votes in the process, thanks to counties like those in Central Florida that had gone for Bush in 2004 but seemed more securely Democratic in 2008. In addition to Florida, Obama won California, Nevada, Colorado, New Mexico, North Carolina, and Virginia – worth a combined 129 electoral votes. McCain carried the rest of the Sunbelt, worth a combined 120 votes.

Four years later, despite record-high budget deficits, a spiraling national debt, and the rise of the Tea Party (a conservative grass-roots movement most active in the Sunbelt, especially in Texas), Obama still easily defeated former Massachusetts Governor Mitt Romney to win a second term in the Oval Office. Despite (or possibly because of) the Tea Party's fiery and divisively anti-liberal rhetoric, Obama was nearly as successful across the Sunbelt in 2012 as he had been in 2008, repeating his victories across the region with the one exception of North Carolina, which went to Romney by just more than 2 percentage points. Reapportionment based on the 2010 census had made several red states including Texas more valuable in 2012 than they had been in 2008, leaving the final electoral vote tally in the Sunbelt at a 142–117 advantage for the Republican. Still, Obama's wins in California, Florida, and

Virginia were suggestive of the Sunbelt's importance and growing status as a battleground region.

The history of American politics in the postwar Sunbelt suggests, among many other things, that the region's political future is anything but certain. Many of the issues that have shaped and defined the region's political culture since the end of World War II – issues such as race and civil rights; the role of religion in public life; the size and scope of the federal government; and the relationships between national security, patriotism, and local economies – have shown few signs of disappearing. At the same time, issues such as immigration reform – long important nationally, but especially relevant in Texas, New Mexico, Arizona, and California – have only grown more crucial to the Sunbelt's overall political culture in the twenty-first century. So has the rapidly increasing population of Mexican Americans and other Hispanics across the region and nation. For this growing population of Latino Americans, however, access to jobs and education is often just as influential on political behavior as is a particular stance on immigration policy. Meanwhile, religious and cultural issues such as school prayer, abortion, and gay rights have, at times, also been powerfully influential. The rising number of Hispanic voters is good news for Democrats, but Democrats should not presume that Latino American voters will be as uniformly loyal as, for instance, African American voters have been since the mid-1960s. Historically speaking, the Republican Party has, at times, succeeded in attracting a fair share of minority voters, for instance, George W. Bush's campaigns for governor of Texas and president of the United States waged from 1994 to 2004. In 1998, Bush carried 40 percent of Texas Hispanics and 27 percent of Texas African Americans – the highest percentage ever for a Republican candidate in a stateside race in Texas – on his way to a second term as governor. Six years later, he carried nearly 45 percent of Latino voters on his way to a second term as president. The Bush example notwithstanding, the surging number of Latino American voters seemed problematic for conservatives after Romney's failure with that group in 2012. Obama carried 71 percent of Latino voters on his way to a second term, prompting many Sunbelt Republicans – including Florida's Marco Rubio – to challenge the GOP's prevailing consensus on immigration reform.[6]

Changing demographics has not only made the Sunbelt seemingly more national; it has also made it more global. As the Sunbelt's population has continued to diversify, so has its economy, though not always for the better. This has been especially true since 1994, when the Clinton administration signed into law the North American Free Trade Agreement (NAFTA). NAFTA was designed to stimulate economic opportunities across both the Mexican and Canadian borders, while reducing poverty in and illegal immigration from Mexico. NAFTA has produced mixed results and the continued influx of migrant workers from Mexico remains a source of intense political debate, especially in the Sunbelt's border states, Arizona and Texas most heatedly. The politics of globalization has been further shaped by issues related to corporate outsourcing and the loss of skilled, white-collar jobs in the region's increasingly postindustrial economy.[7]

The exporting of Sunbelt products, ideas, and tastes adds yet another element to the concept of regional globalization. The Sunbelt's presence in other parts of the world grew substantially during the early twenty-first century. Arkansas-based companies

---

[6] For more on the politics of immigration in the Sunbelt, see Sylvia Manzano, "Latinos in the Sunbelt: Political Implications of Demographic Change," in Nickerson and Dochuk, *Sunbelt Rising*, 335–360; see also John Garcia, *Latino Politics in America: Community, Culture, and Interests* (Lanham, MD: Rowman & Littlefield, 2003); Tomas R. Jimenez, *Replenished Ethnicity: Mexican Americans, Immigration, and Identity* (Berkeley: University of California Press, 2009); and Marc Rodriguez, *The Tejano Diaspora: Mexican Americanism and Ethnic Politics in Texas and Wisconsin* (Chapel Hill: University of North Carolina Press, 2011). More could be said, and more has been written, on other forms of ethnic political identities in the Sunbelt. For instance, for a study of Jews in the Sunbelt, see Deborah Dash Moore, *To the Golden Cities: Pursuing the American Jewish Dream in Miami and L.A.* (New York: The Free Press, 1994). For a well-contextualized discussion of contemporary issues related to immigration and border security in the American Southwest, see, for example, Miguel Antonio Levario, *Militarizing the Border: When Mexicans Became the Enemy* (College Station: Texas A&M University Press, 2012), 120–126.
[7] Ibid.

such as Tyson Foods, Inc., and Wal-Mart have, at times, dictated labor and product markets in other parts of the country and world and have done so with remarkable power. Meanwhile, fast-food chains such as Chick-fil-A, a Georgia-based company; In-N-Out Burger, based in suburban Los Angeles; and McDonald's, also originally a Southern California brand but now as thoroughly global as any brand in the world are just three examples of the region's expanding economic influence. And of course nothing has globalized American values quite like the motion picture industry based in Hollywood, California. Hollywood has been in the business of exporting elements of the idealized Sunbelt since its formation in the early twentieth century. By 2000, there were nearly three times as many workers employed in the motion picture industry in Los Angeles County as were employed in all aerospace industries combined. Less than twenty years earlier, those numbers were nearly reversed, with twice as many Los Angeles County workers employed in aerospace industries in 1983 than were employed by Hollywood. The end of the Cold War did not simply change the nature of geopolitics; it also changed the immediate economic reality in several defense-oriented and fervently hawkish Sunbelt cities and states.[8]

Global issues related to the defense, immigration, labor, and the economic marketplace are also being shaped by issues related to energy. The Sunbelt continues to be influenced by the politics of power development – including the pursuit of renewable energy sources like solar and wind – even as the region also continues to be a source for traditional energy sources like oil and natural gas. Environmental concerns have traditionally intersected with policies related to energy production; that intersection will almost

---

[8] Judis and Teixeira, *The Emerging Democratic Majority*, 80; Richard Pells, *Modernist America: Art, Music, Movies, & the Globalization of American Culture* (New Haven: Yale University Press, 2011); Bethany Moreton, *To Serve God and Wal-Mart: The Making of Christian Free Enterprise* (Cambridge, MA: Harvard University Press, 2009); Eric Schlosser, *Fast Food Nation: The Dark Side of the American Meal* (New York: HarperCollins, 2001); see also chapters by Darren E. Grem and Laresh Jayasanker in Nickerson and Dochuk, *Sunbelt Rising*, 293–334.

certainly continue for the foreseeable future. Related to this is the politics of water and natural resource management, more generally. Finding reliable sources of drinking water remains a pivotal issue at the state and local levels across the Sunbelt, especially in the arid Southwest, and especially as scientists have connected the prospects of potential global climate change to the extreme droughts experienced across the Sunbelt in 2011, 2012, and 2013.[9]

How to solve these problems while preserving the region's economic growth and development has and continues to be a challenge, especially for Sunbelt residents reluctant to see government as a solution to their problems. But then again, the dynamic struggle between libertarian principles and the attractions of subsidized prosperity has always been a central characteristic of the Sunbelt's political culture. One thing, however, seems certain: as it has for more than six decades, the Sunbelt will undoubtedly continue to host many of the nation's most divisive and important political battles, at the same time that it also continues to produce many of the nation's most passionate grassroots uprisings, and some of its most influential and charismatic leaders. In these ways, the contested nature of Sunbelt politics should continue to fascinate journalists, scholars, and pundits for years to come.

[9] For more on energy policies in the Sunbelt, see Andrew Needham, "Sunbelt Imperialism: Boosters, Navajos, and Energy Development in the Metropolitan Southwest," in Nickerson and Dochuk, *Sunbelt Rising*, 240–264.

Index